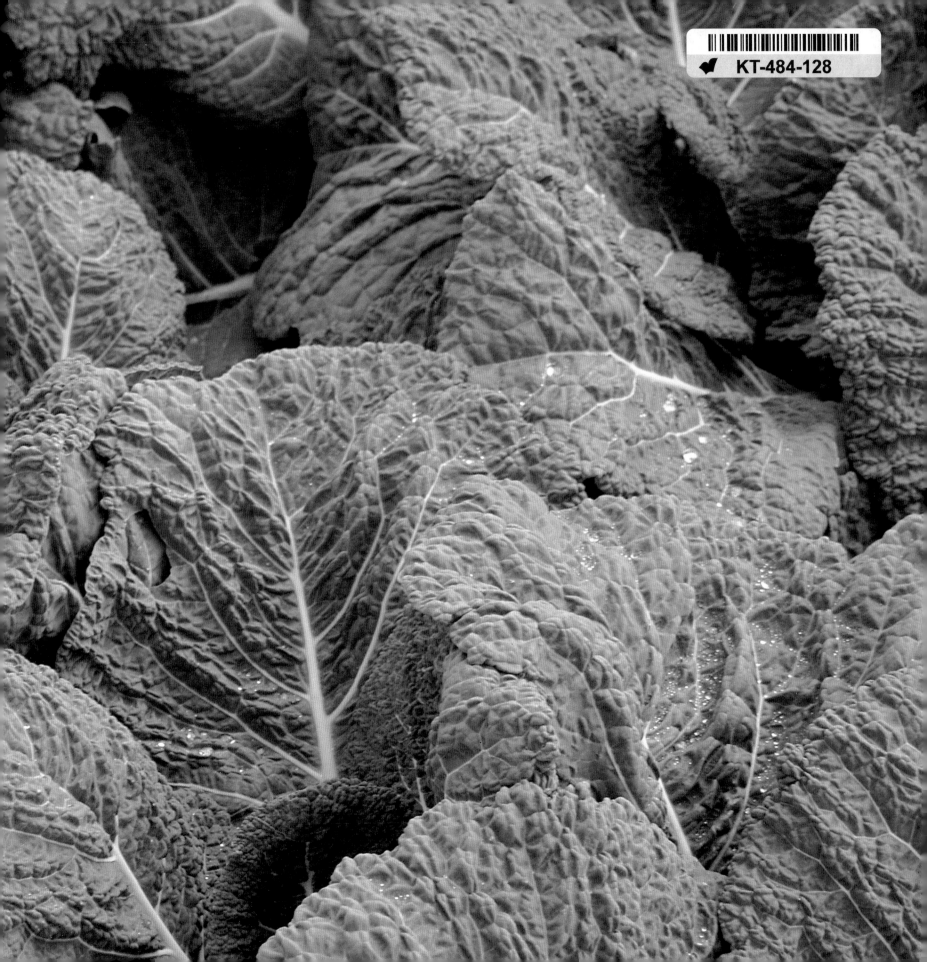

IN AN IRISH COUNTRY KITCHEN

IN AN
IRISH COUNTRY
KITCHEN

CLARE CONNERY

PHOTOGRAPHS BY
CHRISTOPHER HILL

WEIDENFELD AND NICOLSON
LONDON

For Ireland and peace

Text © Clare Connery 1992
Photographs © Weidenfeld & Nicolson Ltd 1992

First published in 1992 by
George Weidenfeld & Nicolson Ltd
91 Clapham High Street
London SW4 7TA

British Library Cataloguing-in Publication Data
A catalogue record for this book is available
from the British Library.

ISBN 0-297-83094-5

Consultant Editor: Vicky Hayward
House Editor: Coralie Hepburn
Designer: Joy FitzSimmons

Phototypeset by Keyspools Ltd, Golborne, Lancs
Printed and Bound in Italy

ENDPAPERS: The cabbage achieved immense popularity during
the famine when it was sown as a safe crop instead of potatoes. It
is now one of the mainstays of Irish cooking.

HALF-TITLE PAGE: Irish apple cake (page 150).

FRONTISPIECE (CLOCKWISE, FROM TOP LEFT): Crubeens, stewed
pork ribs, fried liver and bacon, an Irish fry and Dublin coddle
(pages 60–2).

CONTENTS PAGE (CLOCKWISE, FROM TOP LEFT): Gooseberries;
boiled and pressed ox tongue (page 69); porter cake, seed cake
and almond cheese cakes (pages 139–40); a traditional thatched
cottage; (from left to right) honey biscuits, oatcakes, caraway
biscuits, saffron biscuits and Irish shortbread biscuits.

ACKNOWLEDGEMENTS

In an Irish Country Kitchen began by a chance meeting with Vicky Hayward and an enthusiastic discussion about Irish food and culture. Vicky instigated the book and Michael Dover at Weidenfeld and Nicolson set the project in motion. Without their encouragement and enthusiasm I would never have had the courage to attempt such a project. I am deeply indebted to them both for the opportunity to write about the two great passions in my life, food and Ireland.

My thanks also to Vicky Hayward, Consultant Editor, and Coralie Hepburn for so painstakingly editing the manuscript and whose help and guidance were invaluable throughout.

This book has been a massive project and there are many people I am deeply indebted to for their support and kind assistance.

First, Dr Alan Gailey, Director of the Ulster Folk & Transport Museum at Cultra, Belfast, who not only provided me with study facilities in the museum's comfortable library, but allowed me access to the museum's archive material and in particular for permission to use a number of recipes from the eighteenth-century manuscript receipt book of Bishop Story of Clogher (1742). Full access to the outdoor museum with its excellent facilities and exhibits also enabled me to test many of the recipes in their traditional surroundings and provided the perfect setting for the food photographs. Without the help of the museum, Dr Gailey and his staff, this book would not have been possible.

My grateful thanks in particular go to Dr William Crawford, Keeper of Material Culture, and Dr Jonathan Bell, Assistant Keeper (Agriculture), for their support, enthusiasm, patience and encouragement. It was their knowledge of all things Irish which inspired the structure of the text and ensured that my interpretation of the facts was accurate. Without their help and knowledge I would never have been able to undertake such a task. I am also grateful to Fionnuala Carragher, Assistant Keeper (Domestic Life), for her time and knowledge; Megan McManus, Assistant Keeper (Crafts), for the many lively discussions about kitchenware; Michael McCaughlin, Curator of Marine Transport, for his guidance on all things coastal; and Mervyn Watson and George Crowe, Museum Assistants, for their help and assistance.

In the outdoor gallery my thanks go to Frank Cox, Billy Brennan and, in particular, Irene McGarrey, who coped so graciously with the upheaval in their houses on so many occasions.

In the quiet of my study room in the museum's library, I researched and wrote most of the text and I am especially grateful to Ronnie Adams, Librarian, for solving my many reference problems; to Sally Skilling, Assistant Librarian, for her endless supply of books, information, company and cups of tea, and to them both, for putting up with my constant questions and presence for so long.

To my friends John and Jean Gamble of Emerald Isle Books, my very special thanks for so generously allowing me to use their eighteenth-century manuscript receipt book of Charles Echlin from County Down (1709), which enabled me to add many colourful and exciting recipes to the text, and for their constant support and encouragement over the years. My life and my book are much richer for knowing them.

I also owe my thanks to my friend and colleague of many years, Anne Macfarlane, who helped me with the final recipe testing and whose meticulous attention to detail ensured that every recipe was perfect. My thanks, too, to my chef, Paul Clarke, who brought a young and talented eye to the proceedings and a pair of skilled hands to the preparation of the food for the photographs. His help, and also that of Peggy Hanna, was invaluable.

I also owe a debt of gratitude to my colleague, Elizabeth Kirkpatrick, who so willingly took on the responsibility of my catering company for the last year to enable me to complete the book; and to my faithful secretary, Doreen McBrien, for typing and patiently retyping endless pages of manuscript and forever keeping me in order.

My thanks and appreciation to the Forestry Division at the Department of Agriculture for supplying me with the game for the photographs; to my photographer, Christopher Hill, who captured so perfectly the essence of the past and the present in field and farm and country kitchen; and to my beloved companions at table, Peter and Clare, for their support and patience.

Finally, to the people of Ireland, whose warmth and generosity give me hope for the future.

CONTENTS

INTRODUCTION

Ireland is an island of contrasts and conflicting images. It is a land of fertile rolling plains, immense black bogs and hauntingly beautiful mountains. It is a place of peace and tranquillity, yet also of ancient feuds, warring people, death and destruction.

It is a land which is at once simple and pastoral, yet developed and industrial, with one foot in the soil and the other in the factory. Even Ireland's most sophisticated cities like Dublin, Belfast and Cork have a capacity to merge the quiet and calm of the earth with the harshness and clamour of industry, giving them a rather countrified feel. Yet all too often it is only the negative images of Ireland and its people that are portrayed, colouring opinions and masking the true nature of the country and its inhabitants.

In spite of such images Ireland remains a noble country, a land of milk and honey, of fortitude and courage, where the vast majority of people continue life as normal, retaining their characteristic humour and tenacity of spirit and remaining caring and dignified in spite of their difficulties.

ABOVE: *Turf, cut from the bogs, was the traditional Irish fuel. It was used both to warm cottages and to cook food.*

OPPOSITE: *A lonely coastal headland in County Donegal, now populated by sheep.*

Ireland offers a quality of life that is unsurpassed in the rest of Europe. While continuing to develop along with their fellow Europeans, these traditionally pastoral people still closely adhere to the principles of home and family which are an integral part of Irish life and society. Indeed, within the home, whether it be an elegant town house or a humble country cottage, the importance of the family is just as strong now as in the days when the hearth was at the heart of it and the hub around which all life revolved. Although today the hearth is physically absent from many modern Irish houses, the site of its birth, the kitchen, is still the focus of family life, the centre of activity and the place where body and soul have been sustained and nourished for generations. It was here, in the original Irish kitchen, that life was lived, the day's activities discussed, friends entertained, music played, stories told and the world put to right. It was here that many were born and many would die, and where joys and sorrows were shared.

Amid all these extraneous activities, food was stored, prepared, cooked and eaten. In the most humble homes, food was quite

basically for sustenance and was cooked with whatever equipment was available. In the more remote parts of Ireland, as in many peasant societies throughout the world, this is still the case today. In the houses of those of greater means, whether in town or country, food for sustenance was still an important factor, but in addition eating was a companionable activity, so much so that, from one side of the globe to the other, the Irish have become renowned for their ladened tables and warm generous hospitality.

Although Ireland has never been noted for having a sophisticated eating tradition at any stage in its history, it nonetheless has an enviable reputation for good wholesome dishes made from a wide range of unadulterated, indigenous products, most of which still offer the finest quality to be found in Europe. In recent years too, in both family homes and commercial kitchens, cook and caterer alike have developed a new awareness of the dishes of our ancestors and a confidence not only to recreate and enrich our native culinary tradition, but to develop a new Irish food culture from this island's lavish bounty.

In every town and village there is a local speciality. It may be the bread and cakes of the northern counties, the rich milk and dairy produce of Tipperary and the central plain, or the fine variety of fish and seafood from the rivers and lakes throughout the country and off its shores. Wherever one goes, from the most remote and lonely headland in Donegal, to the towns of the southernmost tip of the island, fine local produce will grace even the most humble of tables.

This book is a celebration of the rich and ancient food traditions of a uniquely beautiful land. It is my tribute to the country of my birth, a country where I am privileged to live.

HISTORY

Man seems to have been a latecomer to Ireland. Many colourful pictures of our early ancestors, during what is called the old Stone Age, have been created for us by the ancient scribes and story-tellers; these portray Ireland as a heroic land of warlike people, steeped in legend, myth and mystery. Delightful they may be, but probably more fiction than fact, particularly since the early history of Ireland, at least up until the fifth century AD, is known only in a very fragmentary fashion.

At one time Ireland was an integral part of the European continent which animals and plants could reach freely, their passage limited only by changing climatic conditions. The Ice Age in particular had far-reaching effects on the plants and animals, considerably reducing them in number and species, and on the landscape as well: as the cold solid mass moved over the earth's surface, it cut into it, resculpturing it and taking much in its path with it. Soil, rocks and shingle were mixed, carried along, then redeposited, forming areas where the water was either unable to drain away, resulting in heavy clay, or areas which could not hold water and sub-

ABOVE: *Croagh Patrick in County Mayo, here shrouded in mist, is climbed annually by pilgrims.*

OPPOSITE: *Throughout history, the sea has provided an essential source of food for those living along Ireland's coast.*

sequently gave rise to land subject to drought. The result was a remodelled landmass with a wide variety of rocks and soils, all either restricting or facilitating the country's development.

It was not until about 10,000 years ago that a further climatic change took place. This enabled plants and animals to move once again, albeit over tortuous lands and rivers. Finally, about 7,500 years ago, the situation changed once more when the basin of the Irish Sea flooded to cut Ireland off from Britain.

Ireland is a small island of some 83,000 square kilometres (32,000 sq miles). Today the striking features of the landscape and the effects of these various climatic changes can still be seen throughout the island. It is ringed by mountains surrounding a large plain, composed mainly of carboniferous limestone. The limestone accounts for the richness of Ireland's soil and the quality of its pastures. Although less dramatic than the mountains, the fertile greenness of the fields in the counties of Tipperary, Meath and Kildare make them just as striking. The highlands and lowlands throughout the

country, from Kerry to Longford, are related by countless bogs and lakes, all majestic and inspiring but none more so than the bogs of Donegal and the lakes of Killarney. Slow winding streams and gushing rivers of unpolluted water flow inland from the mountains before making their way to the sea.

The most distinctive contrasts of landscape are in the north, east and the southwest. In the west there is the most extensive area of mountain, bog, poor land and high rainfall, which has always made it difficult to cultivate and colonise; the east, too, has a landscape of outstanding natural beauty, albeit one which is less vigorous and more

gentle. As nature would have it, here the land is also more fertile and workable and the climate more temperate, factors which have resulted in it being extensively cultivated, populated and industrialised by many different people throughout the centuries.

THE EARLY SETTLERS

Two of the earliest settlements discovered in Ireland, thought to date back to around 7000–6000 BC, are a hut site in Mount Sandel, County Londonderry, and a hunting camp at Brougal, Lough Boora, County Offaly. It would appear from excavation that the small group of people who settled together on these

camps lived in circular huts no more than 6 metres (20 feet) across, made from fairly large saplings covered by hides, reeds and possibly earth, with a hearth set towards the entrance. Outside were large pits and areas where stone tools were manufactured. Among the tools discovered were flints, blades, axes and arrows.

The burnt remains of bones and shells tell their own story and have provided a picture of the possible food eaten at the time: wild boar, hare and dog; salmon, trout, eels, seabass and flounder; pigeon, duck, grouse, capercaillie – a bird of pine forests, now extinct – and one bird of prey, the goshawk;

Strangford, County Down, was one of the first places to be settled by the Vikings.

THE FIRST FARMERS

It was somewhere around 4000 BC that a shift from food collection to food production took place. This happened so abruptly that it seems to have been the result of the arrival of a new group of people, who introduced crop growing and animal rearing to the country. It is thought that these first farmers came across what is now the Irish Sea by boat, bringing with them their families, domestic plants and animals, and introducing species which were up until then unknown to the island. Where these people actually came from is still very much a matter of conjecture: some historians believe it was the south-west of Scotland, others the north of England – the shortest sea crossings. Others are of the opinion that they could have come from the Atlantic, Western and Central European cultures, who at this time were spreading through Britain.

Whatever their origins, it was these early inhabitants who helped to develop the country's culture and mixed economy and formed the basic genetic stock of the Irish people. In order to grow crops and raise animals they had to clear dense areas of oak and elm forests, so that ploughing could be made easier and light could get in to help the crops grow. It was in these clearings that the first houses of Ireland's Stone-Age farmers were constructed: strong rectangular structures supported by thick wooden posts and rafters, covered with thatch. These houses were more substantial than many of those built in the eighteenth and early nineteenth centuries.

Although very little is known about the type and quantity of crops grown or the animals reared, from the number of cattle bones discovered it seems likely that the emphasis was on grazing rather than cereal production. However, the effect of the shallow cultivation methods used by these farmers quickly exhausted the soil and so they moved on, clearing more woodlands and establishing new camps. Such activity had a profound effect not only on the appearance of the landscape, but eventually on its structure, for it was around this time that the climate changed, becoming colder and wetter, and turning many of the forest clearings into peat bogs. These have developed through the centuries, covering large areas of the country.

Over a period of more than a thousand years, these skilled and creative Neolithic people developed a remarkable society, introducing farming, creating field walls, and constructing substantial houses. However, their greatest contribution to the period was the building of large burial tombs and monuments. About a thousand different types still remain, like those in the Boyne Valley, and can be seen all over Ireland.

THE BRONZE-AGE FARMERS

The development and richness of this prehistoric culture and economy continued into the Bronze Age with the exploitation of metallic ores, particularly copper and bronze, to make flat axes, spear heads and other metal objects including simple knives. Gold was panned from some of the rivers and great skill was displayed in the making of metal and gold ornaments and jewellery. Trade in these metals probably took place with other parts of Western Europe.

There can be little doubt that the agriculture introduced by the Neolithic people, particularly that of stock raising, also continued to develop. The study of animal bones has revealed the continued dependence on oxen, pigs and sheep, with a smaller reliance on game and other wild animals. The ancient cooking sites, which are scattered all over the country, have come from this age, too. These consist of sunken troughs called *fulachta fiadha*. Of various lengths and sizes, they were lined with stones or wood and were generally built near water so that they could easily be filled with the large quantity required. A fire was lit beside the pit, large stones were heated in it and these were then

hazelnuts and apples. All of these suggest that the early settlers were hunters and gatherers, living from the natural resources around them.

Tentative archaeological reconstruction of the lifestyle of these early people implies that they did not roam aimlessly over the island, but followed a very definite pattern, moving between campsites in an annual cycle governed by the seasons and the natural migration of birds and animals.

thrown into the trough to make the water boil. Large joints of meat, wrapped in either straw or hide, were then lowered into the water to cook. Similar methods of cooking were also practised in coastal areas, where rock pools were heated in the same way to cook fish.

THE IRON-AGE FARMERS

Towards the end of the Bronze Age and into the period known as the Iron Age, further developments took place. As iron became a regular material, farm implements and tools were improved. Large cauldrons were manufactured along with wheeled carts, musical instruments and bigger wooden ploughs.

Celtic intruders arrived on the island somewhere around 500 BC, but we know very little about Celtic Ireland before the coming of Christianity. However, epic tales and stories written down centuries later, although not strictly history, do give an idea of life immediately before the Christian period. Such tales depict a tribal and rural society of warrior princes, of major and minor kingdoms, and of battles and cattle raids. It was also the time of great pagan religious festivals whose myths and rituals revolved around the land and the seasons. Many of these festivals survived Christianity, becoming incorporated into its beliefs and festivals, albeit in a modified form.

THE FARMERS OF CHRISTIAN IRELAND

During this period the people lived in wooden huts built inside *raths*, circular enclosures of earthen banks or stone walls often erected on a hilltop, which varied in size between 20 and 125 metres (66–410 feet) in diameter. Within these there was space for small farm buildings and an open area where livestock could be penned when necessary. The large wooden huts were probably the homes of the chieftain of the clan and his family, while the smaller ones propped against the inside of the bank or in the outer ditches were those of the

serfs and slaves. The king's residence or palace, the *crannog*, was more elaborately constructed and built on a lake. Villages were probably formed from a group of these *raths* and played an important part in the trade and exchange of goods which had started at the beginning of the sixth century and was now taking place with the Continent. At this time oil and wine in Mediterranean jars were being exchanged for, of all things, wolfhounds.

Soon after St Patrick brought the Christian faith to Ireland in the fifth century, the Church established a monastic organisation whose settlements were to have an important influence on farming methods, food and education. Monastic enclosures were built, which varied as much in size as the houses and *raths*. With the establishment of the larger and more important of these, such as Armagh, Bangor and Kildare, small communities were formed where monks and lay people lived side by side in the same settlements. The inhabitants of these monasteries developed arable farming and a more varied form of vegetable growing specifically to accommodate their diet, which consisted largely of vegetables and grains. They grew cabbages, leeks, onions and celery along with corn, barley, wheat and a little rye. Oats were introduced during this period and eventually became the principle grain crop, with oat bread the common bread of the people, and porridge one of the staple foods. The monasteries also had their own orchards with apples, damsons and other fruits.

The legendary lives of the saints and early laws, such as the Brehon Laws – administered by the Irish Brehons or judges – offered a rich contribution to many branches of historical research and provided valuable information about the life, customs and eating habits of the times, albeit indirectly. The life of St Brigit, a contemporary of St Patrick, makes many references to food in her miracles. In one vision, which she supposedly recounts to St Patrick himself, she

says: 'I saw four ploughs ploughing this island and sowers sowed seed and it grew immediately and began to ripen and streams of new milk filled the furrows and the sowers were clothed in white garments.' In another one, butter and bacon feature: 'Under pressure of poverty and with guests just about to arrive, she changed nettles into butter and the barks of trees into the richest and most delicious bacon.' Beer also features frequently in St Brigit's miracles and appears to have been both a part of the staple diet and a regular item of celebration.

Literary texts of the eighth century, such as the sagas and medical tracts, also contain a wealth of information about the countryside and the farmers of early Christian Ireland. At this time the farming class was required to give food to the chieftains, and detailed lists give an indication of the farm produce of the day. The drawback of these lists is that they show only the aristocratic foods, those of the chieftain and his retinue, and make no reference to what the common folk ate. The items listed include: calves, sheep, pigs, pork, milk, cream, butter and other dairy produce, kiln-dried wheat loaves, malt and herbs. Early medical tracts refer to the growing of peas, beans and flax, which was cultivated for its oil as well as its fibres.

Although it is difficult to estimate the size of the farms at this time, it is known that there were two types: the 'strong' farm and the 'small' farm. The 'strong' farm was fully equipped with a long house and annexe, a sheep fold, a calf pen and a pig sty. For tillage there were all the accessories and facilities with which to sow, harvest and store grain, including a barn and a dry kiln. The farm would also have had a share in the village mill, where grains such as wheat, barley, rye and oats were ground.

Excavation suggests that the emphasis was placed on cattle rearing for dairying rather than crop production, with the meat and hides being used as a by-product. One law tract says that the minimum number of cattle stock on a 'strong' farm should be twenty cows, two bulls and six oxen. On the land there would have been fenced pasture for grazing sheep, but the farmer also had access to the commercial uncultivatable land held by his clan. Calving took place in the spring, and with the early summer flush of milk the cows were driven up to a mountain pasture accompanied by herdsmen and women who lived in temporary huts called booleys. The milk produced at this time was used as a drink, solidified into curds or churned into butter. Surplus butter was buried in the bogs which kept it cool and prolonged its life, so much so that examples of this 'bog butter' have been found even in recent years. The 'strong' farmer also grew barley, made malt and brewed his own beer.

The 'small' farm, in comparison, would have been greatly reduced in scale with fewer animals and less equipment. A plough and other tillage tools would probably have been shared with a few neighbours.

THE FARMERS OF VIKING IRELAND

In the latter part of the eighth century occurred a fresh influx of new peoples, the first since the Celts had entered Ireland. The newcomers quickly established themselves along the eastern and southern coasts, from Strangford Lough to Dublin and at Wexford, Waterford, Cork and Limerick. These were the Scandinavian sea pirates of Northern Europe who became known as the Vikings.

These Scandinavians were, through time, to make their most enduring contribution to Ireland as traders and town dwellers, being the founders of the first towns and contributing to the expansion of trade and communications with the outside world. By the tenth century Dublin city was the focal point of both trade and settlement, with a number of outlying dependencies in Carlingford and

Small field patterns and drystone walls are typical of the rural landscape.

Strangford Lough and important trading towns such as Wexford, Limerick, Waterford and Cork.

Archaeological finds from the refuse of Dublin city suggest that in the eighth century pears, plums, damsons, sloes, cherries, raspberries, strawberries, blackberries and bilberries were eaten in addition to the usual agricultural products. Imported luxuries such as figs, raisins and walnuts were in evidence as well. It would also appear that beef had become an important commodity. The Viking Age in Ireland ended with the Scandinavian settlers becoming completely integrated with Irish society.

THE FARMERS OF NORMAN IRELAND

After a period of isolation, twelfth-century Ireland was drawn back into the mainstream of Western history by the arrival of the Normans, who initially came from Wales as mercenaries to fight for Dermot MacMurrough, King of Leinster. We know from archaeological excavations of Anglo-Norman sites, travel writers of the time such as Giraldus Cambrensis, and from other literary sources that they brought with them a vastly different style of living to that of their Irish peers. They also possessed a strong sense of organisation and development which was to change the landscape, the agriculture and the commerce of the country. They were hungry for wealth especially in the form of arable land. Where they found soils to their liking they erected an earthen motte, later replaced by a stone castle, and settled themselves in the surrounding countryside. They also established manorial estates in south-east Ireland where they grew successful wheat crops.

The basic Anglo-Norman unit was the manor, consisting of about 1,200 hectares (3,000 acres). Here the lord would have his home-farm – often protected by a motte – containing his house, farm buildings and the surrounding fields. His workforce was built up of people from outside Ireland, to whom he gave large farm units linked to him by rent, allegiance or services in kind, as well as the Irish who had formerly occupied the land before his arrival. Their status was, however, usually considerably reduced and although some were allocated plots of land to rent, there was no security of tenure. Others held cottages but no land, and others had land without tenure held mainly by service. The duties of those who serviced the manorial lord included ploughing, harrowing, sowing, weeding, scaring birds, reaping, stacking and thrashing.

The colonists prospered for a time throughout Leinster and East Munster, taking the flat lands, the rivers, the coasts, and the Norse trading towns, leaving the hill country, the woods and the bogs for the natives. They created new resources: silver was mined, and wool and hides were sent in large quantities to France, Flanders and Italy. Wool cloth, linen and furs were exported, while luxury goods such as figs, raisins, sugar and sweetmeats along with marzipan, walnuts, wine, satins, silk and cloth of gold were brought in. The Norman cooks introduced new and exotic dishes, using the spices and seasoning with which they were familiar to make pastry pies of poultry, beef and game. They also stuffed and roasted suckling pig, roasted heads of boar and made custard tarts and mincemeat.

One of the most important literary references to the foods eaten in Ireland in the twelfth century, many probably introduced by the Normans, is an old Irish story known as *The Vision of MacConglinne*. In the vision, MacConglinne, a gluttonous poet, dreams of all manner of fine things to eat and drink. These include milk, butter, cheese and curds – important foods since the first farmers introduced cattle to Ireland somewhere around 4000 BC – oaten bread, wheaten cakes and speckled fruit clusters; bacon and sausages, referred to as puddings; the meat and offal from pigs, cows and sheep; corned beef, lard and salmon; carrots, leeks and kale; porridge and honey in combs; along with mead, wine and ale. It is through the poet's vivid descriptions that we gain a valuable insight into the foods available to a certain section of the community – probably the richest – before 1300.

By the fourteenth century, following continual wars, further invasions, the Black Death and the deterioration in climate, the Anglo-Norman way of life had fallen into a decline from which it never really recovered. Many Anglo-Norman families intermarried with the Irish and adopted a number of their ways, identifying more with Gaelic Ireland than their Anglo-Norman roots. This resulted in the remaining Royal Authority being confined to a few walled towns and an enclave on the east coast called the Pale: an area which ran from Dundalk, through Kells to Kildare and, from there, back east across the northern foothills of the Wicklow Mountains to reach the coast south of Dublin at Dalkey. Here land patterns were changing from the medieval strip holdings to large leasehold farms worked by almost landless labourers. The Pale was well kept and productive. The staple crop was wheat, but barley and rye were also grown, barley essentially for brewing and distilling. Cattle, particularly milk cows, were still highly prized, and milk products of all kinds continued to be eaten. Cattle not used for milk were killed and eaten either raw, boiled or roasted. Meat was also used as an ingredient for soup. Blood was drawn and mixed with milk, butter or grains and made into a concoction called black or blood pudding. Mutton, pork, hens, rabbits and venison were also eaten.

In the poorer lands, particularly in the 'Irish' areas, life was much different and 'booleying', or transhumance, was still widely practised. People were constantly on the move, taking their cattle to the mountains for pasture in summer and returning to the lowlands with them in winter. These people lived mainly on milk products, with perhaps some watercress and wood-sorrel and whatever wild foods that were available.

THE ORIGINS OF MODERN FARMING

This easy-going life of the pastoralists irritated the Tudor monarchs, and in the sixteenth century they set about turning these wandering Irishmen into settled Englishmen – by conquest. The areas that were ultimately taken were those that had originally appealed to the Anglo-Normans, with the addition of the good land in Munster and Wexford. The English Government at this time extended its control over the whole of Ireland and many people from both England and Scotland migrated to Ireland. Although settlement was heaviest in the north, it was also considerable in Munster and Wexford. This influx of people along with the striking growth in trade brought about the most important feature of the period, the development and expansion of agriculture into a market-oriented industry with the emphasis on sheep, cattle and wool as the main exports along with the commercial production of grain. This growth of trade was accompanied by a significant growth in wealth, an increase in travel and the consumption of new and exotic products particularly by the well-to-do. The diet of the common people, with the exception of the poorest, was also comparatively varied with most small cabins having a piece of ground where corn, oats, peas, cabbage and, of course, potatoes were grown.

By the late seventeenth and early eighteenth centuries a pattern of small enclosed fields for arable farming was spreading over the country and in some areas the general standard of living and prosperity seem to have improved. Where there was an emphasis on pasture rather than tillage, cottage industries such as the spinning and weaving of flax and wool became a source of supplementary income. Farms and villages, shops and local industries reflected the growing commercialisation, and an improved system of roads and bridges made transporting such commodities to the main areas of trade much easier. Fairs and markets had now been established throughout the country. Slaughter houses at the docks accommodated the increasing export trade in carcass and salted beef to England and the West Indies. Fish, hides and furs declined in importance, and the shipment of live cattle and sheep was replaced by that of butter for the Continental market, and wool for the English market.

THE POTATO IN IRELAND

Round about the last fifteen years of the sixteenth century, and during one of the stormiest periods in Ireland's troubled history, another form of plantation took place, one which also had a very significant and long-lasting effect on the Irish people. It was the plantation of the potato.

It is not known exactly how or when the potato came to Ireland, but it is traditionally thought to have appeared as the result of a shipwreck off the coast of Galway, though there is no evidence to support this. The first specific reference to the potato occurs in a manuscript in the archives of the Montgomery family of County Down, which gives 1606 as the year when potatoes were grown on Montgomery land. Whatever the date of their arrival, it is thought that they were first grown in gardens or 'haggards' which were attached to cottages, or on small pieces of land neither good enough or large enough to be worked by the plough.

Within fifty years of its introduction, probably around 1670, the potato became the universal and staple food throughout the island, almost displacing the old diet of meat, milk and oatmeal of the labourers, cotters, and small and medium farmers who formed about nine-tenths of Irish society. Amongst the Anglo-Irish landlord class and richer townsmen it probably remained as an extra, to accompany the abundance of meat and poultry already eaten. John Dunton, a seventeenth-century commentator, writes:

> Behind one of these cabins lies the garden, a piece of ground of sometimes half an acre, and in this is the turf-stack, their corn, perhaps 200 or 300 sheaves of oats – and as much peas; the rest of the ground is full of those dearly loved potatoes, and a few cabbages which the solitary calf never suffers to come to perfection.

There were obviously a number of factors which favoured the cultivation of the potato in Ireland and enabled it to play such a significant role in the economic life of the people in such a short space of time. In the main, however, it was the climate, the land and its easy cultivation which made it successful and invaluable. The climate generally is moist and cool, perfect for keeping the potato free of many of the virus diseases which attack and destroy it. The soil is also deep and friable – even in the boglands which up until then were practically uncultivatable – which meant it could be worked by hand. After the mid-eighteenth century, exports of corn began to increase and rents began to rise. Population pressure forced families to sell corn crops to pay rent while relying on potatoes to store over the winter to feed themselves and their livestock, especially their pigs. The potato – although 75 per cent of the tuber is water – provided the carbohydrate, protein and vitamin C required to keep them alive and healthy. The food value of the potato per 0.4 hectares (1 acre) was also more than that of any grain crop. To fulfil their daily nutritive requirements, each person had to eat 3 kg (6.5 lb) of potatoes, the equivalent of a large bag. This is an unthinkable quantity to us, but considering the average consumption could be as much as 3.6 kg (8 lb) per day, it was obviously not a problem.

In addition to all these benefits, the potato took little effort or skill to prepare and cook. Indeed, it could even be cooked and served in

the one pot or cauldron set over the most basic of burning turf fires on the floor of the cottage. If necessary, the potato could be roasted in the ashes of the fire and eaten from the hand without even the need for a pot, plate, knife or fork.

When the potato became a widely grown food crop, it was cultivated on lazy-beds, long narrow ridges that served to drain the land. Throughout the country the poorest farmers subdivided holdings so plots became irregular in size and shape, often with no more than about 0.1 hectares ($\frac{1}{4}$ acre). This cultivation of the land in small parcels reflects the continuous struggle of people who had to scrape a livelihood from the mountains and boglands.

From the seventeenth century on, the writings of the commentators in Ireland confirm the widespread use of the potato as a staple food for the vast majority of Irish people. One of the most important travel writers of the eighteenth century was the agriculturist Arthur Young, whose writings not only offer a vivid description of the importance of the potato in Irish life, but of the style of that life itself. He stresses the prevalence of the potato at nearly every place he stopped at on his travels, such as at Ballynoey, County Cavan: 'The poor live on potatoes and milk, it is their regular diet, very little oat bread being used, and no fresh meat at all except on Easter Sunday and Christmas Day. Their potatoes last them through the year; all winter long only potatoes and salt.' From Gloster, King's County, he writes: 'Their food is potatoes and milk for ten months and potatoes and salt for the remaining two; they have however a little butter.'

It is hard to measure the poverty of the Irish at this time but one example from a visit to a cabin near Ballygawley, County Tyrone, from *Reid's Travels in Ireland* (1823), certainly creates a vivid picture of a

Potato digging.

people who preferred their 'praties with a bone in them'.

The family were at dinner: the repast consisted of dry potatoes only, which were contained in a basket set upon the pot in which they had been boiled; this was placed on the floor in the middle of the cabin. The father was sitting on a stool and the mother on a kreel of turf; one of the children had a straw box, the youngest even sprawling on the floor, and five others were standing round the potato basket. [The potatoes were only half-boiled.] We always have our praties hard, they stick to our ribs and we can fast longer that way.

The potato grew not only in importance but in volume, and all available land was given over to its cultivation. The production of the other staples of the Irish diet, especially milk, consequently went into decline. The population also continued to grow dramatically, to such an extent that the insufficient land was eventually unable to cope with the enormous drain on its resources. The problem was compounded by the primitive agricultural system of the time. Living standards fell below the subsistence level and, in order to survive, the people were forced to move to the higher lands where it was still just possible to produce potatoes, or to move out of the country altogether, either to England or America. This is indeed what happened, even before the famine, so that by 1830 the rate of population growth was beginning to ease. But this was still not enough to alleviate the problem and when, in 1845, potato blight finally caught up with the potato in Ireland, disaster was inevitable.

It was in the aftermath of the famine that the situation for both the land and those who laboured on it began to improve. It became obvious that the land needed to be worked in much larger areas, the small 'parcel' plots being of little use. A more balanced supply of food had to be grown so as not only to

improve the diet of the people, but to help the physical condition of the land which had been completely drained through the desperation of the rural poor. The Society of Friends, in their efforts to offer famine relief, introduced the cultivation of carrots, turnips and parsnips to the small holdings and cottiers' plots. They also encouraged green crops, for field use on the larger farms. There was a return to pastoralisation as many of the farms endeavoured to exploit the grasslands which now cover 80 per cent of Ireland's usable agricultural area. (Even today, they are Ireland's greatest natural resource.) As a result, there was a considerable increase in cattle, sheep and milk production.

Today, although only a small percentage of the population earns its living directly from the land, agriculture and its related industries are still among the most important elements in the economic life of the country. Furthermore, in spite of the fact that approximately one third of the population of the Republic of Ireland lives in Dublin and its immediate surroundings, with half the population of the north of Ireland living within a 32 kilometre (20 mile) radius of Belfast, most people still have strong connections with the country and will certainly have no difficulty in tracing their roots back to the soil.

IRISH MARKETS AND FAIRS

Of all the activities associated with agricultural produce in Ireland, the most important and enjoyable takes place at the local market. Although these are no longer as large or as numerous as they were in the nineteenth century, some form of market trading still goes on in most towns and villages throughout the country. Over the years some markets, like those of Belfast and Dublin, have been enclosed to protect them from the elements, while the large market in Cork is not only covered but has been divided into sections resembling small shops, thus providing more hygienic and comfortable trading conditions. Of all the markets still in existence, it is the one in Cork that shows off the country's produce to the full.

Each market, whether large or small, has its own individual character and specialist stalls: some are renowned for their poultry and eggs, game and meat; others for their fruit and vegetables, bedding plants, linen and hardware. Although the character of many of these has changed over the years, the atmosphere is still one of hustle and bustle, charged with excitement as people buy and sell, exchange greetings, discuss the weather and meet friends.

The markets of today remain as important centres for the social and commercial life of the community. Indeed it was these centres for selling the produce of the countryside that brought about the development of towns and villages and eventually roads which were to link one market town to another. In order for a town to be linked by such a road network it had to qualify as a market town. A patent had to be purchased which gave the right to hold either a weekly market or a fair on certain specified dates. This was usually applied for by a landlord demonstrating his intention to develop a town on his property. So, any landlord wishing to create a town had to attract people from the surrounding countryside to come and sell their produce to the towns-people and purchase goods and services in return. As a result, the towns and villages throughout Ireland were designed to accommodate the market or fair, with the predominant feature being a central square or main street where traders could set up stalls and conduct their business. The existence of addresses such as Market Street, Cornmarket, Haymarket and Fairgreen in many of our towns and villages is a constant reminder of their original function.

The town or village would be divided up into different product areas: the butchers' area for example, known as the 'Shambles', was where carcasses were dissected and sold.

There were also areas for bread and poultry, and for the two most important products, oatmeal and potatoes, both of which were referred to as 'winter food for the poor'. In fact, oatmeal was such an important commodity that in the 1740s it was brought by horse from Louth as far north as Coleraine to be sold in the local markets of the area. In the 1750s bread was brought from Dundalk to County Armagh, again to be sold in the local markets because bakeries were not in operation there at the time.

During the market or fairday the town was completely taken over by the farmers, their livestock and products along with the merchants and dealers who had come to purchase and trade. The items sold at these markets or fairs were, as today, the ordinary produce of the farms of the district. For this reason they varied from one area to another as well as from season to season: potatoes, vegetables, poultry, meat, butter and eggs were on sale alongside fuel and grain. In certain areas, where there were local industries, there was also a supply of wool, woollen yarn and cloth, linen yarn for weaving, linen cloth, baskets, wooden implements, crockery, hides, skins and oak bark for tanning. Generally the markets were larger during the autumn and winter as the cattle were coming off the grass and the crops were being harvested.

Pedlars also came to the market, bringing with them items that were not locally produced, such as salt for preserving butter, dried or salt fish and crocks for storing milk. Some markets also specialised in certain items or skills such as the sale of agricultural tools or the services of coopers, who made tubs and barrels of all shapes and sizes and for a multitude of purposes.

While the main purpose of the market, which was run from once to several times a week, was to ensure a regular supply of commodities for the townspeople, the fair was the place where people from further afield could come to trade in both seasonal and surplus products, particularly livestock.

These fairs were originally organized twice a year and lasted for several days at a time. However, with the growth in trade and industry in the seventeenth century, new patents were issued which specified four annual fairs with the emphasis on May and November, these months being the important ones for the livestock trade which was particularly valuable during this period. During the eighteenth and nineteenth centuries fairs became much more frequent, with some towns even holding them with the markets once a week and calling them 'the big market'. Many of these, however, were run without the necessary patents and were frequently poorly organised and rather boisterous. This eventually resulted in their decline as well-regulated markets and fairs attracted more customers.

Fairs were not only for the sale of goods: games, horseracing and various athletic competitions were held; public and legal business was conducted; dancing competitions took place in the square; ballads were sung on the streets and in the pubs; and matchmaking, courting and eloping went on day after day.

A delightful description of a fair at Castledermot in 1842 was written by the travel writer, William Thackeray, and recreates the typical atmosphere of such occasions:

> The long street of the place was thronged with oxen, sheep and horses and with those who wished to see or to buy. The squires were all together in a cluster at the police house; the owners of the horses rode up and down showing the best paces of their brutes: among them you might see Paddy in his ragged frieze coat seated on his donkey's bare rump and proposing him for sale. I think I saw a score of this humble though useful breed that were brought for sale to the fair. 'I can sell him,' says one fellow with a pompous air 'wid his tackle or widout.' He was looking as grave over the negotiation as if it had been for a thousand pounds.

Working horses are an increasingly rare sight.

Besides donkeys of course there was plenty of poultry and there were pigs without number, shrieking and struggling and pushing hither and thither among the crowd rebellious to the straw rope. It was a fine thing to see one huge grunter and the manner in which he was landed into a cart. The cart was let down on an easy inclined plane to tempt him. Two men ascending urged him by the fore legs, another two entreated him by the tail. At length, when more than half of his body had been coaxed upon the cart, it was suddenly whisked up causing the animal thereby to fall forward: a parting shove sent him altogether into the cart: the two gentlemen inside jumped out and the monster is left to ride home.

The important fairs still fall at the turning points of the pastoral year. The spring fairs of February and March and the Lammas Fairs of July and August were to a large extent concerned with horses, sheep and wool, while those in May and November were the great cattle and hiring fairs. The livestock economy was dominated by the great fairs of Ballinasloe, Mullingar and Banagher. At Ballinasloe in Galway the fair was held from 5 to 9 October. Its size, during the eighteenth century was obviously considerable, as can be seen from a letter written by one of the chief judges:

The whole Province of Connaught is indeed principally pasture ground, as you may judge it is from the quantity of cattle sold at one fair only at Ballinasloe which lasts four days. There is generally sold there between 60,000 and 70,000 sheep and between 20,000 and 25,000 horned cattle . . . 'Tis thought to be the greatest fair in Europe for cattle (except I think it is the fair at Leipzig and Jaginder to which great quantity are brought out of Hungary to supply a large part of Germany).

The Lammas Fairs are believed to be a continuation of the pagan Festival of Lughnasa, one of the quarterly feasts of the old Irish year. It is possible that Lammas was originally a Celtic feast adopted by the Anglo-Saxons and given a Christian name. It means 'loaf-mass' and is derived from the custom of each family presenting to the Church bread made from the first of the wheat. It was a festival of the first fruits and took place at the same time as Lughnasa, on 1 August or within the Lughnasa period of 25 July to 12 August. The Lammas Fairs were popular throughout Ireland and a number of them still exist today, albeit in a greatly modified form. One of the largest and most popular of these, specialising in livestock, is the Puck Fair at Killorglin, West Kerry, held for three days from 10 to 12 August. The first day of the fair was referred to as 'Gathering Day'; the second, 'Fair Day'; and the third, 'Scattering Day'. The fair derives its name from the Gaelic word *poc*, meaning a billy goat. Each year a goat is chosen, decorated with garlands and ribbons, paraded through the town accompanied by music and song, crowned and installed on a high wooden platform where it presides as King of the Fair for the three days, and is fed on cabbages. The procession begins at the bridge of the town on the eve of the fair and comes to rest at the stage erected at the centre of the square. On the evening of 'Scattering Day' the goat is taken down from his platform and carried, on the shoulders of four men, around the town to the shopkeepers who contribute to his 'expenses', after which he is sold by auction.

Another Lammas Fair which greatly resembles the Puck Fair at Killorglin is the Ram Fair at Greencastle in County Down, on the shores of Carlingford Lough. It originally ran for three days, beginning on 12 August, and takes its name from the custom of

Modern baling techniques have yet to reach some parts of the country.

enthroning a great ram on top of old Greencastle's walls, where it presided over what was considered to be the greatest sheep fair in south Down. A very full description of the Ram Fair, as it was in 1881, is given by Michael G. Crawford in *Legendary Stories of Carlingford Lough* (1931):

'Every road led to the Fair, and every road was black with people, hastening thither and the sea, too, was dotted with boats, yawls and yachts, bringing people from the Louth shore, and distant places outside the Bar, far along the coast. Old men and women, bouchals and colleens, all packed together, and calling gaily to each other as the boats passed, and the boatmen rowed their best or tacked and sailed to beat each other to the Mill Bay Feish.' It had all the usual participants and amusements of a country fair: tricksters, tinkers and gypsies, booths and side-shows, platforms for wrestling and boxing bouts, musicians and dancing. A memory of faction-fighting with sticks has come down, and also of another custom which it is of great interest to find here: 'the famous Shillelagh Dance, was executed to the music of the Irish bagpipes, by a number of men armed with sticks, who crossed and re-crossed them, placing them in different positions relative to each other, and presenting the most complicated figures imaginable.'

The Ould Lammas Fair, held on the last Tuesday of August at Ballycastle, is thought to be one of the oldest in Ireland. It was possibly introduced by the McDonnells of Antrim at the end of the fourteenth century as a means of distributing food to members of the clan who as yet were not quite settled in County Antrim. In this century fishermen from Islay used to come to the fair to sell great quantities of dried fish, having sailed to Ballycastle in their luggers. They returned home with various items from the fair including tinware. The fair at Ballycastle sold everything from sheep and cattle to dulse (edible seaweed) and yellowman (hard-boiled sweets). Alongside the stalls were amusements: swings, chairoplanes, hobby horses, a steam organ and entertainment provided by a strong man, a boxing champion and many of the stallholders themselves. Dancing, dealing and much drinking went on all night. Today, although it has changed in character and a much greater variety of goods are displayed for sale, the basic attraction of the fair, with its hustle and bustle, its music and its social activity, still remains.

In July and August there are also many horse and sheep fairs, with the most notable being the Muff Fair in East Cavan; the Moy Fair in County Tyrone; the Banbridge Horse Fair in County Down; the Drogheda Horse Fair in County Routh and the Ballybay Horse Fair in County Monaghan. These Irish horse fairs attracted not only local dealers but people of every nationality, who travelled from all over the country and indeed further afield to buy horses. At the Moy Fair dealers came specifically to buy for the armies of their respective countries. In addition to the horse trading, both dealer and observer enjoyed the other main business of the fair – the drinking and dancing! Indeed, fairs and markets of all kinds throughout the country were notorious for their drinking and fighting, considered by the participants as exercises in vigour and skill. One of the most infamous of all the fairs in Ireland was that held just outside Dublin at Donnybrook.

Hiring fairs were also held in most parts of Ireland and were the main places where farm labourers were employed. Some hiring fairs had special names like The Gallop in Limavady and the Loosing Fair in Newry. Another name often applied to hiring fairs was 'Rabble'. Hiring Fairs are thought to have been introduced during the reign of Edward III, when the English Parliament passed the Statute of Labourers Act which declared that magistrates must fix the wages of farm labourers and that the rates must be made known to all those concerned. The rates were publicised at the Statute Sessions around the beginning of May and in the autumn, usually 12 May (old Mayday) and 12 November (old Hallentide), the dates often varying from town to town to coincide with the normal market day. On these set days, employers and workers alike came to find out what the fixed rates were, after which the hiring of labour took place.

At almost all hiring fairs, people looking for work gathered in the centre of the town or village. Sometimes they identified themselves by holding a stalk of straw, but more often they were recognised by the bundle they carried under their arm, which contained their clothing and other personal effects. Some would also have had their tools with them.

The terms of employment between master and servant were mostly agreed verbally, being sealed at the fair by a token payment of 'earls', which ranged from a shilling to one pound. Generally the workers lived on the farm, either in separate accommodation which might be provided for whole families, or as part of the household. The female workers slept in the house; the men often in the barn. The working conditions and treatment varied greatly from farm to farm and were largely dependent on the attitude of the employer.

Although hiring fairs are a thing of the past, the tradition of holding markets and fairs throughout Ireland still remains – even if it is a little shaky in some places – as a living testimony to the richness of the land and the continued importance of agriculture in the community.

CALENDAR CUSTOMS

Even though much of the Irish population is today concentrated around the major cities, agricultural traditions have not been forgotten. Throughout the year many of the activ-

Bairm brack (page 137).

year, and so it became the time when the people gathered seaweed to fertilise their crops and collected shellfish and other shore produce. In a few places around Galway Bay a live shellfish, such as a limpet or a periwinkle, was placed at each of four corners of the house to bring good luck to the fishermen and a bountiful harvest from the shore. There were celebrations in the house, too, and a special festive supper was always prepared no matter how poor the household. Flummery, a type of oatmeal blancmange, and sowans, an oatmeal drink similar to flummery, were often on the menu and were particularly popular in Derry, while apple cake and apple dumplings were favourite items in the apple-growing county of Armagh. A type of fruit bread called bairm brack is also thought to have been associated with the festival. Butter, freshly churned that day, and buttermilk were served, and main dishes ranged from colcannon, mashed potatoes with spring onions and shredded cabbage, to fowl, bacon and even mutton in the more prosperous farmhouses. It was also customary in some areas to give gifts of butter, buttermilk or pieces of meat to poor neighbours. Indeed, pieces of bread and butter, a cake or dish of porridge were often left out for St Brighid herself.

Shrove Tuesday, the next event in the festive calendar, marks the last day before the beginning of Lent. It was a time for hunting the hare and for feasting, and to fatten up before the Lenten austerities began. The Lenten fast in former times was a very strict occasion, during which no animal product of any kind could be eaten: no meat, eggs, butter, lard, milk or cheese. To dispose of the excess stocks of butter, milk and eggs before the fast began, pancakes were made and became the integral feature of the celebratory meal. In Ireland, Shrove Tuesday is still very much a family festival and tossing the pancakes around the fire or at the

ities and food customs of the farming community are celebrated in the towns and villages, almost as vigorously as in the heart of the country.

Such activities and customs were created in accordance with the calendar year which, in the old Irish calendar, was divided into four quarters: Imbolic (February); Beltane (May); Lughnasa (August); Samhain (November). Each of these quarters had its own specific celebrations, influenced by the pastoral and arable traditions.

Although New Year's Day marks the beginning of the calendar year in most parts of Europe, it has never been a major festival in Ireland. The start of the year in Ireland's rural calendar is 1 February – the beginning of spring, marked by Saint Brighid's Day. It was said that on this day the saint placed her foot in the water and warmed it, giving rise to the belief that from that time on the weather should improve, spring ploughing could begin and milk and butter production would increase.

On the coast, the spring tide closest to the festival was believed to be the greatest of the

Stirabout or porridge (page 153).

stove is very much part of the activities.

The ban on animal products throughout the period of Lent meant considerable hardship to an agricultural community. More seriously, bread – one of the people's staple foods – was also forbidden, for the bread of the Irish is leavened with sour milk or buttermilk and baking soda. Milk was therefore not used for bread-making during Lent, and yeast, barm or sourdough were substituted as leven. The poor, however, had neither the knowledge or the means to produce such bread and had to be content with oatcakes. Their diet was so frugal normally that they were granted a small amount of dispensation by the ecclesiastical authorities, allowing them to eat what they could, when they could get it.

A farming family of slightly greater means would generally have had a meal of dry oatcake or porridge and black tea, morning and evening, with the main meal being at midday and consisting of potatoes, perhaps with a little fish and onions to flavour it. On the coast shellfish and edible seaweed would accompany the potatoes, and the drink, normally sweet or sour milk, was replaced by a fermented drink of water and oats called bull's milk.

All who could afford to do so laid in a stock of salt fish, ranging from a few salt herring or ling, which would be hung from the rafters on a piece of string or withy (flexible willow stick), to a whole barrel full of salt herring in the more prosperous households. But even then the quantities eaten were very sparing and of secondary importance to the potatoes. A portion of meat was also hung up in the rafters and only taken down on Easter Sunday, when it was burned on the fire to give the house a good rich smell.

Good Friday was a very austere occasion, with many people fasting for a large part of the day and having only a light meal of fish in the evening. Good Friday was also an im-

portant day in the farmer's year because it was thought that it was the luckiest day to begin sowing the corn or a few potatoes, but apart from that very little other work was done. It was also the one day in the year when no fishing boats put to sea, and fishing with nets and lines was discouraged. However, those who lived along the coast gathered shellfish and edible seaweed, which they ate as their main meal. Today on Good Friday, hot-cross buns are sold by town bakers throughout the country, but this was not always a traditional custom in Ireland.

Eggs laid on Good Friday were marked with a cross and each member of the family ate one on Easter Sunday.

By Easter Day a superfluity of eggs had accumulated, so it was not surprising that they featured heavily in all the preparations and the festive activities. They were used for all sorts of things – eaten in large amounts for breakfast on Easter Sunday morning, made into cakes, decorated and given as presents.

The Easter Sunday dinner was also a festive meal, second in importance only to that on Christmas Day. Meat was eaten by people who could afford it: roast veal, young lamb or kid. Wealthier farmers may have killed a bullock for the festival and sent presents of portions of it to friends and poorer neighbours. Frequently the beef had been slaughtered in the early winter and salted down for use throughout the year, with special joints being reserved for festivals and important occasions.

On Easter Sunday throughout Ireland, at the crossroads of a town or on a convenient spot of ground or other public place, generally outside if the weather permitted, a cake dance was held. The cake was either a bairm brack, a boxty cake, a griddle cake or a barley or oaten bannock. The cake was ceremoniously set on top of a churn dash, or plunger, and the dance began. When the dance was over, the best male and female dancers were chosen and it was their honour to take down the cake and divide it among all the rest of the dancers.

In a number of towns herring processions or herring funerals were also held by the town butchers to symbolise the demise of the herring and the return of meat eating at the end of Lent. It was reported that in a few towns, such as Drogheda, Dundalk and Cork, the herring was hung on a long rod and carried through the town, being beaten by sticks along its journey until there was very little, if anything, left of it.

The next major festival in the rural calendar is the Gaelic Beltaine or May Day, the day that marks the beginning of the summer. At one time it was particularly important to the housewife, who took pride in being able to provide a dish of 'stirabout' (porridge made from oat or wheaten meal) because it was evidence of her thrifty housekeeping that she had managed to make her corn last through the winter and could begin the summer with a substantial dish. It was a great struggle for poor households to stretch the corn out to this time as they had very little else to eat.

Many superstitions were associated with May Day, particularly those connected to the supernatural world. Witches and fairies were thought to be active at this time and precautions were taken to ward off their evil intentions. Not only were wells, fields, byres and houses guarded, but on May Eve bonfires were lit and both men and women 'leapt the flames' before driving their cattle through the smouldering ashes or between two small fires to protect them from witchcraft. But it was the milk cows that needed the most protection, because their 'white meat' provided the main source of food for the people throughout the year. Milk was poured on the threshold of the house, or at the roots of the fairy thorn, and in the Glens of Antrim it was said that May flowers were crushed to provide a juice which was then used to wash the cows' udders. Sometimes their backs were marked with the sign of the cross and, after milking on May Day, a cross was made with the froth of the milk. A bunch of primroses was tied to each cow's tail as it was thought to ensure protection against the evil spirits. A sprig of rowan was also thought to be one of the best protections against evil: it might be placed on the byre door or on the milking vessel, or hung on the cow's horns. It was also used to protect the arable land, and in some areas was stuck in the ground of the potato crop. Sometimes not even rowan offered protection against the butter-stealing witches and, as a result, no milk was given away on May Day and no stranger was allowed to milk the cows. Much attention was also paid to butter-making and a small quantity of butter made on this day, and known as 'May butter', was kept in the dairy for the rest of the season.

Another important day in the agricultural calendar was the Summer Solstice or St John's Day on 24 June, which was celebrated with a wealth of customs and superstitions, many similar to those observed on May Day. However, midsummer was also an important date in some fishing communities because it was the day that the boats and nets were blessed. At Portballintrae in County Antrim the salmon fishermen of the River Bush celebrated by holding a communal dinner, considered to be the event of the year and known locally as The Salmon Dinner. The menu consisted of fish soup, freshly caught salmon, new potatoes and, naturally, Bushmills whiskey.

The period between St John's Day and the harvesting of the potatoes (before the new early varieties were introduced) was called the Bitter Six Weeks, because it was during this time that most food stocks put away from the harvest the previous year were near their end and as a result rations were short. For this reason, there are also many references to 'The Hungry Month', 'Hungry July' and 'July of the Cabbage'. In past centuries this period ended with the festival that marked the beginning of harvest, the Festival of Lughnasa on 1 August. This has continued in recent times, except that the celebrations connected with Lughnasa, or Lammas Day, are now held on either the last Sunday in July or the first Sunday in August.

It was the aim of the farming community to have the first of the crops ready for harvesting by Lughnasa, so that at least part of it could be used to prepare the festive meal. This generally consisted of new potatoes, skimmed milk, bacon, fowl, fish, beef, mutton or cabbage; whatever the household could afford. Bread and porridge made with the first corn were also served sometime during the day. Another feature of the festive meal was fresh fruit. This might have been garden fruits such as gooseberries or currants, or the wild fruits from the heather hills or woods such as whortleberries, blaeberries, wild raspberries or strawberries.

In addition to the festival meal there were excursions to the hills for picnics, in which both young and old took part. The main event of the picnic was the gathering of blaeberries (bilberries), and for this reason the Sunday before Lammas is often called Bilberry Sunday.

Champ (page 82).

During September and early October frenzied work went on throughout the countryside to ensure that the harvest was safely gathered in. This was followed by a 'harvest home', a celebratory meal given by the farmer and his wife to the workers, which would take place in the kitchen or, in the very large farms of the south and east, in a barn. The size and type of food served at the harvest home depended largely on the size and wealth of the farm, but it generally consisted of normal country fare, albeit in more liberal quantities than at normal meals. Many accounts tell of bread, milk and milk products, with stronger drink provided during the dancing. Some mention a main dish of beef, bacon or chicken, served with cabbage and potatoes; others refer to oatcakes being served with cream; while others mention a meal of rice cooked in sheep's milk. Sometimes the milk traditionally served with everyday meats would be replaced by porter or beer.

In the south-west of Ireland the end of the potato harvest was celebrated by a 'stampy party' for the workers and helpers, so-called because the main dish was cakes of 'stampy', a bread made from grated raw potatoes, squeezed dry and mixed with flour and various flavourings.

Many of these feasts and celebrations pale in significance when compared to the festival which marks the dying, or end, of the rural year on All-Hallows Eve on 31 October – better known as Hallowe'en; Samhain, 1 November in the ancient calendar. Superstitions and folklore abound at this time, and a multitude of special foods are associated with the occasion.

The vigil of the Feast of All Saints has for many centuries been a day of abstinence, that is to say, a day on which no meat was eaten. For this reason, the traditional dishes at Hallowe'en did not include meat and different localities had their own special dishes. County Armagh celebrates with

potato-apple cake and potato-apple dumpling; Counties Tyrone, Cavan, Fermanagh and Derry specialise in boxty pancakes, boxty dumplings, boxty bread, potato pudding and colcannon. Bairm brack, oatcakes, batter pancakes, apple cake and blackberry pies, along with apples and nuts, are also Hallowe'en favourites.

No matter what the dish chosen for the Hallowe'en supper or 'tea', a wedding ring and various other charms, carefully wrapped in greaseproof paper, are baked inside it. This will decide the destiny during the coming year of the person finding it on their plate.

The Christmas season, although one of the most important in the Christian calendar in Ireland, was never a major secular festival, probably because the traditional farming year ended in November. However, there are a number of foods and customs associated with it. Shortly before Christmas some of the family went to the nearby town to 'bring home Christmas'. This was usually on the day of the Christmas market called the Margadh Mor, the 'Big Market'. To this they brought the produce of their farms – butter and eggs, hens, geese, turkeys and vegetables – then, with the money obtained from these, they made their own Christmas purchases of meat and other little luxuries, like dried fruits, spice, sugar and tea. Tea was very much a luxury and was often only drunk on Christmas Day. Whiskey, wine and beer may also have been bought, and toys and sweets for the children.

If presents were given at all, they would have been in the form of food. Bacon, eggs, potatoes and fowl were given by the country people to their relatives and friends in the town, and presents of 'town goods' were received in return.

Christmas Eve was observed as a fast day and many people did not eat until the main evening meal which generally consisted of

Shin and Guinness and beef stew with dumplings (page 68).

fish, such as cod, hake or ling, with white sauce and potatoes. Some waited until midnight, when the candles were lit and the Christmas celebrations began with the cutting of the Christmas cake and the taking of tea punch, whiskey and other drinks. The children were given sweets and apples.

Christmas Day was marked by church services, visits from family and friends and special meals. In Ulster many a poor family had their only meat dish of the year, remembered in the County Down saying 'Glory be to Christmas, the day we get the beef'. More often than not, however, the beef was a goose. Prosperous farmers usually killed a bullock, calf, pig or sheep before Christmas and, as well as enjoying it on their own Christmas table, shared it with their poor neighbours and their work people. Often this was salted beef from the animals killed at Martinmas. Roast or boiled beef seems to have been the most popular Irish Christmas dish, which is remembered today in the spiced beef that is still eaten at Christmas throughout the country. A boiled ox head was a favourite dish in Armagh, Tyrone and Monaghan. Sometimes the dinner would have included chicken or goose, as well as bacon and mutton.

Cakes, puddings and pies were all made well in advance in the more prosperous farmhouses. 'Cutlin pudding' was made on Christmas Eve in County Wexford. This consisted of a thick porridge of wheaten meal, with sugar, spices and fruit added and the whole made into a ball, about the size of a football, which was then wrapped in a greased cloth ready for boiling. Another pudding was made from bread and potatoes and boiled in a calico bag suspended in the cooking pot.

Although today the Christmas pudding is more refined, less stodgy and generally boiled in a pudding basin rather than a bag, many other festive foods and dishes are still the same and are used to celebrate the traditions of our agricultural past.

THE FARMHOUSE TRADITION

It was in the eighteenth and nineteenth centuries that very detailed accounts of agricultural practices became known. It was through the writings of the travel commentators who visited Ireland during this time, observing the countryside and reporting on it and the life of the people, that we are able to form a true picture of life in rural Ireland. It would certainly appear from these, and from the number of government reports written on the state of agriculture in Ireland during this period, that agricultural society was divided into a number of different levels. These ranged from the smallest and poorest farm where the people just managed to scrape an existence from the land, through the middle class or 'strong' farm which was able to afford a comfortable existence, to that of the landowner whose manor and estate clearly displayed considerable wealth and elegance.

Although I was not born or bred in the 'country', my memories of times spent there at the homes of my relatives are just as vivid today as when I was a child. Here I was introduced to many new experiences and an entirely different style of life to the rather

ABOVE: *Hens were an important source of food and income on every farm.*

OPPOSITE: *Traditionally, oatcakes (page 136) were cooked on a griddle over a turf fire and then leant against a metal stand to dry out.*

refined and sheltered one I was more accustomed to in Belfast. The two main farms where I stayed were in County Armagh and County Cavan. These would once have been described as 'strong' farms, for they comprised a substantial house, outbuildings, animals and land. Staying there at different times of the year not only enabled me to experience this level of farm and all its activities, but provided me with the opportunity to see many different examples of Irish farms and houses which varied greatly in size and stature and had changed very little from the time of the eighteenth- and nineteenth-century travel writers. The lowest level of these dated back to the 1840s and consisted solely of a house. It was here that not only the family lived, but where the cow, the pig and the hen were also accommodated. Although this custom was regarded as the sign of a very primitive people by the nineteenth-century travellers, it was in fact practised by many pastoral peoples throughout Europe. The habit, with a few exceptions of course, came to an end earlier this century.

The basic type of farmhouse was generally made from mud, stone or brick, depending on what was most readily available in the area. Mud houses were most common in Leinster, but were also found in the provinces of Munster, Connaught and Ulster, when stone was scarce. Stone houses were built in most places, but principally in mountainous districts, and turf sods, cut from the peat bogs, were used to make homes for the very poor. To protect these houses against the weather they were covered with coats of limewash which were renewed every year. During the nineteenth century brick-making became a local industry and some red-brick houses began to appear, but this was generally only where there was a reforming landlord.

These farmhouses were long and narrow, in fact it was thought to be unlucky if they were more than one room wide. If cows were also to be accommodated they were tethered to the end wall of the house, the one farthest from the hearth. An open drain below their tails ran under one of the side walls and led into a manure pit just outside. A general feature of these 'byre-houses' was two doors, one opposite the other, with flagstones between them. This served as a passage for the cow, which was driven out through the back door after milking. When the cows were removed from the house, the byre area was converted into a bedroom.

Another common feature of many of these simple houses, particularly in the eastern half of Ireland – roughly from Derry to Cork – was the jamb wall, sometimes called the Holland wall in Ulster. This was a screen made of wood, mud or stone, which was built directly in front of the entrance door and coming out from the side of the fire so as to partition it off and reduce the draught from the door. These screen walls were generally built in houses where the door opened directly into the hearth area in the centre of the house, which caused smoke problems when the chimney did not 'draw' well. The jamb wall usually had a small window in it so that the person sitting by the fire could see out. This window also helped to let in the light

from the open half-door (another feature of the Irish farmhouse) which, apart from a few small narrow windows, was the only source of light.

In some houses in the north-west of the country, there was also a small rectangular outshot or annex on one of the side walls at the chimney-end of the kitchen. This was called a *cailleach* and provided the space for a bed beside the warmth of the fire.

The roof, like the thick lime-washed walls, the tiny window and the half-door, was another architectural feature which added variety to these simple houses. There were a number of different types of roof and thatch: some which gave the impression of having no ridge; others with hipped or stepped gables. The timbers supporting the thatch were usually A-shaped couples, traditionally made of bog oak. These coupled rafters held long purlins which supported a layer of branches or laths of bog fir. On top of these were placed strips of scraws (sods) to help keep the damp out and the heat in, as well as forming a base on which the straw could be secured. The first thin layer of thatch was sewn to this using a thatching needle and hay-rope, followed by the outer thatch which could be in one of several regional styles.

The floor of the house was much less sophisticated and was usually made of beaten earth or 'daub', as it was commonly called. Stone flags were greatly favoured and even the poorest homes would have had at least a few around the hearth.

THE HEART OF THE HOUSE

In all of these houses, irrespective of their size and sophistication, the most important place was the hearth. This was not only the focal point of the house but the centre of activity – the very heart of the Irish home and the family. The turf fire which burned continuously on this hearth was the symbol of the continuity of the family and hospitality towards both friend and stranger. It was often said that if the fire went out, the

souls of the people of the house would leave, and for this reason the fire was always kept burning. At night a live turf was buried in the ashes to retain a spark which could be fanned into a blaze of life the next morning.

In the earliest houses the hearth was in the middle of the floor and the smoke escaped through a smoke hole in the roof. Later houses always had the hearth either on the gable wall, in the case of byre-type houses, or in the centre of those of the jamb-wall type. From the sixteenth century onwards the use of chimney flues helped to remove the smoke from the cottages and gave rise to many different regional styles of chimney breast in brick, stone, clay-plastered wickerwork or of lath and plaster. As chimney flues were more constricted, in the nineteenth century it became the practice to build small lofts on each side in front of the chimney. These were used for storage or as additional sleeping accommodation.

The hearth was situated in the main room, or in some cases the only room, in the house. Here the family sat in the evening and discussed the news of the day. There was always space for both family and friends around the fire and, although seats were scarce in these farmhouses, something to rest on could usually be found. In some homes a wooden or stone seat was built near the hearth, and the settle bed beside the fire could also be used as a seat during the daytime. If there were chairs, they were made either of wood or straw or a combination of a wooden frame and twisted straw-rope seat ('suggan' chairs). These upright chairs generally had a short back and legs, but sometimes also had arms and were made into rocking chairs. Because of their shape, they were particularly well suited to the unevenness of the ground. Stools were more common than chairs and the three-legged variety in wood was used everywhere and referred to as a 'creeper'; straw versions were known as 'bosses'. Sods of turf were also used as stools. The most important seats in the house, the seats of honour reserved for the head of the house and guests, were on either side of the fire, the nearest place to the heat.

THE IRISH FIRE

The fire was not only the main source of heat for keeping the family warm, it was the only source for cooking. Consequently, the hearth had to accommodate all that was required, from boiling water to baking bread. The built-in oven never really became a common feature of the Irish home, except perhaps in the case of the larger 'strong' farmhouse and the home of the local cleric. It certainly did not exist in the houses I was familiar with in Cavan and Armagh.

Here, as in nearly every other part of Ireland, the fire was at floor level, not raised in a grate. This meant that portions of the fire could be moved about the hearth, creating several sources of heat. The main one was under the big pot; a smaller one below and on top of the 'bastable', or pot-oven, baking bread; a teapot would sit on another; with maybe a flat iron on the fourth.

From the nineteenth century two methods of suspending cooking pots over the fire were used throughout Ireland: the 'crook' and the 'crane'. The crook, the oldest form of suspension, was hung above the hearth from a beam of wood positioned at a safe distance from the fire. The crook, like the crane, was made of iron, though some made of holly-wood have been known. It terminated in a hook from which the pots were hung. The iron crane is more characteristic of stone fireplaces than those with wattled braces because, being required to carry very heavy pots or cauldrons which could be swung in and out over the fire, the support needed to be strong. Generally a number of hooks were hung from the crane, at least one of these being adjustable to allow pots to be brought nearer to or taken further from the fire. The arm of the crane swung out into the room to enable the cook to remove boiling pots without stooping directly over the fire. It was a heavy, hot and

dangerous activity, which not only required strength but skill – facts I never realised until I began to cook on the open hearth myself.

COOKING EQUIPMENT

The cooking equipment used on this type of hearth generally included a number of cast-iron pots or cauldrons, introduced into the country by the Normans in the seventeenth century. There would be a few three-legged pots with capacities ranging from 2 to 90 litres ($\frac{1}{2}$–20 gallons). The large pots were used to boil food for the pigs and other animals; for boiling water; for washing clothes, and for dyeing wool for home-spinning. The pot-oven – a form of Dutch oven – was primarily used for baking, but also for roasting and boiling. Indeed, the best roast beef I ever tasted, and which I vividly remember to this day, was the Sunday joint cooked in a pot-oven over the glowing embers of my aunt's fire. While this pot hung on one hook from the crane, another filled with boiling potatoes swung from a second hook alongside it. A third and smaller pot, also suspended from a hook, cooked the carrots, parsnips and other vegetables. It was a cross between a balancing act and a piece of Gaudi architecture. I have yet to discover how this elderly lady ever managed to produce such meals for ten of us and get them to the table piping hot, complete with roast potatoes, gravy and an apple tart for afters – also cooked in a pot-oven.

This pot-oven can also be set on a trivet or just left standing on its own feet on the flagstones. The lid is dished so that the turves may be placed on top as well as below, thus giving heat all round which is particularly valuable when roasting meat or baking bread – the other main use of this particular pot.

In addition to the pots, the other cast-iron cooking equipment included a griddle, a flat circular plate about 46 centimetres (18 inches) in diameter with two lugs, or ears, from which to hang it over the fire. It was on this griddle that all the flat breads and cakes,

such as oatcake, soda farls and potato cake, were baked. Bread stands, or sticks, were used for hardening-off oatcakes in front of the fire. A frying pan, kettle, tongs, pot hooks, bellows, poker and brush were also part of the hearth furniture in most farmhouses. Spit stands, however, would only have been found in the more prosperous or 'strong' farmhouses. All of these items were stored at the side of the hearth and when well polished their shiny black surfaces reflected the glow from the fire, creating a very homely atmosphere.

KITCHEN FURNITURE

The rest of the furniture in the Irish farmhouse, like everything else, varied depending on the wealth or poverty of the family, but generally the kitchen would be equipped with a few basic items. There would be a bin made of wood in which the family's supply of grain was stored. This had a sloping lid and, in recent years, was divided into two compartments to hold both oatmeal and flour. There were flat wooden baking boards on which to work griddle bread and cakes, and possibly a rolling pin.

Tables are of a comparatively recent origin and were not part of the furniture of poor homes until well into this century. In such homes the family sat around the fire and ate from a wicker basket set on top of a three-legged pot. Baskets were also used for many other purposes in the Irish kitchen, such as holding the turf for the fire and the potatoes before and after being cooked. Where tables were found they stood against the wall, were made of scrubbed oak and were used for baking and food preparation rather than eating from. In earlier periods small boards were used as tables and hung on the wall when not in use. An extension of this principle was used in the tables hinged to the wall, which had a collapsible leg, or legs, which also made for easy storage. Such tables were very prevalent in Ulster, even in the city houses where space was limited.

Pottery vessels were used in Ireland from the Neolithic period, and wood was turned into all sorts of containers and widely used up until the nineteenth century; horn was made into spoons. It was not until the eighteenth century that delft-ware was used for crocks, bowls, jugs and jars in wealthier homes; these were manufactured locally and imported.

By 1900 most 'strong' farmhouses in Ireland had a dresser in which to hold and display a collection of mugs, plates and dishes, and store food. Such dressers were probably copied from those found in medieval castles. Dressers of different types were to be found throughout Ireland and were the most striking feature of rural homes. Irrespective of the design, they all had two features in common: an upper and lower section. The upper section consisted of two or three shelves on which the dishes and plates rested, with the cups being hung from hooks on the front of the shelves. The lower section was deeper than the upper and had a top which formed a work area and an open space below where water pails, crocks and milking vessels were stored. This bottom section was sometimes used as a coop for the hens.

In my aunt's home there was also a small cold room, a sort of walk-in larder, where the milk, butter, eggs, sides of bacon and pails of water were stored. Behind this lay the dairy where the milk was stored and the cream separated and made into butter. When there was an excess of milk, butter and cheese were also made. This was very much a feature of a 'strong' farm, for in poorer homes, butter was prepared in the kitchen where the butter-making equipment was also kept.

Even in the poorest dwellings, where there was perhaps only one cow, some simple items for collecting the milk and making the butter and curds were required. Milking vessels varied from simple wooden pails to special metal milking cans. A 'tinny', a tin bucket, was also used, though it was originally meant to be a water carrier. Once the milk was brought into the house it was poured into earthenware or wooden bowls, or 'keelers' as they were known in Donegal, where it was allowed to settle. Wooden skimmers were used to remove the cream for butter-making in farmhouses like my aunt's, where the quantity of milk was sufficient to produce enough cream to churn. In most homes, where there were only a few cows, the whole milk would be churned to make butter. Every house had a churn, but its size depended on the number of cattle owned. The most common was the dash, or plunge, churn, a stoutly built wooden vessel, more or less conical in shape, waisted near the top with a splayed neck into which the lid fitted. The staves used to make up the churn were generally made of oak and held together with hoops of split hazel, sally rods or metal. The cream or milk was agitated by a wooden dash, or plunger. This had a long handle which went through the centre of the lid and was plunged up and down to make the butter – a very slow and tiring process. In the nineteenth century the larger farms would have used the barrel churn. This, as its name implies, consisted of a large barrel supported on a stand which was rotated on its axis by means of a crank handle, the milk inside being agitated by means of fixed flanges. After churning, the butter was washed and turned into large wooden bowls where it was salted and worked with either a butter spade – a mushroom-shaped butter worker – or the side of a small wooden bowl. In the early eighteenth and nineteenth centuries the butter was stored until there was enough to fill a firkin, which could be sold at the local market. Nowadays, nearly all the milk produced goes to the creameries, from where it is sold as liquid milk and cream, or processed into butter, yoghurt or cheese.

The kitchen was therefore truly the heart of the house. In the larger farmhouses it was also physically at the centre of the house, with all the additional rooms leading from it. The bedroom would have been at one end, with a room called the parlour at the other. The parlour was usually behind the chimney breast to keep it warm, or it may even have had a hearth of its own. It was often referred to as the west or back room and was reserved for the elderly, guests occasionally, and for laying-out the dead for the wake. In the larger 'strong' farmhouses there might also have been a dining room. Most houses had one or more attics, usually called lofts; one of these may have been used as an additional sleeping space, but in larger houses they were generally always well-furnished bedrooms.

THE 'BIG' HOUSE
In contrast to these simple country farmhouses, the manor houses – of which there were several thousand throughout Ireland – shared not only the architectural features but the lifestyle of their English counterparts. The size and splendour of these dwellings ranged from compact gentleman's residences to extensive mansions, like Russborough in County Wicklow and Carton in County Kildare. The lords of these manor houses spent much of their time away from their estates, socialising in London, Dublin and Europe along with society's international elite. As a result, family life was far removed from the symbolic Irish hearth and the style of living was more elaborate and sophisticated than in the humble dwellings of the vast majority of the Irish people.

One of the main contributions that these manor houses made to the Irish kitchen was the introduction of new culinary ideas and recipes, many of which are to be found in the 'receipt' manuscript books of the eighteenth and nineteenth centuries. The influence of these eventually percolated through the rest of society, combining with the dishes already in existence and creating the Irish cuisine with which we are familiar today.

CLOCKWISE, FROM TOP: *Soda farls (page 133), an Irish fry (page 60) and currant soda (page 132).*

LIVING OFF THE LAND

The agricultural activities generated around the Irish farmhouse were always largely dependent on the type of land on which it was situated, its size, wealth and needs, along with the general economic climate of the time. However, the majority of Irish farms, whatever their size and wherever situated – be it on fertile land or barren and mountainous terrain – generally included a little of both arable and pastoral farming, with the emphasis being placed on whatever the land and other circumstances dictated. Milk production was significant on lush fertile regions such as the Roe Valley, along the Shannon Estuary, the grazing lands of Meath and Kildare, and particularly in the Golden Vale of Tipperary. This area, even today, is one of the most prosperous regions in the country, with the largest farms and the most important centres for commercial milk production.

Although such areas offer the best grazing land, other less fertile and more hilly and mountainous regions also provide grazing for the hardy breed of cattle popular in Ireland. These include the Longhorn, the Kerry and the Moilie cattle, whose ancestors date as far

ABOVE: *Carrots were introduced to the small holdings and cottiers' plots to alleviate the effects of the famine.*

OPPOSITE: *Arable and pastoral farming have long been a twin concern of those living off the land.*

back as the Iron Age. As well as being suited to all types of areas, these breeds could be used for both milk and meat production as required. This meant that farms almost everywhere, even the smallest and most remote, could survive, albeit in many cases at subsistence level.

THE DAIRYING TRADITION

Milk and its products have been of prime importance in the Irish diet throughout history, and to the life of the community certainly up until the introduction of the potato in the seventeenth century.

Many different types of milk and milk products were enjoyed, from sweet milk of thin consistency to thick milk of a sour taste, and from simple curds to cheese. Collectively these products were known as *banbidh* – anglicised by the Elizabethans to 'white meats', using meat in its original sense as a food.

Milk

Fresh or 'sweet' milk, as it is often referred to in Ireland, is the milk straight from the cow, hot and frothy with a warm comforting

IN AN IRISH COUNTRY KITCHEN

smell. I can remember only too well the many futile attempts I made to milk a cow, precariously balanced on a three-legged stool in the byre, with my experienced country cousins finding the entire proceedings too amusing for words. I never did manage to perfect the art, but acquired many a wet milky face through trying. This fresh milk was originally taken as it was as a drink, combined with oats to make porridge, or used to make butter, curds, whey and cheese. In later times it was also used to make puddings and sauces, or combined with other foods to produce the popular dishes of the day. In earlier agricultural Ireland milk was also drunk sour. This sour milk was a thick milk, *bainne clabair* – referred to by the English travel writers as 'bonny clabber' – and although sour to the taste, had not yet separated into curds and whey. It was soured either naturally – in other words, by just letting it sit around until it went 'off', which would not have been difficult considering there were no means of preserving it – or by putting fresh milk into a vessel that had previously contained sour milk, which in turn soured the fresh milk.

Butter

One of the main uses of milk was in the production of butter. For this, either the whole milk or the 'ripe' (slightly sour) cream was used. If the butter was to be eaten immediately, with very little or no salt added to it, it was referred to as 'fresh' butter. If, however, salt was added, generally as a preservative, it was considered an inferior product. The Irish Laws, popularly known as the Brehon Laws, stated that the sons of inferior grades, or farmers, were to have 'salted' butter (*gruiten*) with their stirabout, or porridge, while it was laid down that the sons of chieftains should have 'fresh' butter (*im ur*), and the sons of kings, honey.

Salt or 'preserved' butter was stored in firkins, baskets, or bags of cloth or leather. Many examples of these have been found throughout the peat bogs of Ireland and are referred to as 'bog butter'. It is fairly generally accepted that these containers of butter were deliberately placed in the bog, where it was cool and moist, as a simple method of preserving them during the summer months when there was an excess, to be retrieved again in times of scarcity. It is also possible that butter was kept in the bog during the summer months until it could be sold at the end of the season, when the herders and butter-makers returned from the summer pastures on the mountainside.

By the end of the nineteenth century, owing to the modernisation of Irish agricultural methods combined with changes in land use and ownership, this summer pasture system had all but disappeared and with it many ancient dairying practices. As far as the original methods of making butter are concerned, information is scant, but it is thought that churning probably took place either by stirring the cream in a dish or tub with a stick, shaking it in a closed container, or working a dash or plunger in a stationary vessel until lumps of butter formed (see page 34). This procedure of agitating cream until lumps of butter are produced is more rough-and-ready than the modern form of butter-making which involves churning the butter to a grain and then washing out the buttermilk.

The making of butter, both for family consumption and for trading, played a very important part in the economic development of Ireland in the nineteenth century. On a small scale, butter was used by families as a means of exchange for other food items and commodities, or sold at local markets to produce a meagre income for the household. Where production was greater, the butter was taken to the nearest major town or butter centre, where it was sold locally or exported. Cork city, because of the strong trading association it had set up, was considered to be the great emporium of the Irish butter trade and the main export outlet for

the whole country.

The need for the butter industry as a whole to produce a more standardised and hygienic product brought about its transformation from what was a simple farm activity into the more centralised and commercial system of the Irish Co-operative Dairy Movement. This movement helped to establish the dairy industry as one of the major industries in Ireland today, renowned for its quality and exporting throughout the world.

Buttermilk

One of the by-products of butter is the milk left over after the butter is removed from the churn. This buttermilk, until quite recently, was highly prized in Ireland as a drink and was served with almost every meal. In my aunt's home one of the favourite meals at any time of the day was a big plate of boiled potatoes in their skins with lots of fresh butter, washed down with a mug of buttermilk. In most houses, particularly country farmhouses, buttermilk also played an important part in the making of curds and cheese. In addition to this it was one of the essential ingredients in many of the traditional Irish breads and remains so to this day.

In Ireland just after World War II, when buttermilk was not so readily available, milk from a 'buttermilk plant' – a plant-like structure composed of yeast and bacteria – was used. Florence Irwin, in her book *The Cookin' Woman: Irish Country Recipes and Others*, recounts a charming story in which an Irishman and his wife, who owned a hotel in Southampton, obtained a buttermilk plant in 1938 while travelling on a train through Central Europe. They were in a carriage full of nuns fleeing from their convent and after helping them one nun gave them her most valued possession – a buttermilk plant. The plant was carefully brought back to England and eventually, for safety, taken to County Down during the war.

Florence Irwin also describes how the

Dairy farming is one of Ireland's major industries.

plant, which she says resembles a lumpy milk food, should be washed every two to four days depending on the ambient temperature; the skim-milk in which it grew was to be strained off for use every fourth day; the plant container then washed; more skim-milk added and the process continued again. As the plant increased in size it was shared with others. When my grandmother no longer lived in the country she cultivated one such plant, so that she would always have a ready supply of fresh 'buttermilk' with which to make her favourite soda bread and pancakes.

A good substitute for buttermilk today, if it is not available, is natural yoghurt. For bread-making either this or 'sweet' milk can be used as long as a chemical raising agent, such as baking soda (bicarbonate soda) and cream of tartar (tartaric acid) or commercially prepared baking powder, is first sieved with the flour.

Curds

Although milk was used to make butter it would appear that originally its main use was in the preparation of curds (*gruth*), one of the most important foods of the Irish certainly up until the introduction of the potato in the seventeenth century. The Brehon Laws describe curds as a condiment for bread; as being used as a form of currency by the 'inferior' grades of society to pay rent; as the summer food for men on sick maintenance, and as a fine for the trespass of dogs. Curds also became part of the normal monastic diet, and a medieval poet even suggests that the weary warriors returning from their circuit of Ireland in AD 942 were refreshed on their home-coming with 'three score vats of curds, which banished the hungry look of the army'. In *The Vision of MacConglinne* 'curds', 'real curds' and 'old curds' feature many times in the lists of foods.

These curds were prepared by letting them form through the natural souring of the milk, or by speeding up the process with the addition of rennet from a calf's stomach, or by souring the new milk with buttermilk. The latter method was described by the travel commentator John Dunton in *Iar-Choacht* in 1698: 'The next morning a greate pott full of new milk was sett over the fire, and when it was hott they pour'd into it a pale full of butter-milk which made a mighty dish of touch curds in the middle of which they placed a pound weight of butter.'

Curds for immediate consumption were

called *gruth*; sour milk curds, *tath*; sweet milk curds (those made from fresh milk) *millsen*; buttermilk curds, *mulchan*; and curds made from *biestings* (the first milk of the cow), *maethal* and *gruthnuis*.

Cheese

Curds were not only eaten just as they were, but it seems that, with varying degrees of pressure, they were turned into cheese (*cais*), carrying in some instances the names of the type of milk used in their production. Production is probably too sophisticated a word for a process which more likely than not just happened as an accident of curd-making, perhaps the result of leaving soured milk too

long, thus precipitating much harder, tougher curds. These heavy curds, either pressed or unpressed, were known as 'curd cheese'.

From early Irish texts we know that many different types of cheese were produced, but apart from their names and a few references to their texture it is hard to know exactly what they were like. Their names were often taken from the curds themselves. It seems that *tath* was a cheese made from sour milk; *millsen*, a sweet cheese made from sweet milk; and *maethal*, as its name suggests (soft, tender, yielding), a soft cheese. In the life of St Kevin, reference is made to a number of women who are said to have carried these

cheeses (*maothla*) in the corners of their cloaks; a number of texts suggest that they were round and quite large in shape. *Mulchan* was a cheese made from buttermilk curds and seems to have been of a similar texture, shape and size to *maethal*, since in texts the words seem to be interchangeable. It also seems to have remained popular until the eighteenth and nineteenth centuries. *Tanach*, or *tanag*, was a hard-pressed cheese made from skimmed milk.

A wide range of cheese was produced from the milk of cows, goats and sheep. A survey of Kilkenny carried out in the early nineteenth century refers to the making and selling of sheep's cheese:

It is their practice [the farmers'] to milk the ewes for two months, and even three, after the lambs are weaned. They say it does not injure the ewes, who generally breed for five years, and are then fattened. Of the milk, cheeses are made, which are sold to persons who come about for the purpose of buying them and retailing them in the market of Kilkenny. The cheese weighs about two pounds, and is sold for one shilling by the farmers.

Although written information on both pressed and unpressed cheese and their production is limited, it is clear that milk curds

Sheep are farmed for their milk as well as for their wool and meat.

and curd cheese formed a substantial part of the Irish diet. However, the importance of cheese as a food began to decline around the seventeenth century, so that by the end of the nineteenth century cheese-making had become virtually unknown as a local or vernacular activity.

It is only in the last twenty-five years that the Irish dairy industry has once again been producing cheese, concentrating mainly on the Cheddar type. In the last ten to twelve years, however, there has also been a revival in the production of farmhouse cheese, which is fast establishing itself on the international market, having not only style and taste, but a very distinctive and fine quality. Although these farmhouse cheeses are produced in many small units throughout the country, the main areas of production are concentrated around the Atlantic coastline of West Cork and Kerry, in the lush dairy pastures of the Midlands, around the lakelands of Lough Erne, in the valleys of Connemara, in the Drumlin hills of County Clare, and on the larger farms in the south-east.

These cheeses are no longer made in the style of those recorded in the early Irish manuscripts and law books, but with the help of traditional recipes and skills learned from notable cheese-making countries throughout the world – such as Switzerland, Holland and France – what was once an important part of the life and food pattern of the Irish people, is now gradually being re-established.

One of the most notable Irish farmhouse cheeses currently being produced is the award-winning Mileens, a soft cheese with a strong distinctive flavour, sometimes compared to Camembert. Mileens comes from the Beara Peninsula in County Cork and is made by Veronica and Norman Steel, pioneers of the revival in Irish cheese-making. Gubbeens, from the same county and the same town of Schull, is another award-winning

cheese, made by Giana and Tom Ferguson from the milk of their Friesian and Jersey herds. This semi-soft cheese with a pinkish brown crust has a unique flavour and texture which varies slightly with the seasons, being softer and creamier in the spring and summer than in the winter. Giana and Tom also produce a delicious semi-hard cheese smoked with local oak wood. In contrast to these, a much harder and more mellow Gruyere-type cheese known as Gabriel is made by Bill Hogan with milk from several small local herds that graze between Mount Gabriel and the sea. Not too far away in County Tipperary, Jane and Louis Grubb produce perhaps the finest cheese in the country, a semi-soft blue cheese called Cashel Blue, made from the raw milk from their own dairy herd. The Webb family of Woodford Dairy in Belfast produce a fine blue-veined goat's cheese, similar to Roquefort, called Rathgore, and from the dairy of John McBride comes a delightful sheep's cheese called Drumiller. All of these, and many more throughout Ireland, are establishing themselves as an integral part of the modern Irish table.

THE MEAT TRADITION

From the early laws, the lives of the saints and the literary writings of the seventeenth century, it is also known that the vast bulk of the cattle population, from the Neolithic period to the Middle Ages, consisted of cows, and that although male animals were reared it was only in small numbers and then mainly for breeding and draft purposes. When beef was eaten it probably came from unwanted bull calves, old cows past their prime and animals which had met their deaths by injury or misadventure. Meat was also available round about November, when dry stock was killed because there was not enough fodder to feed them over the winter as well as those still producing milk or those required for breeding. It was, however, unusual to kill those cattle still supplying milk, even if the family was starving. As one sixteenth-century travel writer explained: 'Flesh he hath, but if he kill it in winter, he shall want milke in summer, and shortly want life.'

When large cattle were slaughtered, because of the volume of meat supplied and the lack of long-term storage facilities needed for its preservation, much of it would have been salted or distributed amongst the family, neighbours and household.

As certain areas of the country went through periods of prosperity, and with the development of an export market, beef as a food commodity grew in importance. During the thirteenth century salted beef, along with pork, was one of Ireland's major exports. However, it was not until the sixteenth century that a more substantial trade in hides and, to a small extent, live cattle was able to take place, with exports going to France, Spain and, by the end of the century, to England. The seventeenth century saw a considerable expansion in exports of live cattle to Britain, so that the London government was forced to ban imports of Irish cattle into England to protect farmers in the stock-raising regions. Ireland was able, however, to switch back into the provision trade for victualling Atlantic fleets and the slave plantations in the West Indies.

During the eighteenth century the Irish provision trade entered its greatest period of prosperity and development, with the largest export of any single industry in Ireland being that of livestock.

At the same time, with the establishment of the large country houses belonging to the landed gentry, meat became an important feature of the wealthy family's menu. A well known socialite at the time, Mrs Delaney, the English wife of Doctor Patrick Delaney, the Dean of Down, on a visit to Newton Grange, near Killala, County Mayo, on 12 June 1732 found the following:

He [Mr Mahone] keeps a man cook and has given entertainments of twenty dishes of meat! The people of this country don't seem solicitous of having dwellings or more furniture than is absolutely necessary – hardly so much, but they make it up in eating and drinking! I have not seen less than fourteen dishes of meat for dinner, and seven for supper, during my peregrinations; and they not only treat us at their houses magnificently, but if we are to go to an inn, they constantly provide us with a basket crammed with good things; no people can be more hospitable and obliging, and there is not only great abundance but great order and neatness.

This style of eating, however, was the privilege of the gentry and was certainly not typical of the eating habits of the vast majority of the population, who still had to exist on oatmeal, milk and potatoes, supplemented in the more fortunate homes by eggs, fowl, fish and game when available.

After a considerable period of decline during the famine years, the beef industry once more continued its steady growth and, by the latter part of the nineteenth century, a considerable export trade to Britain in live cattle was taking place from all the major ports. This trade continued until the middle of this century when the first carcass beef was exported. The first person to set up a beef-processing plant in Northern Ireland was W.P. O'Kane, a poulterer from Ballymena in County Antrim. He tells of the first carcasses being shipped out of his abattoir in coal lorries, arriving at their destination safely, if a little dirty. Fortunately, things have changed greatly over the last forty years and today the animal is closely monitored from farm to table. Quality of hygiene and handling on the farm, at the abattoir, at the processing plant and during transportation, are strictly controlled by Government and European Community legislation to ensure a first-grade product.

About 60 per cent of the carcass meat now leaving Ireland does so with the bone removed and in vacuum packs. More changes are on the way as the beef industry, one of Ireland's major industries, adjusts and prepares for new demands in the ever-changing and expanding marketplace.

Pig Meat

While beef was often reserved for the wealthy and the landowners, or for a special occasion such as Christmas, pork was enjoyed by most households in Ireland throughout the centuries. Until the early part of this century, it would have been rare to visit a farmhouse in Ireland, of any size, that did not have at least one pig.

Sagas, tales, law tracts and the lives of the saints frequently mention the pig as a meat, either in its 'fresh' state as pork or salted as bacon. It would also appear from the many references to swineherds in early literature, and from the direct references to pigs in the law, that such meat was regarded as an important food for both the economy and the people, and one requiring special provision: 'Swine must sleep in a style secured with four strong fastenings by night, and must have a swineherd with them by day.' *The Vision of MacConglinne*, in particular, mentions it numerous times. For instance:

The fort we reached was beautiful,
With walls of custards thick,
Beyond the loch,
New butter was the bridge in front,
The rubble dyke was wheaten white,
Bacon the palisade.

The pig or pigs were kept either in the garden, a yard, a piece of field or in the woods. Oak woods were particularly favoured as the pigs enjoyed the oak-mast (acorns), an important food known for fattening pigs from earliest times. The right to

CLOCKWISE, FROM TOP: *Stuffed pork fillet, pressed ox tongue, Irish spiced beef, jellied lamb and savoury meat loaf (pages 61–72).*

*Boiled bacon with traditional
vegetables (page 58).*

heart was stuffed and pot-roasted or sliced and stewed. In order to be able to keep the rest of the meat longer it was salted.

In preparing the sides of the pig for bacon, the two undercuts from the sirloins – known as pork fillets – were removed and generally stuffed and pot-roasted. The flesh was then removed from the ribs to produce what is known as 'spare ribs'; these were generally stewed with onions, either 'fresh' or after they too had been salted. The sides were then trimmed and the trimmings called 'griskins'; sometimes these were combined with the spare ribs and heart and made into a stew. The hind legs produced two hams, and the fore legs, boned and rolled, were turned into what is known as shoulder bacon. The lard was rendered and made into 'slim-cakes' or kept for frying. The ham and the flitches of bacon were then salted and sometimes smoked by hanging them from the rafters in the kitchen close to the turf fire. The pig, when prepared this way, provided meat for the family for many months, or was divided up among neighbours.

By the nineteenth century the pig was playing an important part in the Irish economy and it was not until the failure of the potato crop that the export trade collapsed. By 1900, however, the pig industry had recovered and the bacon and curing industry once more played an important part in the economy of the country. The main centres for the bacon-curing industry were Waterford, Cork, Limerick and Belfast, with those at Waterford and Belfast being the largest and most important. The method of handling the pigs was different in Ulster to the other counties: the pigs for the Belfast market arrived as dead carcasses, having been killed on the farm, while those for the other markets arrived alive, to be killed and cured at the provision stores. The type of 'cure' also varied from area to area, giving the special

pasture pigs in oak, beech or chestnut woods was an important aspect of any agreement between tenant and overlord in the Middle Ages.

When the potato was introduced at the end of the sixteenth century it formed the major part of the pigs' diet. Nursing sows, in addition, were fed dairy and household refuse and sometimes sour milk with chopped boiled cabbage mixed in it, and just before being sold they were fattened with extra potatoes. Since the pigs also required warmth, particularly when suckling or being fattened for market, they were frequently brought into the house to share the fire with the rest of the family, which is probably why the comment about the Irish 'keeping pigs in the parlour' arose. My mother's cousin remembers piglets being tied up in a sack and hung from a hook at the side of the range to keep warm, and on many of my jaunts to County Cavan I often enjoyed feeding the

weaker members of the pig's family from a baby's bottle also at the side of the open fire.

It was around the Feast of St Martin, on 11 November, that the rent was due and the 'family friend' was made ready for market. For many years, particularly in the north of Ireland, the pig was slaughtered on the farm either by the local butcher or pig killer. Once killed, the pig was bled and scalded, the hairs and innards removed, and the carcass transported to market by horse and cart.

If the pig had been killed for family use, not a bit of it was wasted: the head and feet were made into brawn; the feet (crubeens) used on their own were boiled and roasted and considered a great delicacy; the stomach bag was stuffed and roasted to become what is known as mock or poor-man's goose; the intestines were stuffed with a mixture of meal, lard and blood and called puddings; the liver was fried and served as part of an Irish 'fry', or boiled and served with potatoes; the characteristics distinctive to each region. The hams cured in Limerick and Belfast were highly prized both on the home and export market – a distinction that still exists today.

Sheep

Travelling through Ireland today, along lonely roads and through mountainous areas like Mourne, Donegal, the Burren and Killarney, one cannot fail to notice the sheep. Set against the landscape, they roam in straggling flocks, delicately planting their feet on what would often seem to be impossible terrain – bracken and gorse, heather and bog, rock and pasture, verdant meadows and wind-swept salt marshes.

Although originally kept primarily for their wool, their meat and milk were also occasionally used, but the method of farming involved was obviously a fairly casual one. In a survey of County Down in the 1800s, the commentator Mr Dubourdieu reported that:

> The sheep system in this country, except among a few gentlemen who have flocks, would make a person used to a grazing country smile, or rather wonder, how the towns in this part of the world are supplied with mutton, the sheep which produce it being mostly bought singly or in pairs, by the butchers from little farmers, who purchase them in the same way when lambs, and keep them one or two years, as they find it profitable and convenient; of course the mutton must be young, in most cases being not more than one or two years old. The lambs are brought from the breeding countries, and are to be met with in all the summer fairs. Sheep thrive remarkably well on dry soil; by the small farmers they are fattened in the house on boiled potatoes, oats and hay; the mutton is remarkably sweet.

It is certainly no exaggeration to say, even today, that sheep fattened near the sea or salt marshes or on the heather covered mountains have a very special flavour. It is not only how or where the sheep are reared that gives them their succulent taste, but also the way in which they are cooked. Stewing, roasting or frying were at one time the main ways of cooking the meat, but Mrs Delaney noted in her writings a curious mutton dish she was given during an elaborate picnic near Killala in County Mayo on 4 June 1732:

> For our feast there was prepared what they call 'a swilled mouton', that is a sheep roasted whole in its skin, scorched like a hog. I never ate anything better; we sat on the grass, had a rock for our table; and though there was a great variety of good cheer; nothing was touched by the mutton.

By the nineteenth century the number of sheep raised for meat had greatly increased and mutton had become more widely used both at home and as a product for export.

Although the sheep industry is a small part of the meat industry as a whole, it does however make a considerable contribution to the table, not only in this country but to those it is exported to, mainly France and England where it is hailed for its fine quality and delicate distinctive flavour, particularly that grazed on the salt marshes throughout the country.

POULTRY

While we have been able to determine the length of time cattle, pigs and sheep have been part of the agricultural tradition in Ireland, it is unclear when domestic poultry arrived. It is assumed that hens have been here for a long time and were not only an important food but a source of income even for the poorest families. They could be bought, bartered or stolen and once acquired cost practically nothing to keep. They fed

Chicken 'frigasse' (page 78).

almost entirely on household scraps and potato skins, a diet supplemented by insects, worms and whatever else they could pick up either round the house, in the yard, garden, field or wherever they felt free to roam. In my aunt's home in Armagh they spent the night perched on a rope hung across a shed in the yard, before they had their own hen house to keep them safe from the fox. A neighbour, however, had a pole hung across the kitchen from eave to eave where they were able to roost. They laid their eggs in a variety of places: a sheltered part of the hedge, the cow's manger, the nest provided in the hen house or the kitchen. In some farmhouses handsome nesting baskets of woven straw, such as those found in County Limerick, were provided. Many kitchens, including my aunt's, also had a dresser with a plate rack on top and a coop for hatching hens at the bottom. In County Down the hen was often found sitting in a stove box beside the fire.

Hens were not only an item of food for the household, providing a valuable supply of protein from both eggs and bird, but were also an important source of income for the woman of the house. Indeed, in the nineteenth century the poultry industry in Ireland was dominated by women, with the exception of the export of eggs and fowl. Poultry keeping enabled women of the labouring and small farmer classes to contribute substantially to the household economy, while in poorer parts the sale of poultry provided the bare necessities of life when eggs were often taken in exchange for other groceries. At this time, even the smallest farm may have had upwards of 100 hens. In 1911 it was noted that women on small farms in certain areas earned between £20 and £60 a year raising poultry. 'In many cases, indeed, the receipts from eggs have been sufficient to pay the rent and also provide the household with groceries.'

Within the domestic situation both the eggs and the fowl would be used, but the fowl only when its laying life had come to an end.

At this time it probably found its way into the pot, which was the best way to tenderise it and make it palatable; often a young rabbit or piece of bacon would have joined it.

With the improvement of roads and transportation, coupled with a demand for eggs from England, the poultry industry was able to increase the number of eggs it exported from eleven million in 1850 to a staggering forty million in 1900. In the early years of the twentieth century the structure of the industry changed, with the purpose of becoming more efficient and cost effective, not to mention improving the quality of the product. The eggs were taken under the control of the creameries and the farmer paid for them along with the milk; a situation which not only changed the industry but removed the financial benefits from the farmers' wives, thus cutting off their main form of income and independence.

Geese

Like hens, geese could be found on all types of farm, even if sometimes the numbers were limited to only one or two. Goose eggs, like those of the turkey and duck, were highly prized and usually reserved for the head of the household or given to the children as a special treat.

Goose was the bird generally eaten on festive occasions in Ireland, particularly on two days of the year – Christmas and Michaelmas, 29 September. Indeed, there is an old saying that 'if you eat goose on Michaelmas Day you will never want for money all year round'.

Michaelmas, from Norman times, was in some parts of the country a hiring or rent day and the day for presenting the landlord with a goose. It is recorded that in Carlow in 1305 a goose was worth twenty old pennies, and in some places it was customary for the landlord to accept either the money or the goose for the rent. It was also one of the days of the year on which farmers killed an animal to give to their poor neighbours; when there was

a flock of geese it was usual to give one of them as the gift.

The tradition of eating goose on Michaelmas Day probably had something to do with the fact that the geese were in their prime at this time of year. Since hatching in the spring they were fed on the summer pastures until September or when the grain was cut. From this habit they took the name 'green geese' and when killed and eaten at this stage, before they were turned on to the stubble of the grain fields to scratch for the remaining grains, they were considered a great delicacy. Once the birds had grazed on the grain fields they were called 'stubble geese', the old term 'wayz geese' being taken from the Anglo-Saxon for 'sheaf'.

Dean Swift's poem from *The Progress of Poetry* gives a wonderful description of the goose and its habits:

The farmer's goose who in the stubble,
Has fed without restraint or trouble,
Grown fat with corn and sitting still,
Can scarce get o'er the barn door sill;
And hardly waddles forth to cool
Her belly in the neighbour's pool;
Nor loudly cackles at the door;
For cackling shows the goose is poor.

In some places it was also the custom to keep the geese in a barn for the last ten to fourteen days of their lives and feed them only on milky foods and potatoes. This would ensure that their flesh would be pale and delicate and of course delicious to eat.

Like the pig in Ireland, nothing of the goose was wasted: its quills were made into writing implements and fishing floats; the large wings were used as brushes with which to dust the flour from the griddle; the down and feathers were used to fill mattresses, pillows and eiderdowns; its fat was used for all manner of things, from rubbing it on the chest as the remedy for a cold, to using it as a polish to 'bring up the shine' on a black kitchen range. The best use for the fat, however, has always been for the roasting of potatoes. It enhances their flavour.

The goose was traditionally cooked in the bastable or pot-oven over the open turf fire and would have been boiled, braised or roasted. My grandmother recalls it being put in the pot, which was half-filled with cold water then hung over the fire until the water boiled. It was then taken off the hook and placed on a trivet beside the fire. Hot turves were then placed under it for about an hour, being replaced as they cooled down. The goose was basted from time to time and after an hour some parsnips were added. The lid was put back on and hot turves were placed on top, until both the bird and vegetables were cooked.

When roasted, it would have been stuffed with potato and onion. If served at Michael-mas in Munster and South Ulster, it would also have been served with a baked apple and a glass of cider, as this time of year marked the beginning of the apple harvest.

As a Christmas bird, goose has been in decline now for a number of years having been replaced by its modern rival the turkey. However, it will still be enjoyed on the farms where geese are bred or by those in the cities who feel able to afford them.

Geese are not reared in Ireland as a major industry but are produced on small farms and marketed either directly from there or sold to the local butcher or poultry shop. A small number of companies are now rearing geese and other types of birds such as phea-sants and guinea fowls on a slightly larger scale. These are being sold in consumer packs at good delicatessens and enlightened supermarkets.

VEGETABLES

Although vegetables were known to have been eaten in both their wild and cultivated forms since as far back as prehistoric times, they certainly do not seem to have played such an important role in the food patterns of the community. The monasteries were, of course, the exception, having their own gar-dens in which to grow the requirements for their mainly non-meat diet.

From early written sources, such as the lives of the saints, early literature and the Brehon Laws, it would appear that a species of plant called *cainnenn* – variously trans-lated as leek, onion or garlic – was in common use, mainly as a flavouring. The early Irish laws specified its use in small amounts, 'a handful' or 'two handfuls', and as a condi-ment or relish for food. In the twelfth-century poem *The Vision of MacConglinne*, onions are also mentioned:

A forest tall of real leeks
Of onions and of carrots, stood
Behind the house.

It would also seem that although these vegetables grew wild they were also culti-vated in rows and widely used. In later times, leeks and onions are frequently mentioned in Anglo-Norman documents and in 1591 there is a record of onion seed coming into Clonmel. Dean Swift, writing in 1795, said this of onions:

They make the blood warmer,
You'll feed like a farmer;
For this is every cook's opinion
No savoury dish without an onion.
But lest your kissing should be spoiled,
Your onions must be thoroughly boiled:
Or else you may spare
Your mistress a share.
The secret will never be known:
She cannot discover
The breath of her lover,
But think it as sweet as her own.

Another vegetable eaten from early times was a root vegetable called *meacan*. Although this name was applied to many plants, scholars have assumed that it refers to the parsnip and carrot.

Peas and beans also seem to feature as vegetables grown in Ireland and, although it is not known exactly when they arrived, it is thought that they were introduced by the monks in the fifth century but only became established as cultivated crops after the Norman Invasion in the twelfth century, and then mainly in areas under Norman in-fluence. From then on, peas and beans seem to have been an important food and many references are made to them in state papers. Indeed, they were even included in the list of goods on which toll might be levied in the charter granted by Edward III to New Ross in 1374. The large whole dried peas would have been those most widely used in former years. Traditionally, they would have been served with salt pork or beef and when masked were known as 'mushy' peas. It is thought that peas were also used to make a type of bread.

Globe artichokes also seem to have been grown in Ireland since the Norman Con-quest, while cabbage, regarded along with potatoes as the mainstay of Irish cooking, did not arrive in the British Isles until the late sixteenth or early seventeenth centuries. It would appear that in the 1770s, cabbage, grown from Scottish seed, was mainly culti-vated as a crop to be fed to sheep and cattle. Arthur Young in *A Tour in Ireland* (1776–9) writes about the agricultural practices of the time and on many occasions reports on the growing of the cabbage, particularly in favour of the turnip.

Cabbages Lord Farnham has cultivated three years; in 1774 he had 4 acres manured with lime and earth and of different sorts, flat Dutch, early York-shire, and green borecole, the seed was sown in the Spring, and planted out in June in rows 3 feet asunder, and horse-hoed clean; found them for milch cows much better than turnips; ... the cab-bages came to a good size, and the crop paid extremely well.

Eventually the cabbage and, indeed, the turnip were both enjoyed as vegetables for the table rather than the farmyard. The cabbage became particularly popular even

though it was the vegetable most frequently destroyed by overcooking which is not surprising when one of the most popular Irish dishes involved boiling it with bacon and ham for two to two and a half hours.

The potato, Ireland's best-known vegetable and the one indelibly linked with her history, although thought to have been introduced in Ireland around the late sixteenth century, did not become widely used until about 1670 when it almost entirely displaced meat and eventually nearly all the other major foods. The majority of the people of Ireland became totally dependent on it for sustenance, which resulted in the deaths of 1.5 million people in the 1840s when the potato crop was destroyed by blight.

Traditionally, potatoes were boiled in their jackets, or skins as we say, not only to preserve their nutrients, but for convenience. In coastal areas the potatoes were boiled in sea water, which was thought to prevent the skins from cracking and to stop the mineral content from being lost, no matter how floury the potatoes. This is possibly why salt is generally added to the boiling water.

In many poor homes in the seventeenth and eighteenth centuries, particularly in the west of Ireland, the potato would have been tipped into a bowl or eaten directly from the pot set in the middle of the floor. Arthur Young in *A Tour of Ireland* gives a vivid description of this activity:

> Mark the Irishman's potatoe bowl placed on the floor, the whole family on their hams around it, devouring a quantity almost incredible, the begar seating himself to it with a hearty welcome, the pig taking his share as readily as the wife, the cocks, hens, turkeys, geese, the cur, the cat, and perhaps the cow – all partaking of the same dish.

CLOCKWISE, FROM TOP LEFT: *Potato soup, nettle broth, carrot soup, watercress soup and leek and oatmeal broth (pages 52–4).*

Another description of eating potatoes can be found in an account of life in north-west County Donegal early this century, given by Fred Coll to Dr Jonathan Bell in *Ulster Folk Life*:

> Apart from beds, there were a couple of hard chairs, stools, and a very small table. The mother, father and grandfather, if he was about, would sit there to eat, and the children would sit round a board set in the middle of the floor. This was known as *'clar na lasaide'*. They would dip their potatoes in the salt and pepper, and if they were lucky enough they got *'blathach'*, buttermilk, as well. That was the staple diet.

In some houses the potatoes were tipped into a flat osier basket, or 'skib', from which the moisture could escape quickly. This was set in the middle of the table and everyone helped themselves from it. In middle-class homes these plainly boiled potatoes would be served in a wooden bowl, while in the grander households the potatoes would be placed inside a beautifully ornamented silver potato ring and then set on a folded napkin to absorb the moisture. Such rings are now highly prized and are generally used for fruit and flower arrangements.

In the late 1800s, although the potato was still grown and regarded as an important vegetable, it was no longer the mainstay of the people. In the early 1900s a new agricultural movement of improvers encouraged the development of cottage gardens as a means of providing an additional source of food and a more varied diet. Here a wide selection of both vegetables and fruit could be grown according to the size of the area and involve the entire family in a productive activity.

Such gardens are now features of cottages and farmhouses throughout the country and, indeed, some of my most vivid and cherished memories are of my grandmother's kitchen garden in County Down. Here on a tiny patch of land, no more than 0.05 hectares

(eighth of an acre), she lovingly grew most of her food as her ancestors had done before her and her successors do today. She planted and harvested the 'old' vegetables – onions, garlic and leeks – the ubiquitous potato and the hardy carrots, parsnips and turnips. She tied up peas and beans, lined up sorrel, spinach and chard, along with the more familiar members of the cabbage family, and cauliflower, marrows, artichokes and courgettes. In summer there was a wonderful selection of both basic and exotic salad leaves, and clumps of herbs – thyme, marjoram, sage, fennel and oregano – would decorate the borders and flowerbeds. A rosemary bush, a bay tree, and several varieties of mint, raised in enamel buckets, were also to be found there.

The fruit garden, which was equally rambling, also played an important part in the overall scheme of things. Fruit bushes were in abundance: several varieties of gooseberries and a multitude of black and red currants. Every July I gazed at these in wonder and marvelled at the brightness of their colour as they stretched their heavy fruit-laden branches towards the rich rows of raspberry and loganberry canes. There was also a strawberry patch, with the fruit and leaves cushioned from the elements on mats of straw. At the farthermost side of the garden grew the grand old apple trees, one variety for eating and, of course, Bramleys for cooking. There was a plum tree, a cherry tree and a rather deformed old quince, which leaned precariously over a bank linking the kitchen garden to the 'front' of the house. It was a truly informal and delightful cottage garden, with everything that was required to produce simple nutritious meals along with a variety of herbal teas and remedies. For a while, in many parts of the country, this form of self-sufficiency seemed to die away. However, today, as in the early 1900s, a move towards the rejuvenation and wider cultivation of these cottage gardens is once again taking place.

SOUP RECIPES

LEFT TO RIGHT: *Potato soup (page 53), Irish farmhouse broth (page 53) and watercress soup (page 52).*

Soup has always played a very important part in the diet of the Irish from the earliest times to the present day. It was often served at every meal, both winter and summer, and in rural districts it would have been a 'poor' household that did not have a pot of soup or broth on the stove every day. In many homes soup would form the basis of the main meal. Sometimes it would be enriched with meat and, of course, the ubiquitous potato, which generally floated on top. Indeed, Irish soups are often so substantial in their composition that they are referred to as 'atin' and 'drinkin' soups.

As a staple food, soup was made from whatever ingredients were available, from the hedgerows, fields and gardens, or from the market. Wild herbs, leaves, vegetables, seeds, nuts and grains, along with meat, fish, shellfish, game birds and fowl – when they were free or could be afforded – were all used. In coastal districts the main ingredients would have been seaweeds, such as dulse, sloke, laver or carrageen.

One of the earliest and simplest forms of soup was made from ground oatmeal boiled in water with chopped vegetables. This produced a thick porridge-like mixture. When meat was boiled in it, it was referred to as a broth and would have been served to retainers or servants at feasts and special celebrations. It is likely that such a soup was made with all types of vegetables, but the most widely used were probably leeks, nettles and potatoes.

In 1847, following the failure of the vital potato crop, famine was sweeping Ireland. The government of the time, in its efforts to relieve the situation, sent to Ireland Monsieur Alexis Soyer of the Reform Club in London to provide soup for the starving millions. On 1 March 1847 Soyer arrived in Dublin and set up his model soup kitchen in front of the Royal Barracks, not far from the entrance to Phoenix Park. Although his effort obviously provided some relief for a few people, it was minimal when compared to the scale of starvation facing almost the entire population of Ireland at this time. According to O'Rourke's History of the Great Irish Famine of 1847, *Monsieur Soyer, after many difficulties, considerable misunderstandings and much ridicule, made a quick retreat to the more congenial atmosphere of his London club. However, his good works were not forgotten, and soup runs and soup kitchens were set up in the same style in many famine-stricken areas throughout the country. Those set up by wealthy Protestant landowners on their estates for the starving peasants, many of them Roman Catholics, were accused of using soup as a proselytising medium. As a result, anyone who changed his religion at this time was called a 'souper', and to this day Protestants bearing a Roman Catholic name are said to be descended from soupers.*

NETTLE BROTH
Brat Neantóg

Nettles were one of the earliest foods of the Irish. They were particularly sought after by the poor and during periods of famine. Nettle soup is generally made in the spring when the nettle tops are young and tender. They should be pulled before the end of May and from an unpolluted area away from traffic and crop sprays. When picking nettles, wear gloves and cut the tops with scissors.

SERVES 10
MAKES 2 litres ($3\frac{1}{2}$ pints)
50 g (2 oz) butter or vegetable margarine
25 g (1 oz) flake oatmeal
175 g (6 oz) leeks, white and green parts
225 g (8 oz) nettle tops, chopped
350 g (12 oz) potatoes, peeled and roughly diced
900 ml ($1\frac{1}{2}$ pints) vegetable stock or water
300 ml (10 fl oz) milk
Salt and freshly milled black pepper

Melt the butter or margarine in a large saucepan and fry the oatmeal until well toasted. Stir in the leeks, nettle tops and potatoes and continue to fry for a few minutes. Stir in the liquid and the seasoning. Bring to the boil, then reduce the heat and simmer very gently for about 30 minutes until the vegetables are tender and the oatmeal cooked. Stir frequently during the cooking to ensure that the potato and oatmeal do not burn. Sieve or liquidise the soup, adjust the seasoning and serve very hot.

WATERCRESS SOUP
Anraith Biolair

Wild watercress has played a very important part in the diet of the Irish since ancient times and is frequently mentioned in early manuscripts. It still grows in many rivers and streams throughout Ireland and is free for the picking, as long as the water is clear and unpolluted.

SERVES 6–7
MAKES 1.5 litres ($2\frac{1}{2}$ pints)
150 g (5 oz) watercress, approx. 2 bunches
50 g (2 oz) butter
1 large onion, finely chopped
40 g ($1\frac{1}{2}$ oz) plain flour

1 litre (1¾ pints) vegetable stock, milk or water
Salt and freshly milled black pepper
150 ml (5 fl oz) cream

Wash the watercress well, removing any yellow leaves and fine hairs, but leave on the stalks. Shred finely. Melt the butter in a large saucepan, add the onion and watercress, tossing to coat in the butter. Cover with greaseproof paper and sweat over a low heat for about 10 minutes to develop the flavour and draw out the juices. Remove the paper and stir in the flour. Pour in the stock, milk or water, bring to the boil, season and then simmer for 20–25 minutes until the vegetables are completely tender. Sieve or liquidise. Return to the saucepan, adjust the seasoning and add the cream. Reheat gently, stirring to blend well and serve either hot or chilled.

LEEK AND OATMEAL BROTH
'Brotchán Roy' – Brachán Rua
'Broth fit for a king'
This was one of the original pottages made by the ancient Irish. The name is taken from the Gaelic word for broth, with the 'Roy' a derivation of the Irish 'Ri' meaning king. The soup is also referred to as Brotchan foltchep after the main ingredient, leek. This is definitely a meal soup, wholly Irish and indeed a bit like a vegetable porridge.

SERVES 6–7
MAKES 1.5 litres (2½ pints)
225 g (8 oz) leeks (2 medium size), white and green parts
50 g (2 oz) butter
50 g (2 oz) flake oatmeal
900 ml (1½ pints) vegetable stock or water
450 ml (15 fl oz) milk
Salt and freshly milled black pepper
Pinch of ground mace
2 × 15 ml (2 tablespoons) parsley, finely chopped

Trim and wash the leeks well to ensure that all the grit and soil has been removed. Shred finely across their length. Melt the butter in a large saucepan and add the oatmeal. Fry gently until well toasted, then stir in the stock and milk. Bring to the boil and add the leeks and seasoning. Simmer for 30–45 minutes until the leeks

are tender and the oatmeal cooked. Adjust the seasoning and serve sprinkled with parsley.

SPINACH AND OATMEAL SOUP
Anraith Min Choirce agus Spionáiste
This soup is particularly good in the spring when the young spinach is at its most tender and flavoursome. It is thickened like many of the earliest Irish soups with oatmeal. It can also be made with sorrel or a mixture of the two.

SERVES 6–7
MAKES 1.5 litres (2½ pints)
350 g (12 oz) spinach
25 g (1 oz) butter or vegetable margarine
1 medium onion, finely chopped
25 g (1 oz) flake oatmeal
75 g (3 oz) potatoes, peeled and diced
900 ml (1½ pints) vegetable stock or water
Salt and freshly milled black pepper
65 ml (2½ fl oz) cream or milk

Wash the spinach, remove any tough spiny stalks and chop the leaves roughly. Melt the butter or margarine in a large saucepan and fry the onion until soft but not coloured. Add the oatmeal and continue to cook until the mixture is beginning to colour slightly. Stir in the spinach. Add the potatoes, stock and seasoning and bring to the boil. Reduce the heat and simmer for about an hour. Sieve or liquidise until smooth. Return to the pan, adjust the seasoning and stir in the cream or milk.

IRISH FARMHOUSE BROTH
Brat Traidisiúnta
Broth to the Irish means a substantial soup, flavoured with meat, enriched with pulses and root vegetables, and thickened with cereal. The earliest broth was thickened with oats giving a porridge-like texture, but nowadays barley is more popular. The meat is generally beef, mutton, boiling fowl or turkey and is either boiled and served with the vegetables or used to make a well-flavoured stock to which the vegetables and cereal are then added, the meat being reserved for a separate meal, or cut into pieces and used to enrich the soup.

In many poor farmhouses meat broth was the Sunday dinner, and often the only fresh meat dish of the week, bacon being used the rest of the

time. For a more substantial meal, cooked boiled potatoes were served in the middle of the soup, broken up and eaten with a spoon.

Today, broth is created out of whatever is to hand, often with either meat bones, brisket or shin used to flavour the basic stock.

SERVES 14
MAKES 2.75 litres (5 pints)
350–450 g (¾–1 lb) shin or brisket of beef on the bone
2 litres (3½ pints) cold water
50 g (2 oz) split green peas
50 g (2 oz) red lentils
50 g (2 oz) pearl barley
2 leeks, approx. 225 g (8 oz), white and green part, chopped
2 medium carrots, peeled and diced
50 g (2 oz) soup celery, chopped
Salt and freshly milled black pepper
2 × 15 ml (2 tablespoons) parsley, finely chopped

Put the meat and water into a large pot and bring to the boil. Skim off the foam from the surface, then add the root vegetables along with the peas, lentils and barley. Return to the boil, then reduce the heat and simmer for 2–3 hours until the meat is tender and the soup thick. Season with the salt and pepper. Remove the meat from the pot, cut into thin fingers or pieces, then return to the hot broth. Serve sprinkled with chopped parsley.

BOILED AND ROAST BRISKET OF BEEF If a larger piece of brisket of beef is used to make the broth, perhaps about 1.5 kg (3 lb), it is often reserved and served as a small joint for another meal. In this case, the fat is coated in browned breadcrumbs and roasted in a hot oven at 220°C (425°F, gas mark 7) for 20–25 minutes until the outside is crisp and golden brown. It is then served in slices with cabbage and potatoes. A joint about this size will serve 4 people.

LENTIL AND BACON BROTH
Brat Bagúin agus Lintilí
Pork and bacon were the most important types of meat eaten in Ireland throughout her history, and still play an important part in the daily diet of the people all over the country. Since every part of the pig is put to good use it appears on the table in many different guises, from

sausages to soup. One of the most popular and substantial soups is lentil and bacon broth. The liquid part of the soup is often drunk first, followed by the meat which is served as a second course with vegetables.

SERVES 6–7
MAKES 1.5 litres (2½ pints)
1 ham shank up to 1 kg (2 lb) in weight, or 1 ham bone, or 1 kg (2 lb) shoulder or collar bacon
175 g (6 oz) split red lentils, rinsed
2 large onions, finely diced
2 large carrots, finely diced
225 g (8 oz) turnip, finely diced
450 g (1 lb) potatoes (approx. 3 large), finely diced
Salt and freshly milled black pepper
Parsley, finely chopped to garnish

Soak salty ham in cold water overnight. The next day, pour off the water and put the meat into a large saucepan and cover with 1.5 litres (3 pints) of fresh cold water. Bring to the boil. Pour off this first boiling water, then rinse the pan and start again with another 1.5 litres (3 pints) of fresh water. Add the rinsed lentils along with all the diced vegetables except the potatoes, which are added 20 minutes before the end of the cooking. Bring to the boil, then reduce the heat and simmer for 2 hours until the meat is tender and the broth rich and thick. Remove the ham or bone from the broth, take the skin off the meat and cut into small cubes. Return these to the broth, check the seasoning and garnish with chopped parsley.
NOTE If the ham joint is being used for a main course, skin and press toasted breadcrumbs into the fat with a little brown sugar. Stick a few cloves in the surface of the meat, set in a small roasting dish with a little oil and cook in a hot oven at 220°C (425°F, gas mark 7) for 15–30 minutes until crisp and brown. A 1 kg (2 lb) joint will serve 4 as a main course.

PEA AND HAM SOUP
Anraith Piseanna agus Bagúin
It is thought that the pea was introduced to Ireland in the early Christian period but only became established as a cultivated crop after the Norman invasion, and then mainly in areas under Norman influence. Dried peas, either whole or split, are often used along with ham or bacon to produce a tasty and satisfying soup.

SERVES 6–7
MAKES 1.5 litres (2½ pints)
25 g (1 oz) butter
2 thick rashers bacon, rind removed and diced, or a ham bone
1 small onion, chopped
1 small carrot, peeled and sliced
175 g (6 oz) split peas (yellow or green) or whole peas, soaked overnight
1 small bay leaf
1 litre (1¾ pints) water or ham stock
Salt and freshly milled black pepper
1 × 15 ml (1 tablespoon) parsley, finely chopped
1 rasher bacon, finely chopped and crisply fried

Fry the bacon, onion and carrot in the melted butter in a large saucepan over a gentle heat until the vegetables are soft. This will take about 15 minutes. Add the peas, bay leaf and stock. Bring to the boil, then reduce the heat and simmer for 1 hour if using dried split peas, and 2 hours if using whole dried peas. Sieve or liquidise the soup until smooth. Season with pepper and salt if necessary, return to the saucepan, bring to the boil and serve sprinkled with the chopped parsley and fried bacon.

POTATO SOUP
Anraith Prataí
Apart from being used as the sole vegetable in soup, as here, the potato combines well with other vegetables, such as leeks, lovage and watercress, and also with fish and shellfish, to produce a wide variety of interesting and flavoursome dishes.

SERVES 6–7
MAKES 1.5 litres (2½ pints)
25 g (1 oz) butter
1 large onion
450 g (1 lb) potatoes, peeled and roughly chopped
450 ml (15 fl oz) water or vegetable stock
450 ml (15 fl oz) milk
Salt and freshly milled black pepper
65 ml (2½ fl oz) cream
4 rashers streaky bacon, chopped and crisply fried
1 × 15 ml (1 tablespoon) snipped chives

Melt the butter in a large saucepan and soften the onion without colouring. Add the potatoes along with stock, milk and seasoning. Bring to the boil, then reduce the heat and simmer for 45 minutes, stirring occasionally to prevent the potatoes from sticking to the bottom of the pan. Sieve or liquidise the soup until smooth. Return to the pan, adjust the seasoning and stir in the cream. Heat through gently and stir in the bacon. Serve sprinkled with snipped chives.

CHICKEN OR TURKEY BROTH
Brat Sicín nó Turcaí
This soup was originally made when boiling fowls were easy to obtain and full of flavour. It is not only served throughout Ireland as part of the traditional Christmas meal, but is produced for every other occasion. As in Jewish cookery, chicken soup is also regarded as the cure for all illnesses and is the symbol of a welcoming table. Today chicken or turkey broth is more frequently made with the remains of either the chicken or turkey carcass.

SERVES 6–7
MAKES 1.5 litres (2½–3 pints)
FOR THE STOCK
1 boiling fowl, 1.25–1.5 kg (2½–3 lbs) and giblets or the carcass of a cooked chicken or turkey
1 large carrot, washed, peeled and cut in quarters
1 large onion, peeled and quartered
1 stick celery
6 peppercorns
3.5 litres (6 pints) water to cover
FOR THE BROTH
1.75 litres (3 pints) chicken or turkey stock
2 large carrots, washed, peeled and diced
1 large onion, finely chopped
1 leek, washed and thinly sliced
2 sticks celery, washed and thinly sliced
1 bay leaf
50 g (2 oz) pearl barley
Salt and freshly milled black pepper
2 × 15 ml (2 tablespoons) parsley, finely chopped

First make the stock. If using a boiling fowl, wash under cold running water removing any lumps of fat from its inside. Put either the whole chicken or the chicken/turkey carcass into a large saucepan with the vegetables, peppercorns and enough water to cover. Bring to the boil, removing any scum. Cover, reduce the heat and simmer for 2–3 hours until the chicken is tender and all the flavour has been drawn out of the bones and vegetables. Strain the stock into a bowl, reserving the liquid and discarding the bones and vegetables. Skim to remove any scum and fat. This is more easily done when the stock is cold. The fat will then lift off in a solid piece. The stock can be frozen in convenient portions for future use, or used immediately.

Put the 1.75 litres (3 pints) of stock into a large saucepan and add the remaining ingredients, with the exception of the parsley. Bring to the boil, then reduce the heat and simmer for 1½ hours until the vegetables and barley are tender and the flavours well blended. Correct the seasoning and serve sprinkled with the chopped parsley.

NOTE This broth was often served with cooked boiled potatoes floating on the top.

CARROT SOUP
Anraith Meacan Dearg

It would appear from scholarly research that a vegetable called meacan *has been eaten in Ireland since prehistoric times. In modern Irish, this word is translated as carrot and parsnip, and although there is, as yet, no evidence to suggest how widely these vegetables were cultivated and used, it can be assumed that they were certainly part of the Irish diet. Today, they feature among our most widely used vegetables, either served as an accompaniment to meat, combined with it in stews, or made into soups, salads and even cakes.*

SERVES 6–7
MAKES 1.5 litres (2½ pints)
2 × 15 ml (2 tablespoons) butter or oil
1 large onion, finely sliced
1 clove garlic, crushed
450 g (1 lb) carrots (4 large) peeled and sliced
900 ml (1½ pints) vegetable or chicken stock
Sprig of thyme, bay leaf, parsley stalks
Pinch of ground mace
Salt and freshly milled black pepper
150 ml (5 fl oz) cream or milk
Croûtons of fried bread
1 × 15 ml (1 tablespoon) parsley, finely chopped

Heat the butter or oil in a large saucepan, add the onion, garlic and carrots. Cook gently over a low heat until the onions are soft but not coloured. This will take about 10 minutes. Stir in the vegetable or chicken stock. Add the herbs for the bouquet garni, held together with string, along with the mace and seasoning. Bring to the boil, cover and cook gently for 45–60 minutes until the carrots are very tender. Sieve or liquidise the soup until smooth. Return to a clean pan and bring to the boil. Adjust the seasoning and stir in the cream. Reheat, this time without boiling to prevent the cream from curdling. Serve sprinkled with chopped parsley and croûtons.

MUSSEL SOUP
Anraith Diúilicín

*Mussels (*Mylilus edulis*) are one of the most prolific and widely available of all the shellfish to be found around the coast of Ireland. They are highly prized by both the local and export market for their size and flavour and are frequently used in stews and soups. In this recipe saffron, a popular spice in the eighteenth century, is used both to colour and flavour the soup, along with home-made fish stock which helps to intensify the flavour of the sea.*

This soup can be made the day before and kept in the refrigerator as long as all the ingredients were very fresh. It also freezes well.

SERVES 4
MAKES 1.2 litres (2 pints)
40 mussels, approx. 1 kg (2 lb) weight
175 g (6 oz) onion, finely chopped
175 g (6 oz) leek, white part only, finely shredded
175 g (6 oz) carrot, finely diced
½ celery stalk, finely sliced
50 g (2 oz) butter
2 small bouquet garni (consisting of sprig of thyme, bay leaf, parsley stalks)
100 ml (4 fl oz) dry white wine
2 cloves garlic
100 g (4 oz) tomatoes, peeled, seeds removed and chopped
750 ml (1¼ pints) fish stock (see page 109)
Pinch of saffron
150 ml (5 fl oz) double cream
2 branches of chervil
Freshly milled black pepper

Wash and scrape the mussels removing the beard and any barnacles that may have attached themselves to the shell. Rinse under running water. Discard any mussels that are open or damaged. Using a saucepan large enough to hold all the mussels, sweat one third of the onion and leeks in 25 g (1 oz) butter until soft, closely covered with a greaseproof paper lid. Add the mussels and 1 bouquet garni. Pour on the white wine (I generally use a Sauvignon Blanc). Cover with the saucepan lid and cook on a high heat for about 4–5 minutes. Stir the mussels from time-to-time to make sure that those at the top go to the bottom of the pan and get a full blast of heat. When all the mussel shells have opened, drain through a piece of muslin lining a sieve set over a bowl to catch all the cooking liquor. This will be needed later. Remove the mussels from their shells, discarding any mussels whose shells did not open. Store in a covered bowl in the refrigerator until required.

Peel and crush the garlic and sweat in the remaining butter with the onion, celery, leeks, carrot, tomatoes and bouquet garni until soft but not coloured, covered tightly with grease-proof paper as before. This will take about 5 minutes. Remove the paper and pour on the fish stock and the reserved mussel liquor. Reserve 20 mussels for garnishing the soup and put the rest into the pot with the remaining soup mixture. Bring to the boil, then reduce the heat and simmer for about 20 minutes. Add the saffron and let it bubble up once. Stir in the cream and blend in a liquidiser or food processor until smooth, then push through a sieve. There should only be about 2 tablespoons of 'debris' which will not go through. Return the soup to the saucepan, correct the seasoning and reheat very gently, adding the reserved mussels just before serving. Sprinkle with some fronds of chervil and serve immediately. Wheaten bread (see page 132) makes a delicious accompaniment.

MEAT RECIPES

LEFT TO RIGHT: *Beef stew with dumplings (page 68), mutton and haricot bean stew (page 71) and shin and Guinness (page 68).*

Although cattle were originally bred for their milk, and sheep for their wool, their meat was also highly-prized by the country's kings and noblemen in early times and was served at formal banquets and feasts. Here, the importance of meat was such that the rank and status of the guests was determined by the pieces of roast meat they were offered. Eventually, as the country developed and grew in prosperity, beef and mutton increased in importance as more general food commodities and were widely enjoyed by the landed gentry, the prosperous merchants and those who reared the animals. For the poor, however, such meat still remained a luxury and generally was only eaten when given as a gift. The vast majority of the population subsisted on oatmeal, milk and potatoes, with the occasional addition of eggs, old hens, bacon, fish, and game when freely available.

When a bullock, sheep or pig was killed on the farm, it was shared with neighbours or those less fortunate. In 1600 the carcass was divided among the neighbours as follows: the head, tail and feet to the blacksmith; the neck to the man who killed the beast; two small ribs to the tailor; the liver to the carpenter; and the sweetbreads to the woman with child.

Fresh meat was enjoyed as long as possible and the remainder was salted down for future use. When sheep meat was eaten, it was generally as mutton and was used for stews or pies. Today mutton is hardly ever seen, having been replaced by lamb.

Until recent years pork and bacon formed the staple diet of both the poor and wealthy of Ireland, and as a result there are more recipes for the various parts of the pig than for any other animal. While some parts, such as the fillet, kidneys, heart, liver, sweetbreads, stomach, feet, head and sometimes the leg, were eaten fresh, most of the pig was salted and cured to make it keep longer. The sides of the pig were known as the 'flitch' and cured as bacon, while the hind legs, the prime cut of the pig, were cured as ham. Although the type of cure varied from area to area, that most commonly used was a dry cure. This involved the flesh being rubbed with a mixture of salt, sugar and saltpetre for up to two weeks. It was then dried and often smoked over a mixture of turf and oak.

Dry-cured bacon, however, is now almost a thing of the past, as most Irish bacon and ham is processed in large factories and wet-cured in brine before being smoked by various chemical means. Unfortunately, this has not resulted in an improvement in quality, but rather the reverse.

Today, many people would consider a meal incomplete if there was not meat of some description on the plate.

BOILED BACON OR HAM
Bagún Bruite

This, at one time, was a very popular dish with most families and although not cooked so frequently now, is still very much part of Ireland's culinary repertoire. The cuts of bacon most widely used are the shoulder, the collar or a piece of unsliced streaky bacon from the flitch. The type of bacon used and the quantity is largely dependent on what can be afforded. Ham is cooked in the same way, but because of its superior quality and higher price it is generally reserved for special occasions. Both the bacon and ham can be bought pale (unsmoked) or smoked. If a small joint is being used make sure it is tied securely into a neat shape.

SERVES 8
1.75 kg (4 lb) joint of bacon or ham
A selection of root vegetables such as:
1 onion, 1 carrot, 2 sticks celery
2 bay leaves
A few parsley stalks
8 peppercorns
6 allspice or juniper berries

Soak the joint of bacon, or ham, overnight in cold water in the refrigerator or a cold larder. The next day, drain the ham and put into a large saucepan with enough fresh cold water to cover it. Bring to the boil, then throw off this first boiling water along with the scum that will have formed. Wash out the pan, rinse the joint, and begin again, covering the meat for a second time with fresh cold water.

Add the washed, peeled and quartered vegetables along with the herbs and seasoning. Bring the water to the boil, then reduce the heat until the liquid simmers. Cover and cook for 25 minutes per 450 g (1 lb) until the meat is tender and the skin can be easily removed. Allow the bacon or ham to cool slightly in the cooking liquor, then remove from the pot and peel off the skin. Serve in slices with parsley sauce (see page 59), cabbage and potatoes.
NOTE A 1.75 kg (4 lb) joint of ham or bacon will yield approximately 10–20 slices depending on whether the meat is carved hot or cold, plus a 150 g (5 oz) tail piece which is ideal for chicken and ham pie (see page 78).

BOILED BACON OR HAM WITH CABBAGE
Bagún Bruite le Cabáiste

When boiled bacon or ham is served with cabbage, the tight-headed, green Irish cabbage is traditionally used.

The cabbage is cut into wedges, the core removed and the pieces cooked with the meat for the last 20–25 minutes. This gives the cabbage additional flavour. Alternatively, the cabbage can be finely shredded and cooked, in just enough of the liquor from the bacon or ham to keep it from burning, for 3–4 minutes until tender. The cabbage is then drained and tossed in butter or bacon fat and seasoned with freshly milled black pepper.

BAKED IRISH HAM
Bagún Bácáilte

Boiled bacon or ham, after cooking and skinning, is often coated in brown sugar or a mixture of sugar and breadcrumbs, studded with cloves and baked in the oven. This is the traditional way of serving boiled bacon or ham at Christmas or on other festive occasions.

Press 4 × 15 ml (4 tablespoons) of demerara sugar into the fat. Sometimes this is mixed with 3 × 15 ml (3 tablespoons) of dry mustard and a few breadcrumbs to give a spicy toasted crust. The fat is then studded with whole cloves and set on a roasting dish with a little ham stock or cider, then baked in a pre-heated oven at 220°C (425°F, gas mark 7) for 20 minutes until the coating is crisp and brown. If the joint of bacon or ham is being baked from cold, use a lower oven temperature (about 180°C, 350°F, gas mark 4) and cook for about 30–45 minutes, depending on the size of the joint, covering loosely with foil if it begins to brown too much.

Serve carved in slices with boiled or braised red cabbage and boiled jacket or roast potatoes.

PARSLEY SAUCE
Anlann Peirsile

This is one of the most popular sauces in Ireland. It is the perfect accompaniment to boiled bacon or ham, boiled tongue, mutton or chicken, as well as poached or baked salmon and other fish. For the very best results, where possible the liquid used should be from the meat or fish being cooked with the addition of a little milk to enrich it.

350 ml (¾ pint) stock, mutton, ham, beef, chicken or fish as appropriate
150 ml (5 fl oz) milk
Small piece of onion
1 bay leaf
Blade of mace
6 peppercorns
50 g (2 oz) butter
50 g (2 oz) plain flour
1 × 5 ml (1 teaspoon) lemon juice
3 × 15 ml (3 tablespoons) parsley, finely chopped
Salt and freshly milled black pepper

Mix the stock and milk together and add the onion, bay leaf, mace and peppercorns. Bring to the boil then remove from the heat and leave to infuse for 15 minutes. Strain.

Melt the butter, stir in the flour and gradually blend in the warm milk to form a smooth sauce. Bring to the boil, then reduce the heat and continue to cook for a few minutes to thicken the sauce and to cook out the flour. The consistency should resemble thick cream. Stir in the lemon juice and parsley and season to taste.

SPICY REDCURRANT SAUCE
Anlann Cuiríní Dearga le Spiosra

A sweet spicy sauce which makes an excellent accompaniment to boiled tongue or ham.

175 g (6 oz) redcurrant jelly
1 orange and 1 lemon, grated rind and juice
1 × 5 ml (1 teaspoon) dry mustard powder
1 × 15 ml (1 tablespoon) horseradish sauce
1 × 5 ml (1 teaspoon) freshly milled black pepper
1 × 1.25 ml (¼ teaspoon) powdered mace
2 × 15 ml (2 tablespoons) tarragon vinegar
250 ml (8 fl oz) tongue stock
175 ml (6 fl oz) red wine
2 × 15 ml (2 tablespoons) port

Combine all the ingredients in a saucepan stirring to dissolve the redcurrant jelly. Bring to the boil and cook briskly for about 20 minutes until reduced by about one third. Serve hot or cold.

Dublin coddle (page 60).

DUBLIN CODDLE
Codal Duibhlinneach

This savoury stew of bacon and sausages is associated with families who have lived for generations in Dublin and who regard the city as their local village. It has been popular since the eighteenth century and we are told that it was greatly enjoyed by Sean O'Casey, Dean Swift and many other literary figures. It was traditionally served on Saturday nights as a supper dish, accompanied by soda bread and washed down by glasses of stout, when the men came home from the pubs.

I have included potatoes in the dish, and although not absolutely correct it certainly makes the dish more acceptable to our sophisticated palates. I often fry the sausages, bacon and onion before combining them with the water and seasoning, as this gives the dish a more attractive colour and additional flavour.

SERVES 4
2 large onions, peeled and sliced
6 thick rashers bacon, approx. 225 g (8 oz),
each cut into 3 or 4 pieces
6 large pork sausages, cut in chunks
750 g (1½ lb) potatoes, peeled and sliced
Salt and freshly milled black pepper
3 × 15 ml (3 tablespoons) parsley, finely chopped
300 ml (10 fl oz) water

Mix the onions, bacon, sausages and potatoes in a saucepan, season with pepper and add half of the parsley. Pour on the water and bring to the boil. Cover tightly with greaseproof paper and a lid, reduce the heat and simmer for 1–1½ hours until the liquid is greatly reduced, and the potatoes are very tender but not mushy. Sprinkle with the remaining parsley, adjust the seasoning and serve hot with slices of soda bread (see page 132) and stout.

AN IRISH FRY
An Friochadh Gaelach

One of Ireland's most famous dishes, and probably the one most frequently eaten in homes throughout the country, is the 'fry'. It embraces the best of Irish produce and is served at any time of the day. For breakfast it generally consists of rashers of bacon with eggs and sausages; traditionally it would also have in-cluded a slice of black or white pudding. At other times of the day, when something even more substantial is called for, kidneys, liver and even steak or chops are added along with fried tomatoes and mushrooms.

A slightly different version is made in the northern counties and includes a selection of the traditional breads such as soda farls, potato cakes, and sometimes pancakes or slices of wheaten bread fried in the hot bacon fat. Served like this, it is known as an Ulster fry. Lard or bacon fat was traditionally used for frying, but in the interests of health I use oil.

An Irish fry.

SERVES 1
2 bacon rashers, back and streaky
2 sausages
2 slices black or white pudding
½ farl of soda bread (see page 133)
1 potato cake (see page 135)
1–2 large eggs
4 × 15 ml (4 tablespoons) oil for frying

The secret of preparing a good fry is to cook the food in the right order, starting with that which requires the longest cooking time, then gradually adding the rest of the ingredients at intervals, so that in the end everything will be ready at once.

Fry the sausages in a little of the oil over a gentle heat until almost cooked through, then increase the heat and add the bacon with its rind removed. Fry until the bacon fat is beginning to crisp, then remove both it and the sausages from the pan, drain on kitchen paper to remove the excess fat and keep warm. Fry the slices of pudding for a few minutes to warm through, then drain and keep warm with the bacon and sausages.

Cut both the soda farl and potato cake in half and fry in the remaining bacon and sausage fat until crisp and well toasted, adding a little extra oil if necessary. Remove from the pan, drain and keep warm. Add the remaining oil to the pan, allow it to warm but not to become sizzling hot, break the egg into the pool of fat and leave on the heat until the white is just beginning to set, then tip the pan away from you and spoon some of the hot fat over the yolk. This will give an attractive milky appearance to the top of the egg and ensure that both top and bottom are cooked at the same time. When the egg is cooked to your liking, arrange the bacon, sausages, pudding and bread on a large plate, then lift the egg carefully from the pan using a flat egg or fish slice. Drain on kitchen paper and place on the hot plate with the rest of the ingredients. Serve with sliced wheaten bread (see page 132) and strong tea.

FRIED LIVER AND BACON
Ae agus Bagún Friochta

Fried liver was often served as part of an Irish 'fry' (see opposite) along with bacon, eggs, sausages, puddings, and soda and potato bread, or as part of what the Irish might call a more 'substantial' meal consisting of kidney and chops – along with all the other ingredients, of course. When served with only the meat, it was known as an Irish grill. Liver was also more modestly served with fried bacon and onions.

SERVES 1
2 rashers of bacon, rind removed
½ large onion, thinly sliced
225 g (8 oz) calf's or lamb's liver, sliced
2 × 15 ml (2 tablespoons) plain flour

Salt and freshly milled black pepper
3 × 15 ml (3 tablespoons) hot water
2 × 15 ml (2 tablespoons) parsley, finely chopped

Fry the bacon until cooked and beginning to crisp. Transfer to a serving plate and keep warm. Fry the onion in the bacon fat until soft and beginning to brown; put on the plate with the bacon. If necessary, when frying the liver add a little fat or oil to the pan.

Combine the flour and seasoning in a polythene bag, add the slices of liver and toss to coat evenly with the flour. Shake off any excess and fry quickly until brown on both sides and lightly cooked through (overcooking results in hard tough liver). Transfer to the serving plate and arrange with the bacon and onions. Add the water to the sediment in the pan and stir to make a little gravy. Bring to the boil, season and pour over the liver.

Serve sprinkled with chopped parsley and accompanied by boiled or mashed potatoes.

PORK OR LAMB CISTE
Císte Muiceola nó Uaineola

This interesting dish has all the qualities of a stew with a bread-like topping. 'Císte' in Irish means cake, a word often used for bread. The topping is similar to a suet dumpling or cobbler and though seldom made today is very tasty.

SERVES 4
4 pork or lamb chops, trimmed of fat but with the bones left in
4 pork kidneys or 225 g (8 oz) pig's liver or lamb equivalent
2 large onions, peeled and sliced
1 large carrot, peeled and sliced
2 × 15 ml (2 tablespoons) parsley, finely chopped
1 × 2.5 ml ($\frac{1}{2}$ teaspoon) fresh thyme, finely chopped
Salt and freshly milled black pepper
450 ml (15 fl oz) water
FOR THE CISTE
225 g (8 oz) plain flour
1 × 1.25 ml ($\frac{1}{4}$ teaspoon) salt
1 × 5 ml (1 teaspoon) baking powder
100 g (4 oz) grated suet
2 × 15 ml (2 tablespoons) sultanas (for the pork dish only)
250 ml (8 fl oz) milk

Stand the chops, with the bones pointing upwards, around the edge of a medium-size saucepan (they will fall slightly to the side). Chop the kidney or liver and layer in the centre with the onions and carrots, herbs and seasoning. Add the water, which should almost cover the kidney and vegetables. Put the lid on and bring to the boil, then reduce the heat and simmer for about 20 minutes.

Meanwhile prepare the ciste. Sieve the flour, salt and baking powder together into a large bowl. Stir in the suet and, if using pork, the sultanas. Mix to a stiff dough with the milk.

Stuffed pork fillet.

Turn on to a floured surface, knead lightly and roll out to a circle, the same size as the top of the saucepan. Lift on top of the stew, pressing down on to the ingredients and allowing the chop bones to poke through. Leave about 5 centimetres (2 inches) around the top of the saucepan to allow the ciste to rise. Cover with buttered greaseproof paper and the saucepan lid. Return to the heat and cook gently for a further $1\frac{1}{4}$–$1\frac{1}{2}$ hours until the cake is risen and the meat and vegetables tender. It can also be cooked in the oven at 180°C (350°F, gas mark 4) for the same length of time.

Finally, loosen the edges of the ciste with a knife, cut into four wedges and serve each with a chop, kidney, or piece of liver, and vegetables.

STUFFED PORK FILLET
Filléad Muiceola le Búiste

In the days when the farmer killed his own pigs for home consumption the fillets were fried or stuffed and roasted, and considered a great delicacy. Today, they are still stuffed and roasted and served for Sunday lunch or on other special occasions. The roasting can be done either in the oven or in a pot on top of the cooker. Although not one of the cheaper cuts of meat, pork fillet is popular because of its leanness and lack of waste. Nowadays, the fillet is also cubed and casseroled, or cut into flat pieces and grilled or fried.

SERVES 4
MAKES 12 slices
2 pork fillets of even size and weight, approx.
350 g (12 oz) each
50 g (2 oz) butter
150 ml (5 fl oz) water
FOR THE STUFFING
1 medium onion, finely chopped
50 g (2 oz) butter
100 g (4 oz) fresh white breadcrumbs
1 × 5 ml (1 teaspoon) fresh thyme, finely chopped
1 × 5 ml (1 teaspoon) fresh sage, finely chopped or
2.5 ml ($\frac{1}{2}$ teaspoon) each of dried thyme and sage
2 × 15 ml (2 tablespoons) chopped parsley
Finely grated rind of half a lemon
Salt and freshly milled black pepper
FOR THE GRAVY
1 × 15 ml (1 tablespoon) plain flour
300 ml (10 fl oz) stock
Salt and freshly milled black pepper
OVEN TEMPERATURE 180°C (350°F, gas mark 4)
OVEN TIME 1–$1\frac{1}{4}$ hours

Prepare the fillets by splitting them down the centre along their length, but without cutting right through them. This will enable you to open out the fillet so that it will eventually lie flat. Follow this first cut with two more on either side, and continue making cuts like this until the fillets are opened out into a flattish-rectangular shape. At no time should the cuts go completely through the meat.

Prepare the stuffing by first softening the finely chopped onion in the butter. Then stir in the breadcrumbs, herbs and seasoning until they begin to bind together. Some people like to add a beaten egg to the stuffing at this stage, but I find it makes it rather solid. Arrange the stuffing on top of one of the prepared fillets, turning in the tails at either end. Cover with the second fillet, wrapping the long sides round the first fillet to encase the stuffing. Tie firmly at regular intervals along the fillet's length with fine string. Gently fry in the other 50 g (2 oz) of butter in a roasting dish or cast-iron casserole until the fillets are brown on all sides.

Pour round 150 ml (5 fl oz) water, cover with aluminium foil and roast in the oven, or cover with a lid and cook on top of the cooker, for 1–1¼ hours. While pork must be well cooked, over-cooked pork fillet is apt to be dry and stringy. The water in the roasting dish will help to prevent this and also provide some tasty stock for the gravy.

When the fillet is cooked, remove the string and transfer to a warm serving dish. Cover and keep warm while making the gravy.

Remove all but 1 × 15 ml (1 tablespoon) of pork fat from the roasting pan, or pot, and sprinkle the flour on the remaining sediment and juices. Stir to blend, then add the well-flavoured stock and bring to the boil stirring continually. Season with salt and black pepper and cook for a few minutes to thicken.

Serve the fillet carved in slices with the roast gravy, apple sauce and a selection of fresh vegetables.

NOTE When economy is a consideration, often only one fillet is used. This is split in the same way, but the stuffing is spread across half its width and the other half of the fillet folded over on top of it. almost completely enclosing it. It is then tied and roasted in the same way. It does not look quite as elegant when carved, but tastes just as good.

STEWED PORK RIBS
Stobhach Easnacha Muice

Butchers specialising in the sale of pork and pork products, with windows piled high with pig's trotters, knees, shanks, fillets, sausages and black and white puddings, rails of bacon and hams and hanging curtains of ribs, were at one time a common sight in all the towns and villages throughout Ireland. Today, although pork is still a popular food, these specialist shops have, with a few exceptions, been almost entirely replaced by the more clinical butchery departments of the supermarket. Belfast, however, is still lucky enough to have an excellent, traditional pork butcher's situated in one of the better-known districts of the city – Sandy Row. It is here that I am reminded of many of the traditional dishes of Ireland, and the cooking of my mother and grandmother who had perfected the art of these simple savoury meals. Stewed spare ribs is one of my favourites and is just as tasty as the 'barbecued' variety more common today.

SERVES 4
1kg (2 lb) spare ribs
450 ml (15 fl oz) water
2 large onions, peeled and sliced in rings
Salt and freshly milled black pepper
1 × 15 ml (1 tablespoon) cornflour
2 × 15 ml (2 tablespoons) parsley, finely chopped

Wash the ribs and cut into manageable portions. Put into a large saucepan and add the water. Bring to the boil and skim. Add the onions and seasoning, cover, reduce the heat and simmer for 2¼–2½ hours until the meat is tender and begins to leave the bones. Blend the cornflour in a little water, then add to the juices in the pan, stirring to mix and prevent lumps from forming. Boil for a further 5 minutes until the liquid has thickened. Add the chopped parsley and serve with soda bread (see page 132) or boiled potatoes and a glass of stout.

CRUBEENS
Crúibíní

Crubeens, or pig's trotters, is one of the great traditional Irish dishes. The delicate little front feet of the pig are thought to be more meaty than the back, having succulent bits of meat concealed around the bones, unlike the back feet, which are all bones and gristle and only used to give flavour and setting strength to brawns or galantines. Crubeens were a favourite in the pubs of Ireland on a Saturday night, when they were eaten in great quantity with soda bread (see page 132) and stout.

They are boiled, gently, in enough water to cover, for 2–3 hours, along with a large onion, a carrot, a bay leaf, a bunch of parsley, a sprig of thyme and 12 peppercorns, until the meat is tender.

Crubeens are eaten in the fingers, either hot or cold, and are very tasty. They can also be coated in breadcrumbs and fried, grilled or roasted in the oven until crisp and brown on all sides.

BLACK OR BLOOD PUDDINGS
Putóga Fola

Traditionally, blood puddings would have been made from cow's blood; then later, sheep's; and today, almost invariably pig's blood. Although the recipes vary a great deal from region to region, and indeed from butcher to butcher, the basic ingredients remain the same: blood, fat, milk or cream, some kind of cereal – generally oatmeal – herbs such as tansy or thyme, and spices and seasoning. In appearance, black puddings resemble very plump sausages and are generally shaped in skins, although in some areas, particularly Cork, they are sometimes made in bowls.

Black puddings are served either hot or cold, cut in 5 mm–1 cm (¼–½ inch) slices. Generally, they are fried in bacon fat or lard and form an integral part of an Irish 'fry' (see page 60).

The black puddings of Cork are a great speciality and are called drisheens (in Irish, 'drisín'). They are made from sheep's blood only, and are larger in diameter than the usual black pudding, resembling a blown-up bicycle tyre. They have a wonderful texture, rather like that of a baked egg custard, and are traditionally flavoured with tansy.

In the covered market at Cork you will find one of the few remaining specialist shops which sells nothing but drisheen and tripe. Most black and white puddings, with the exception of those from a few specialists in Cork, Portrush and Dublin, are now commercially produced. Since animals are no longer slaughtered on the farm, and blood is not readily available from the abattoir, they are no longer made at home.

White puddings (putóga bána) are very similar to black puddings, except they are not made with blood. They contain only oatmeal, lard, onion, herbs and seasonings.

KIDNEYS
Duáin

Lambs' and sheep's kidneys, like calves' kidneys, have a more delicate flavour and texture than those of the ox and pig. The former are ideal for grilling, while the latter are more suitable for stewing.

A popular way of preparing lambs' kidneys for breakfast was to cook them whole in their 'jacket' fat, or suet, in the oven. This ensured that all the juices stayed in and the kidneys remained moist and succulent. It is, however, very much an acquired taste, and probably too strong for most twentieth-century palates. The cooking method used is also less likely to remove any impurities.

KIDNEYS IN THEIR JACKETS
Duáin ina gCraicne

Allow 2–3 kidneys per person, wipe – without removing the suet they are encased in – and set on a baking dish. Cook in a pre-heated oven at 220°C (425°F, gas mark 7) for 40–45 minutes until the fat is crisp and cooked. Cut each kidney through the centre, from the rounded side, without completely separating each half. Open out like a book and lay on top of a piece of freshly toasted bread, each kidney slightly overlapping the other. Garnish with parsley.

GRILLED KIDNEYS
Duáin Gríoscaithe

Once again allow 2–3 kidneys per person, but this time remove the fat and silvery-blue skin. Split them open on the rounded side, but without separating the two halves. Remove the central core either with a knife or a pair of scissors. Put on a skewer so that they will remain flat and open during the cooking. Season with salt and freshly milled black pepper and brush with oil or melted butter. Lay on a grill rack under a pre-heated grill and cook, turning several times, until they are done. This will take about 8 minutes. Do not overcook the kidneys as they will dry out and become tough like overcooked liver. Serve on toast, in the same way as the kidneys in their jackets, with grilled bacon or as part of a mixed grill.

LIVER AND BACON CASSEROLE
Casaról Ae agus Bagúin

The most delicately flavoured liver is either from the calf or the lamb and is perfect for frying because it is so tender. Ox liver is coarser, both in texture and flavour, and is only suitable for stewing. Pig's liver is superior to ox liver and is of a particularly high quality in Ireland. It can be fried, stewed or stuffed and baked.

SERVES 4
225 g (8 oz) bacon, rind removed
1 × 15 ml (1 tablespoon) fat or oil
450 g (1 lb) pig's liver, sliced
3 × 15 ml (3 tablespoons) plain flour
Salt and freshly milled black pepper
1 large onion, peeled and sliced
450 ml (15 fl oz) water, or bacon or ham stock
2 × 15 ml (2 tablespoons) parsley, finely chopped

Cut the bacon slices into two or three pieces and fry in a hot frying pan until the fat begins to run. Remove and drain on absorbent kitchen paper. Dip the slices of liver in the flour, seasoned with salt and pepper, and fry in the bacon fat until brown on both sides, adding a little extra fat or oil if necessary. Remove from the pan and fry the sliced onion. Layer the bacon, liver and onions in a saucepan or casserole, seasoning well between the layers with salt, pepper and parsley. Pour over enough stock to cover, bring to the boil, then reduce the heat and simmer for about an hour until the liver is tender, all the flavours well blended and the sauce thickened. The casserole can alternatively be cooked in the oven at 180°C (350°F, gas mark 4) for the same length of time. About 50 g (2 oz) of sliced and fried mushrooms can also be added to this dish.

Serve sprinkled with a little extra chopped parsley and boiled potatoes in their skins.

TRIPE AND ONIONS
Triopas agus Oinniúin

This is another famous Saturday night dish which is greatly enjoyed by many Irish people, although tripe is one of those foods that you either love or hate. Since Tripes à la mode de Caen *is one of the great peasant dishes of Norman France, it is possible that the Irish liking for this food was acquired from the*

Normans when they came to Ireland.

Tripe is the stomach tissue of cud-chewing animals, usually cows, but also pigs, sheep or calves. It is sold by the butchers as 'dressed' tripe, which means it has been thoroughly cleaned and given a long initial cooking to tenderise it. There are several different types of tripe: the flat or ridged variety of the first stomach, and the honeycomb-patterned tripe of the second stomach, which is slightly more tender. Dressed tripe, although partially cooked, still requires another 2–3 hours simmering to make it completely tender.

SERVES 4–6
1 kg (2 lb) dressed honeycomb tripe
1 kg (2 lb) onions, peeled and sliced
600 ml (20 fl oz) milk
1 bay leaf
Pinch of grated nutmeg
Salt and freshly milled black pepper
25 g (1 oz) butter
25 g (1 oz) plain flour
250 g (8 oz) streaky bacon, chopped and fried until crisp
65 ml (2½ fl oz) cream
50 g (2 oz) breadcrumbs
1 × 5 ml (1 teaspoon) parsley, chopped

Wash the tripe and simmer in enough salted water to cover for 2 hours. Drain and refresh in cold water. Cut the tripe into large pieces and put into a saucepan with the onions, milk, bay leaf, nutmeg, salt and pepper. Bring to the boil, cover and simmer gently for about an hour.

Melt the butter in another saucepan. Add the flour and cook for a minute. When the tripe is cooked, strain off the milk and gradually add to the butter and flour mixture to make a smooth sauce. Pour on top of the tripe and onions and stir in the bacon and cream. Adjust the seasoning and pour into a shallow serving dish. Sprinkle the breadcrumbs on top and brown under the grill. Dust with finely chopped parsley before serving.

MINCED BEEF
Mairteoil Mhionaithe

Minced beef, made from the trimmings of the carcass and the less tender cuts such as shin, leg and neck, is one of the most frequently used meat products. When minced finely with only a little fat left in to keep it moist, minced beef can be used for stews, pies and beefburgers. Four dishes which are favourites in most homes, including my own, are minced beef, carrots and onions; savoury minced beef tart; mince in pastry; and meat loaf. These recipes were passed down to me by my grandmother and two are included here.

SAVOURY MEAT LOAF
Builín Feola

This traditional meat loaf would have origin-ally been cooked in an earthenware jar in a pot of boiling water over the open fire. It is still boiled in this way in many homes today, but on the cooker rather than over the turf fire. How-ever, it is more frequently baked in a loaf tin in the oven. It slices beautifully and is delicious hot or cold with tomato sauce and salad.

Savoury meat loaf.

SERVES 4
Oil for brushing
2 × 15 ml (2 tablespoons) browned breadcrumbs
FOR THE MEAT FILLING
1 small onion, finely chopped
25 g (1 oz) fat or oil
450 g (1 lb) minced beef
100 g (4 oz) breadcrumbs
1 egg beaten
1 × 15 ml (1 tablespoon) tomato ketchup
1 × 5 ml (1 teaspoon) Worcester sauce
1 × 5 ml (1 teaspoon) mixed herbs
1 × 5 ml (1 teaspoon) chopped parsley
Salt and freshly milled black pepper
1 loaf tin, 19 × 9.5 × 5.5 cm (7½ × 3¾ × 2¼ in)
OVEN TEMPERATURE 190°C (375°F, gas mark 5)
OVEN TIME 1 hour

Grease the loaf tin and dust with the browned breadcrumbs. Soften the onion in the hot fat, add the minced beef and continue to cook until browning. Stir in the rest of the ingredients. Pack tightly into the prepared tin, cover with aluminium foil and bake in the oven for 1 hour until firm to touch.

If boiling in an earthenware jar, pack in tightly, leaving no air spaces and also cover tightly with aluminium foil. Submerge in a large pot of enough boiling water to almost cover and cook for 1–1½ hours. When cooked, turn out and serve, either hot or cold, cut in slices and accompanied by tomato sauce.

MINCED BEEF, CARROTS AND ONIONS
Mairteoil Mhionaithe le Meacain Dhearga agus Oinniúin

A stew of best-quality minced beef flavoured with onion and carrot and served with boiled potatoes and peas. A popular Irish week-day meal.

SERVES 4
450 g (1 lb) minced beef
1 large onion, finely chopped
1 × 15 ml (1 tablespoon) fat or oil
1 large carrot, diced
300 ml (10 fl oz) cold water or beef stock
1 bay leaf
Salt and freshly milled black pepper
1 × 5 ml (1 teaspoon) arrowroot or plain flour, blended in a little cold water

Fry the minced beef and the onion in the hot oil in a large saucepan over a high heat until the meat browns. Add the carrot, water or stock, bay leaf and seasoning. Stir well and bring to the boil, then reduce the heat and continue to cook gently for 20–30 minutes until the meat is cooked, the vegetables tender and the flavours well blended. Remove the bay leaf and thicken with the blended arrowroot. Cook for a further few minutes. Correct the seasoning and serve with potatoes and peas.

POT ROAST OF BEEF
Mairteoil Photrósta

It was only in the early part of this century that ranges and cookers became part of the standard kitchen equipment. Up until then food was cooked over the fire in an open hearth or grate. Indeed, in some of the more remote parts of the country this method of cooking is still practised, albeit rarely. All roasting, however, was done in a pot-oven, a flat-bottomed pot standing on three legs (see page 33).

The tradition of pot-roasting meat did not die out with the demise of the three-legged pot as it was replaced by the saucepan and cast-iron casserole, along with the range and the more modern gas and electric cookers. Neither was the pot-roast confined to country homes: in my family home in Belfast the pot-roast of beef was the traditional Sunday lunch, although it never tasted quite the same as its country cousin. Pot-roasting is still carried on in many homes today, because small joints of meat can be used, and it is often more convenient and economical than oven-roasting.

MAKES approx. 10 slices
A 1.5 kg (3 lb) joint will serve 4–6.

Well hung silverside or topside are the cuts of beef most frequently pot-roasted and are tied into a neat shape before cooking. A little dripping – beef fat – is heated in a large saucepan and the meat is quickly browned in this on all sides. The heat is then turned down very low, the lid put on and the meat cooked for about 2–2½ hours. I generally allow 40–45 minutes per 450 g (1 lb). The joint is then carved in slices and served with boiled carrots and potatoes.

Gravy can be made from the meat juices blended with 1 × 15 ml (1 tablespoon) cornflour. The meat, when cooked slowly, should produce about 350 ml (12 fl oz) of juice.

BRAISED BEEF, CARROTS AND ONIONS
Mairteoil Ghalstofa le Meacain Dhearga agus Oinniúin

This traditional braised dish, like the pot roast, was originally cooked in a saucepan or casserole, either on the top heat of the range or cooker, or in the oven. It differs from pot roasting in that it is a combination of both roasting and stewing. Joints or thick slices of meat are browned before being cooked on a bed of vegetables. Liquid is also added, which not only enhances the flavour, but means that the less tender cuts of meat such as silverside, topside or thick plate can be used, the meat being tenderised by the liquid and the slow cooking.

Braised steak (page 67).

Rolled top breast, sometimes referred to as brisket, is also suitable for braising. It comes from the point, or meaty end, of the boned and rolled brisket and resembles the whole fillet of beef but with fat round the outside. Although it looks tender, it is one of the toughest pieces of meat from the beef carcass and takes longer to cook. Fortunately, the long wait is worth it as the cooked joint not only tastes delicious but also carves beautifully.

SERVES 6
MAKES approx. 12 slices
1.5 kg (3½ lb) joint of beef
1 large onion
2 large carrots
225 g (8 oz) turnip (optional)
1 × 15 ml (1 tablespoon) fat or oil
600 ml (20 fl oz) beef stock or water
Sprig of thyme, bay leaf, parsley stalks
Salt and freshly milled black pepper

Tie the meat into a neat shape. Peel and quarter the onion, peel the carrot and cut into four. Peel the turnip and cut into pieces, about the size of the carrots. Brown the meat in the hot fat or oil, then remove from the pan. Add the vegetables and toss in the fat for a few minutes to colour slightly. Add the stock or water and stir to remove any sediment from the bottom of the pan. Replace the meat, setting it on top of the vegetables. Tuck the herbs, tied together, down one side and season with black pepper. Bring the liquid to the boil, cover and then reduce the heat and simmer for 2–2½ hours for topside, silverside or thick plate, and 4–5 hours for the brisket. Alternatively, the meat can be brought to the boil on the top of the cooker, then transferred to a pre-heated oven at 180°C (350°F, gas mark 4) to complete the cooking.

When ready, lift the meat on to a hot serving dish, remove the string and keep warm while preparing the gravy. Strain the liquid from the braising pot into a smaller saucepan. Remove any excess fat and thicken with 2 × 15 ml (2 tablespoons) of cornflour blended with a little cold water. Return to the boil and boil for a few minutes, adjust the seasoning and serve with the beef.

Traditionally, the vegetables would have been served with the beef, but after such long cooking they are inclined to have lost their

65

colour, texture and flavour. Nowadays, it is more common to serve freshly boiled carrots and turnips along with the joint.

CORNED BEEF
Mairteoil Shaillte

Owing to the lack of long-term storage facilities in the past, most meat was preserved, generally through salting. Beef preserved in this way is known as salt beef, pickled beef, or corned beef.

Nowadays, meat is usually salted for flavour and variety rather than preservation. When individual joints of meat are to be prepared in this way it is best to choose compact meaty joints such as silverside or topside, or the brisket of beef which can be on or off the bone. One end of the brisket is fat and lean in layers and is generally cooked on the bone, while the other is more fleshy and makes an excellent meaty joint; when boned and rolled, it is sometimes referred to as the top breast of brisket. The difference between these joints is not only their fat content but also their cooking time. Silverside and topside take 2–2½ hours, while the brisket requires 4–5 hours to make it tender – a fact often omitted in recipe books, but vitally important to the successful cooking of the meat. Tongue can also be prepared in the same way. Both beef and tongue can be bought ready salted from most butchers.

FOR THE PICKLE
450 g (1 lb) coarse salt
2.75 litres (5 pints) cold water
100 g (4 oz) sugar, white or brown
25 g (1 oz) saltpetre
3 bay leaves
FOR THE MEAT
1 × 1.75–2.75 kg (4–6 lb) joint of beef or 1 ox tongue
100 g (4 oz) coarse salt

Boil all the ingredients for the pickle together in a large pot for about 10 minutes. Leave to go quite cold. When cold, test the pickle to see if it is strong enough by dropping in a whole uncooked egg still in its shell. If the egg floats, then the pickle is ready. If it sinks, more salt must be added and the boiling, cooling and testing repeated once more.

Wipe the meat, removing any clots of blood and gristle but do not wash it. Then rub with the salt, making sure that it reaches all the cracks, crevices and seams. Put into a large sterilised glass or earthenware container and completely cover with the pickle. If necessary, place a plate or board on top, weighted with a flat stone. Store in the refrigerator or cold pantry for 10–14 days, turning every few days.

The meat should be soaked in cold water overnight or for at least a few hours before cooking, depending on the saltiness of the pickle.

CORNED BEEF AND CABBAGE
Mairteoil Shaillte le Cabáiste

This, like Irish stew (see page 72) and shin and Guinness (see page 68), is one of Ireland's classic beef dishes. It is made with corned or salt beef and is served with its flavouring vegetables, cabbage and often suet dumplings. Cabbage achieved immense popularity during the famine when it was sown as a safe crop instead of potatoes.

SERVES 6–8
1.5–1.75 kg (3½–4 lb) salted silverside, topside or brisket of beef
Cold water to cover
1 large onion stuck with 4 cloves
Sprig of thyme, bay leaf, parsley stalks, tied together
6 small onions, peeled
2 large carrots, peeled and quartered
1 large cabbage, quartered
Freshly milled black pepper

Soak the salted meat in cold water overnight, or for at least 2 hours to ensure it is not excessively salty when cooked. Put into a large saucepan and cover with fresh cold water. Add the onion stuck with the cloves and the bouquet of herbs. Bring to the boil, then reduce the heat, cover and simmer for 1½ hours if using silverside or topside; if using brisket simmer for 4 hours.

Meanwhile, prepare the vegetables keeping them roughly the same size. Add the onions and carrots to the pot after the silverside or topside has been cooking for 1½ hours and the brisket for 4 hours. Cook for another 30 minutes until both the meat and vegetables are tender. Add the cabbage 15 minutes before the end of the cooking time.

If dumplings are being made, add to the pot along with the cabbage 15–20 minutes before the end of the cooking time (see page 68).

Serve the meat on a hot dish surrounded by the dumplings and vegetables, and accompanied by boiled potatoes.

IRISH SPICED BEEF
Mairteoil Spiosraithe

Spiced beef is traditionally served in Ireland at Christmas as a change from salt beef and along with roast beef; boiled salt beef was the forerunner to the turkey. It originated in the time when it was difficult to obtain freshly killed beef at Christmas, most of it having been salted after the pre-winter slaughter.

Although spices are known to have been imported into Ireland from as early as the twelfth century, they were regarded as luxuries. Spiced beef, therefore, would only have been served in wealthy homes, where the spices could be afforded, acquired in exchange for other goods, and where beef was available.

Spiced beef can be prepared in a number of different ways, using an infinite variety and combination of spices. The two methods I use for freshly killed, unsalted beef use both a dry and wet spice. I find the wet spicing method slightly more convenient and certainly less messy, but both taste equally good.

SPICED BEEF I
Using dry spice and salt (begin preparations 2–3 weeks before use)

SERVES 6–12
1.75–2.75 kg (4–6 lb) beef – silverside, topside or brisket, boned and rolled
FOR THE SPICED PICKLE
450 g (1 lb) coarse salt
25 g (1 oz) saltpetre
1 × 2.5 ml (½ teaspoon) powdered cloves
1 × 2.5 ml (½ teaspoon) powdered allspice
1 × 5 ml (1 teaspoon) black peppercorns
1 × 1.25 ml (¼ teaspoon) powdered ginger
1 × 1.25 ml (¼ teaspoon) powdered mace
1 × 5 ml (1 teaspoon) powdered bay leaves
12 whole dried juniper berries
¼ onion, finely chopped
350 g (12 oz) soft brown sugar

Irish spiced beef.

Trim the meat if necessary and wipe with a damp cloth. Combine all the ingredients for the pickle in a large glass or earthenware bowl or crock and mix well. Set the beef on top and rub the spicing mixture well into the flesh, making sure it gets into all the crevices. Cover and keep in the refrigerator or other cold place. Turn the meat each day, rubbing in the spices. Do this for 14–17 days depending on the size and thickness of the joint.

When the meat is sufficiently pickled, remove it from the bowl and wash in cold water. Tie firmly into a neat shape and put into a large saucepan. Cover with cold water. Bring to the boil, skimming well. Add a peeled onion stuck with 3–4 cloves, a carrot cut into pieces, a stick of celery, 12 whole peppercorns and a big bunch of fresh herbs including parsley, thyme and a bay leaf. Return to the boil, then reduce the heat and continue to cook, with the pot covered, for 2–2½ hours. If brisket is used, cook for 4–5 hours. During the last 30 minutes of cooking, 300 ml (10 fl oz) of Guinness can be added which gives a very rich distinctive flavour.

Remove from the cooking liquor and roll tightly in waxed or greaseproof paper and aluminium foil to set the shape. Leave to go cold before slicing and serving with pickles. Spiced beef can also be served hot, but it is more usually served cold.

NOTE Spiced beef is sold in many butcher's shops throughout Ireland, particularly at Christmas when it is often tied with red ribbon and decorated with a sprig of holly. It makes an excellent present.

SPICED BEEF II
Using a wet spiced pickle (begin preparations 1 week before use)

SERVES 6–12
1.75–2.75 kg (4–6 lb) beef, silverside, topside or boned-and-rolled brisket
FOR THE SPICED PICKLE
450 g (1 lb) coarse salt
25 g (1 oz) saltpetre
2 × 5 ml (2 teaspoons) ground bay leaves
1 × 5 ml (1 teaspoon) ground cloves
2 × 5 ml (2 teaspoons) ground mace
1 × 5 ml (1 teaspoon) ground black pepper
2 cloves garlic, crushed in salt
2.5 ml (½ teaspoon) allspice
2 × 15 ml (2 tablespoons) brown sugar
1 litre (2 pints) water

Trim the meat if necessary and wipe with a damp cloth. Combine all the ingredients for the pickle in a large glass or earthenware bowl or crock and mix well. Set the beef in this liquid, making sure there is enough to cover it. Cover and keep in the refrigerator or other cold place, turning daily for a week. When the meat is sufficiently pickled, remove from the bowl. Tie firmly into a neat shape and cook as for the previous recipe.

BRAISED STEAK
Stéig Ghalstofa
A quickly prepared dish of individual portions of braising beef, such as topside, silverside and thick plate, cooked with mushrooms and onions in a rich sauce flavoured with mushroom ketchup, a seasoning which was extremely popular in the eighteenth and nineteenth centuries. The recipe for mushroom ketchup appears in many manuscript cookery books of that period. One from the recipe book of the Echlin family of County Down is given on page 84. Today, however, it can also be bought ready-made from good delicatessens or supermarkets.

SERVES 4

750 g–1 kg (1½–2 lb) topside, cut into individual
portions 2 cm (¾ in) thick
50 g (2 oz) plain flour, seasoned with salt and
freshly milled black pepper
2 × 15 ml (2 tablespoons) oil for frying
100 g (4 oz) mushrooms, button or field, sliced
1 large onion, peeled and sliced
1 × 15 ml (1 tablespoon) mushroom ketchup
1 × 15 ml (1 tablespoon) brown sauce
300 ml (10 fl oz) water

Put the meat in a large polythene bag along with the seasoned flour and shake well to coat it. Fry in the hot oil in a large saucepan or ovenproof casserole until brown on both sides. Add the mushrooms, either whole if they are the small button variety, or sliced if large or if field mushrooms. Add the onion along with the remaining ingredients. Bring to the boil, cover, then reduce the heat and simmer gently for 1½–2 hours until the meat is tender. Alternatively, the dish can be cooked in a pre-heated oven, after having been brought to the boil on top of the stove, at 180°C (350°F, gas mark 4) for the same length of time. Serve with peas and boiled jacket potatoes or soda or wheaten bread (see page 132).

GAELIC STEAK
Stéig Ghaelach

This is a modern recipe which has become a favourite, particularly in hotels and restaurants, throughout the country. It combines the best of Ireland's natural produce – beef, cream and of course whiskey – in a tasty and quickly prepared dish. Sirloin or fillet steak are used most frequently, but it can also be made with rump steak flattened out to 3 mm (⅛ in) thick.

SERVES 1

1 × 225 g (8 oz) fillet or sirloin steak, or 1 thin
piece of rump steak
Freshly milled black pepper
1 × 15 ml (1 tablespoon) butter
1 × 15 ml (1 tablespoon) oil
2 × 15 ml (2 tablespoons) onion, finely chopped
1 measure Irish whiskey
3 × 15 ml (3 tablespoons) double cream
Pinch of salt
Watercress, to garnish

Trim the excess fat off the meat and season well with the milled black pepper. Combine the butter and oil in a frying pan and heat to blend. Add the onion and fry gently until soft but not coloured, scrape to the sides of the pan, increase the heat and when very hot add the steak. Fry very quickly, sealing on both sides, until cooked as required. Add the whiskey to the pan and set alight. Remove the meat on to a warm serving plate and keep warm while finishing the dish. Add the cream to the pan and mix with the onion and meat juices. Bring to the boil, reducing slightly. Taste for seasoning and pour over the meat. Serve garnished with watercress.

BEEF STEW WITH DUMPLINGS
Stobhach Mairteoil le Domplagáin

Stews made from beef, mutton and pork, combined with the traditional vegetables of the country – onions, carrots, parsnips, turnips and leeks – provide an unending variety of dishes throughout the year. Frequently, potatoes are also added, to enrich and thicken the stew and to enable the entire meal to be cooked in the one pot. In years gone by, in the poorer farmhouses, this was particularly important as there was probably only one pot, and this had to be used for everything.

Dumplings, made from flour and suet, were also often added to the stew, as in this traditional recipe.

SERVES 6
FOR THE STEW

750 g–1 kg (1½–2 lb) stewing beef: chuck steak,
thick plate or shin
2 × 15 ml (2 tablespoons) fat or oil
450 g (1 lb) carrots, peeled and sliced
1 large onion, peeled and chopped
1 × 15 ml (1 tablespoon) plain flour
450 ml (15 fl oz) water or beef stock
Salt and freshly milled black pepper
1 × 15 ml (1 tablespoon) parsley, finely chopped
FOR 8 DUMPLINGS
750 g (4 oz) self-raising flour
50 g (2 oz) shredded suet or butter
2 × 15 ml (2 tablespoons) parsley, finely chopped
Salt and freshly milled black pepper
1 egg, size 2
4 × 15 ml (4 tablespoons) cold water

Cut the meat into 2.5 cm (1 in) cubes, and brown in the hot fat or oil in a large saucepan or ovenproof casserole. Add the carrots and the onion and mix in the flour. Pour on the water or stock and bring to the boil. Season with salt and milled black pepper. Cover and simmer for 1¼–1½ hours until the meat is almost tender.

Meanwhile prepare the dumplings. Combine the dry ingredients in a mixing bowl and, if using butter rather than suet, rub it in until the mixture resembles fine breadcrumbs. Mix together the egg and water, pour on to the dry mixture and mix to form a sticky dough. Using a wet dessertspoon, drop spoonfuls of the dough on top of the simmering stew. There should be eight dumplings. Cover and cook for a further 30 minutes. Serve sprinkled with parsley.

SHIN AND GUINNESS
Spanla Mairteola agus Leann Dubh

This rich stew has been popular since the nineteenth century and combines beef and root vegetables along with one of the national drinks – Guinness. Originally, porter or stout – a weaker, darker beer than Guinness – was used along with shin of beef which produced a rich, highly flavoured stew. Nowadays, a stewing cut of beef, such as thick plate or chuck steak, is preferred as this has less fat and gristle and there is no weight loss because of the bone. However, the flavour is not quite as good. Sometimes the beef is also cut into individual slices, rather than cubes, which gives a different presentation. The dish is then referred to as braised beef and Guinness.

SERVES 4

1 kg (2 lb) shin of beef
50 g (2 oz) plain flour, seasoned with salt and
pepper
2 × 15 ml (2 tablespoons) fat or oil
1 large onion, peeled and sliced
1 large carrot, peeled and sliced
300 ml (10 fl oz) Guinness
450 ml (15 fl oz) water
1 bay leaf
50 g (2 oz) prunes, soaked in water to cover
Salt and freshly milled black pepper
1 × 15 ml (1 tablespoon) parsley, finely chopped

Trim the meat from the bone, removing any

Oxtail stew.

excess fat. Cut into cubes, approximately 2.5 cm (1 in), and put into a polythene bag along with the seasoned flour and shake well to coat. Heat the oil in a large saucepan or ovenproof casserole and fry the meat until golden brown. Add the onion and continue to cook for a few minutes until it also begins to colour. Stir in any remaining flour along with the carrot, Guinness and water. Stir to combine, scraping any sediment off the bottom of the pan to prevent burning. Add the bay leaf, bring to the boil, then reduce the heat and simmer gently for 2 hours until the meat is tender.

Alternatively, after the stew has been brought to the boil it can be cooked in the oven at 180°C (350°F, gas mark 4) for the same length of time. It is important not to overcook

the meat as it will become stringy. Half an hour before the end of the cooking time, add the prunes. These give a particularly rich flavour to the finished dish. Remove the bay leaf, adjust the seasoning, sprinkle with parsley and serve with boiled potatoes in their jackets. Do not forget that the stones are still in the prunes!

OXTAIL STEW
Stobhach Damh-Eireabaill

Oxtail, like all other stewing cuts of meat including the shin, brisket and neck, was frequently combined with whatever root vegetables were available to produce a rich, tasty stew. Oxtail, although once widely used, in recent years seems to have become less popular than many of the other cuts of meat which is a great pity as it has a particularly delicious flavour. The following recipe was the one used in my grandmother's home.

SERVES 4
1 large oxtail, cut into 5 cm (2 in) lengths
50 g (2 oz) plain flour, seasoned
2 × 15 ml (2 tablespoons) fat or oil for frying
1 large onion, peeled and thinly sliced
2 large carrots, peeled and sliced
2 × 15 ml (2 tablespoons) tomato purée
Pinch each of ground mace and allspice
Sprig of thyme, bay leaf, parsley stalks, tied together
600 ml (20 fl oz) beef stock
Salt and freshly milled black pepper
2 × 15 ml (2 tablespoons) parsley, finely chopped

Put the pieces of oxtail into a large polythene bag with the seasoned flour and shake to coat each piece. Brown in the hot fat or oil in a large saucepan. Add the prepared vegetables and continue to fry for a further few minutes. Stir in the tomato purée. Add any remaining flour from the bag along with the ground spices and bouquet of herbs. Stir in the stock and bring to the boil. Reduce the heat, cover and simmer for 2½–3 hours until the meat is falling off the bones. Skim off any excess fat and adjust the seasoning. Sprinkle with the parsley and serve with mashed or boiled jacket potatoes.

BOILED AND PRESSED OX TONGUE
Damh-theanga Bruite Brúite

In Ireland, tongue is generally served cold after being pressed, but sometimes it is served hot with a spicy, Cumberland-type sauce which is also delicious cold. The best tongue to use is a salted ox or calf tongue.

SERVES 6
1 salted ox tongue, 1.5–2.75 kg (3–6 lb)
Cold water to cover
1 large onion
4 cloves
1 large carrot
1 stick of celery
6–8 peppercorns
2 bay leaves
A few parsley stalks and a sprig of thyme
2 × 5 ml (2 teaspoons) gelatine powder

Soak the tongue in cold water overnight to remove any excess salt. Drain and rinse, then put in a large pot with enough cold water to cover. Bring to the boil, then throw off this first

Irish stew (page 72).

boiling water. Rinse the tongue and wash out the pan. Begin again with fresh cold water, this time adding the onion stuck with the cloves, the celery stick cut into large pieces, the peppercorns and the herbs tied together to form a bouquet garni. Bring to the boil and simmer for about 4 hours until very tender. To test if cooked, try to pull out the small bone at the base of the tongue; if it comes away easily, the tongue is ready. Also test by sticking the point of a knife into the thickest part of the tongue, just above the root; it will slip in easily if the tongue is cooked.

Cool slightly in the liquid, then remove and put into a bowl of cold water. This will make it easier to skin. Peel off the skin, cutting away a little of the root and removing any bones. If serving cold, curl the tongue round to fit into either a tongue press, a deep round cake tin or a soufflé dish. The tongue must fit very tightly into the container so that it will mould into a neat shape when pressed. Reduce the stock by boiling, to concentrate the flavours, then strain off about 275 ml (9 fl oz). Sprinkle the gelatine powder into a little cold water in a cup set in a small pan of simmering water. Melt it until absolutely clear before adding to the 275 ml (9 fl oz) of stock. Pour over the tongue. If no purpose-built press is available, set a saucer or plate on top along with a weight. Leave in the refrigerator overnight to set before turning out and serving, cut in slices with Cumberland sauce, or redcurrant or quince jelly.

If the tongue is to be served hot, it can be left unpressed. Carve in slices and serve with a spicy redcurrant sauce (see page 59) or if pressed, cut in thick slices and re-heat in the sauce.

ROAST LAMB
Uaineoil Rósta

Today, in Ireland, roast leg or shoulder of lamb is associated with spring and is often served for Easter Sunday lunch with a selection of small spring vegetables including new potatoes, roast gravy and mint sauce. Redcurrant or quince jelly are also favourite accompaniments.

In Ireland, all meat would traditionally have been roasted in the pot-oven over the open fire. However, since the advent of wall-ovens, ranges, and gas and electric cookers, roasting is generally done in a roasting dish in a hot oven.

To roast a shoulder or a leg of lamb, put it into a pre-heated oven at 230°C (450°F, gas mark 8) and cook for 30 minutes, then turn down the heat to 180°C (350°F, gas mark 4) and cook for 30 minutes to the pound.

A SHOULDER OF LAMB AND OYSTERS
Gualainn Uaineola agus Oisrí

Although much of the mutton originally prepared in Irish houses was stewed, the chops were also fried, and whole joints were both boiled and roasted. This fascinating recipe, adapted from the eighteenth-century manuscript recipe book of the Echlin family from County Down, is for a shoulder of mutton stuffed with oysters and served with an oyster sauce. Originally the shoulder of mutton was boiled, but since mutton is no longer readily available I have used lamb, which is much more tender and lends itself more readily to roasting. I have also altered the quantity of ingredients, but without changing the proportion, in order to make it more suitable for today's smaller families and taking into account the high price of oysters.

The shoulder can be left on the bone and a pocket made on one side of the blade bone to contain the stuffing. However, I prefer to have it boned. I can then stuff, roll and tie it into a neat shape, which makes carving and serving relatively easy. It is a wonderful dish with a stunning taste and is perfect for a special occasion.

SERVES 6
MAKES 7–8 slices
3 kg (7 lb) shoulder of lamb, boned but not rolled
2 × 15 ml (2 tablespoons) butter or oil
Salt and freshly milled black pepper
FOR THE STUFFING
1 large onion
2 × 15 ml (2 tablespoons) butter or oil
10 fresh oysters, removed from their shells and the juices reserved
225 g (8 oz) breadcrumbs
Grated rind of half a lemon
1 × 2.5 ml ($\frac{1}{2}$ teaspoon) fresh thyme, finely chopped
2 × 15 ml (2 tablespoons) parsley, finely chopped
1 × 1.25 ml ($\frac{1}{4}$ teaspoon) ground cloves
1 × 1.25 ml ($\frac{1}{4}$ teaspoon) ground mace
1 × 1.25 ml ($\frac{1}{4}$ teaspoon) ground nutmeg
Salt and freshly milled black pepper
FOR THE OYSTER SAUCE
1 small onion, finely chopped
50 g (2 oz) butter
100 g (4 oz) mushrooms, sliced
2 anchovies, chopped
1 × 5 ml (1 teaspoon) capers
10 fresh oysters, removed from their shells and the juices reserved
85 ml (3 fl oz) oyster juice
275 ml (9 fl oz) mutton or lamb stock
1 × 15 ml (1 tablespoon) cornflour
3 egg yolks
1 × 15 ml (1 tablespoon) vinegar
1 × 15 ml (1 tablespoon) parsley, finely chopped
OVEN TEMPERATURE 180°C (350°F, gas mark 4)
OVEN TIME $3\frac{3}{4}$ hours

Begin by preparing the stuffing. Fry the onion in the butter or oil until soft but not coloured. Roughly chop the oysters and add to the pan with the breadcrumbs and seasonings. Allow to go completely cold before using to stuff the lamb.

Lay the meat, skin side down, on a board and place the stuffing down the centre. Roll the meat as neatly as possible into a log shape. This is not terribly easy as the shoulder is an awkward shape. Tie at intervals with string. Weigh the joint once it has been stuffed, so that an accurate time can be calculated. It will be approximately $2\frac{1}{2}$ kg ($5\frac{1}{2}$ lbs) weight. The timing works out at 40–45 minutes per lb depending how well cooked you like your lamb. I find 40 minutes perfect. Place the meat in a roasting tin and rub with the 2 × 15 ml (2 tablespoons) butter or oil. Season with salt and pepper. Set on the top heat and lightly brown all over before transferring to the pre-heated oven. After $1\frac{1}{2}$ hours, cover the joint loosely with foil. Baste occasionally during the cooking time.

While the lamb is cooking, prepare the sauce. Fry the onion in the hot butter until soft but not coloured, then stir in the mushrooms and continue to fry on a high heat for a few minutes. Add the anchovies, capers and oysters, stir in the oyster juice and stock and bring to the boil. Reduce the heat and simmer gently for a few minutes to cook the oysters. Put the cornflour and egg yolks into a bowl, add the vinegar and beat lightly to combine. Remove the pan from the heat and carefully add the yolk mixture, stirring all the time to blend. Return the pan to the heat and cook gently to thicken. Stir in the parsley and keep warm.

Transfer the lamb from the roasting tin to a serving dish, remove the string, cover and keep warm. Drain off all the fat from the roasting pan and scrape off the sediment and meat juices, making sure they are not burnt. Add to the sauce. Stir to combine. Heat thoroughly and adjust the seasoning. Carve the lamb, garnish with watercress and serve in slices with the sauce.

MUTTON AND HARICOT BEAN STEW
Stobhach Caoireola agus Ponracháin

Mutton was used to make a variety of savoury stews, some combining the most basic ingredients available such as potatoes and onions. One of the simplest of these, Irish stew, is enjoyed throughout the country and indeed far beyond its shores. Other stews, in addition to the basic root vegetable, included barley, haricot beans, herbs, spices and even oysters to make very rich and sophisticated dishes.

In this stew, haricot beans are combined with onion, carrot, turnip and juniper berries. I normally use stewing lamb as mutton is not so readily available. The dish is particularly good when shoulder chops are used.

SERVES 4

750 g (1½ lb) shoulder mutton or lamb, boned
2 × 15 ml (2 tablespoons) fat or oil
1 large onion, peeled and sliced
25 g (1 oz) plain flour
600 ml (1 pint) stock or water
1 carrot, approx. 175 g (6 oz) peeled and diced
225 g (8 oz) turnip, peeled and diced
50 g (2 oz) haricot beans
4 juniper berries, crushed
Sprig of thyme, bay leaf, parsley stalks, tied together
750 ml (1¼ pints) lamb or vegetable stock
Salt and freshly milled black pepper
2 × 15 ml (2 tablespoons) parsley, finely chopped

It is not necessary to soak the haricot beans overnight, but wash them well under running water and put into a large saucepan with 1.75 litres (3 pints) of cold water. Bring to the boil and boil for 10 minutes. Remove from the heat and leave the beans to soak in the liquid for about an hour.

Trim the excess fat off the meat. Cut the meat into large cubes. Fry in the hot fat or oil until browning, then remove from the pan. Fry the onion until soft and golden brown. Pour off the excess fat. Stir in the flour and cook until it is just beginning to colour. Stir in the stock to blend. Return the meat to the pan. Dice the carrot and turnip and add to the pan along with the beans, juniper berries and the bouquet of herbs. Bring to the boil, cover and reduce the heat. Simmer for 1½–2 hours until the meat and beans are tender. Season with salt and pepper. Remove any fat from the top of the stew and serve sprinkled with parsley.

IRISH STEW
Stobhach Gaelach

There are many different recipes for this famous Irish dish. Some people suggest that mutton was originally the main ingredient, others believe it to have been kid. Nowadays, since mutton is hardly available, lamb chops from the neck or shoulder, or stewing lamb taken off the bone are used. Although it is not truly authentic, many restaurants and indeed homes, including my own, serve what they call Irish stew but made with stewing beef. It would also appear that in the north of Ireland another type of Irish stew was made, using spare pork ribs instead of the mutton or lamb chops.

Basically, Irish stew is a peasant dish, made with the cheapest and most readily available ingredients. The meat is combined with onions, potatoes, parsley, seasoning and water and when correctly made should be rich and thick and not watery like soup.

Irish stew is traditionally served on its own with mushroom ketchup (see page 84) or with pickled red cabbage (see page 85) and accompanied by a glass of stout. This is my version:

SERVES 4

1 kg (2 lb) neck of lamb, cut into rings about 1.5 cm (¾ in) thick OR 1 kg (2 lb) stewing lamb cut into large pieces
2 large onions
1 kg (2 lb) potatoes
2 × 15 ml (2 tablespoons) parsley, finely chopped
Salt and freshly milled black pepper
400 ml (14 fl oz) water

Wipe the lamb, peel the onions and cut into rings. Wash and peel the potatoes and cut into 5 mm–1 cm (¼–½ in) slices. Layer the meat and vegetables in a deep pan, seasoning well with salt, pepper and parsley between each layer, and ending with potatoes. Pour over the water and cover with a piece of buttered paper, either greaseproof or aluminium foil, and then the lid. Bring to the boil, then reduce the heat and cook for 2–3 hours until the meat is tender and the liquid well absorbed. Alternatively, the stew can be cooked in the oven at 160°C (325°F, gas mark 3) once it has come to the boil.

Serve with additional chopped parsley and a glass of stout.

NOTE Many people also add sliced carrots to the stew, although they are not thought to have been part of the original ingredients and are rather frowned upon by the purists. Their addition does, however, produce a very tasty stew.

JELLIED LAMB
Uaingoil i nGlóthach

In the early part of this century one of the best and most popular ways of using up leftover pieces of lamb was to combine them with hard-boiled eggs and peas and to set the mixture in a mould with gelatine. This was turned out, cut in slices and served with salad leaves – a perfect example of the influence of Victorian Britain.

SERVES 5–6
MAKES 10–12 slices

225 g (8 oz) cold lamb off the bone
11 g (0.4 oz) gelatine powder
600 ml (20 fl oz) stock made from the lamb bones
4 × 15 ml (4 tablespoons) mint sauce
50 g (2 oz) tender young peas, lightly cooked
2 hard-boiled eggs, sliced
1 × 15 ml (1 tablespoon) parsley, finely chopped
Salad leaves and fresh herbs to garnish
15.5 × 10 cm (6 × 4 in) round cake tin, scalded

Trim the lamb of any excess fat and chop finely. Use the bones to make a rich, well-flavoured stock. Leave this to go cold before using, so that all the fat can be easily lifted off.

Put the gelatine into a small saucepan and add 2 × 15 ml (2 tablespoons) stock. Dissolve over a very gentle heat, shaking the pot rather than stirring. Once the gelatine has gone clear, add to the remaining stock, stirring all the time to prevent small lumps forming as the gelatine comes into contact with the cold liquid. Stir in the mint sauce. Taste for flavour, adding a little more mint sauce if necessary. Pour about 1 cm (½ in) of the stock into the bottom of the cake tin. Leave until set. Now arrange several rings of peas around the outside of the tin. Lay some slices of egg in the centre, then pour over enough stock to cover. Mix the chopped lamb with the parsley and the remaining peas. Chop the remaining egg and add to the meat with some freshly milled black pepper. Pour on the remaining stock. When on the point of setting, pour into the mould. Cover with a plate or foil and leave in the refrigerator to set.

Turn the mould out on to a serving dish, garnish with salad leaves and herbs, and serve cut in slices.

Jellied lamb.

POULTRY
RECIPES

CLOCKWISE, FROM LEFT: *Pot roast chicken,
chicken 'frigasse', barmacue chicken and
chicken and ham pie (pages 76–8).*

POT ROAST CHICKEN
Sicín Potrósta

At one time chickens were regarded as a luxury and although even the poorest country families would have kept a few, it was for their eggs rather than for their flesh. When they were eaten it was generally only on Sundays, feast days and special occasions, and even then it would have been the birds which had come to the end of their useful laying life.

They were cooked in the heavy iron pot hung over a fire of glowing embers. The pot was used, not only because it was one of the few pieces of cooking equipment available in many Irish homes, particularly before ranges and ovens became popular, but because it was also the most practical way to cook a bird which was old and tough. Pot roasting made the flesh tender and palatable, and the surrounding onions, carrots and herbs helped the flavour. Sometimes a young rabbit or a piece of bacon would also have been added.

SERVES 4–6
1.5-2 kg (3½-4½ lb) chicken
2 × 15 ml (2 tablespoons) fat or oil
225 g (8 oz) bacon, in a piece
12 button onions, peeled
2 large carrots, approx. 450 g (1 lb), peeled and cut in chunks
1 small turnip, approx. 225 g (8 oz), peeled and cut in chunks
1 clove garlic, crushed
Sprig of thyme, bay leaf, parsley stalks, tied together
150 ml (5 fl oz) dry white wine
450 ml (15 fl oz) chicken stock
Salt and freshly milled black pepper
1 × 15 ml (1 tablespoon) butter
FOR THE STUFFING
50 g (2 oz) butter
1 medium onion, finely chopped
75 g (3 oz) coarse oatmeal
3 × 15 ml (3 tablespoons) parsley, finely chopped
Salt and freshly milled black pepper
FOR THE SAUCE
1 × 15 ml (1 tablespoon) butter
1 × 15 ml (1 tablespoon) plain flour
Salt and freshly milled black pepper
OVEN TEMPERATURE 180°C (350°F, gas mark 4)
OVEN TIME 1–1½ hours

If there are giblets with the bird remove them, wash well and use to make some well-flavoured stock along with a piece of onion, carrot, bay leaf and a few peppercorns. This will take about 30 minutes.

While the stock is cooking, the stuffing can be made. Wipe the bird inside and out with kitchen paper, removing any lumps of fat from inside the carcass. Fry the chopped onion in the melted butter until soft but not coloured. Stir in the oatmeal, parsley and seasoning. Gather together into two pieces and use to stuff both the breast and the body cavity. Secure the neck flap underneath the bird using a skewer; this will keep the breast stuffing in place. Then truss the bird firmly, keeping the wings and legs close to the body so that it keeps its shape; this can be done using string or skewers.

Cut the bacon into large cubes and fry with the onions in a large frying pan in the hot fat or oil until both are beginning to brown. Using a draining spoon, remove from the pan and put into a large pot or casserole. Next fry the chicken, turning it several times to brown all over, just as you would for a pot roast of beef (see page 64). Remove from the pan to the large pot with the onions and bacon. Add the carrots, turnip and garlic, arranging the vegetables around the chicken. Pour over the wine and stock and tuck the bunch of herbs at one side. Season well with milled black pepper. Bring to the boil, cover, then reduce the heat and cook gently for 1–1½ hours until the chicken and vegetables are tender. Baste several times during the cooking. The chicken can also be cooked in a pot in a pre-heated oven for the same length of time. When the chicken is cooked, remove it from the pot, draining it well. Put on a large warmed serving dish and surround with the well-drained vegetables and bacon. Discard the bouquet of herbs. Keep the chicken warm while making the sauce.

Bring the liquid in the pot to the boil over a high heat and reduce by about one third. Blend the butter and flour together to make a paste and gradually whisk in a little at a time to thicken the sauce. Taste to correct the seasoning. Carve the chicken in slices and serve with the vegetables and stuffing, pouring the sauce over the meat and vegetables.

BARMACUE CHICKEN
Sicín 'Barmacue'

One of the most interesting recipes I discovered in the 1709 manuscript of the Echlin family from County Down is for 'Barmacue' chicken. This is a roast chicken with a stuffing which combines walnuts, mushrooms and mushroom ketchup, popular ingredients in many Irish country kitchens in the eighteenth century.

SERVES 6–8
1 × 2.5 kg (5 lb) roasting chicken
25 g (1 oz) butter
150 ml (5 fl oz) chicken stock
FOR THE STUFFING
1 medium onion, finely chopped
50 g (2 oz) butter
225 g (8 oz) mushrooms, finely chopped
100 g (4 oz) fine white breadcrumbs
1 × 5 ml (1 teaspoon) mushroom ketchup (see page 84)
3 × 15 ml (3 tablespoons) parsley, finely chopped
100 g (4 oz) shelled walnuts, finely chopped
1 × 15 ml (1 tablespoon) tomato ketchup
Freshly milled black pepper
1 × 15 ml (1 tablespoon) rum or walnut liqueur
1 bunch watercress, to garnish
FOR THE GRAVY
2 × 15 ml (2 tablespoons) plain flour
1–2 × 15 ml (1–2 tablespoons) rum or walnut liqueur
300 ml (10 fl oz) chicken stock
OVEN TEMPERATURE AND TIME
180°C (350°F, gas mark 4) for 30 minutes, then reduce to 140°C (300°F, gas mark 2) and cook for a further 2 hours

Begin by making the stuffing. Soften the onion in the 50 g (2 oz) of butter, add the mushrooms and fry until cooked and beginning to brown (this will take about 10–15 minutes). Stir in the remainder of the ingredients. Leave to go cold.

Loosen the skin around the breast of the bird with your hands, so that the stuffing can sit in an even layer just below it on top of the flesh. Push the stuffing into this space and flatten all over the breast of the bird. Press the last of the stuffing over the breast, or wishbone, and into the neck cavity. Fold the neck skin underneath the bird without stretching it and hold in place with a skewer. Truss the bird, keeping the legs and wings close to the body. Set on a roasting dish and spread the 25 g (1 oz) butter over the bird's breast and legs. Pour round the stock and cook in the pre-heated oven for 30 minutes, then reduce the oven temperature, cover the breast of the bird loosely with a small piece of foil and cook for a further 2 hours.

When the chicken is cooked transfer it to a warm serving dish, remove the skewer and trussing string and keep warm while preparing the gravy. Drain off all but 1 × 15 ml (1 tablespoon) of the fat from the roasting dish, then stir the flour into the pan and mix with the sediment and cooking juices. Add the liqueur and cook for a few minutes before stirring in the stock. Bring to the boil to thicken the gravy, season with salt and freshly milled black pepper and strain into a sauceboat.

Garnish the chicken with a bunch of watercress and serve carved in slices with the stuffing and sauce, a selection of fresh vegetables and a variety of pickles.

CHICKEN GALANTINE
Sicín Cnámhaithe

During the eighteenth and nineteenth centuries, when the large houses and estates were established in Ireland and the inns were serving food, many elegant dishes and concoctions, both sweet and savoury, were to be found. Indeed, in 1732 Mrs Delaney, the English wife of Dr Patrick Delaney, the Dean of Down, in an account of a visit to Newton Grange, near Killala, tells us:

> *He [Mr Mahone] keeps a man cook and has given entertainments of twenty dishes of meat! The people of this country don't seem solicitous of having good dwellings or more furniture than is absolutely necessary – hardly so much, but they make it up in eating and drinking! I have not seen less than fourteen dishes of meat for dinner, and seven for supper, during my peregrinations; and they not only treat us at their houses magnificently, but if we are to go to an inn, they constantly provide us with a basket crammed with good things; no people can be more hospitable or obliging, and there is not only great abundance but great order and neatness.*

One dish which was popular in the homes of the landed gentry at this time, and is greatly enjoyed today for special occasions, cold buffets and Christmas celebrations, was the galantine. This is a dish made from boned poultry, or other meats, stuffed and shaped into a roll, then cooked in stock, either in a saucepan or in the oven.

The following recipe suits most tastes because the stuffing ingredients are neither highly spiced nor unusual. However, for variety, I sometimes add 75 g (3 oz) walnuts, finely chopped, 175 g (6 oz) mushrooms, finely chopped, and 1 × 15 ml (1 tablespoon) mushroom ketchup (see page 84) and the same of dark rum.

MAKES 22 slices
1.75–2.25 kg (4–5 lb) roasting chicken, boned with the skin left unpunctured
2 large slices frying ham, cut about 3 mm ($\frac{1}{8}$ in) thick
350 g (12 oz) pork sausage meat
300 ml (10 fl oz) chicken stock
50 g (2 oz) butter
FOR THE STUFFING
1 large onion, finely chopped
2 × 15 ml (2 tablespoons) butter or oil
225 g (8 oz) fine white breadcrumbs
2 × 15 ml (2 tablespoons) parsley, finely chopped
Salt and freshly milled black pepper
1 egg, size 3, beaten
OVEN TEMPERATURE 190°C (375°F, gas mark 5)
OVEN TIME 2 hours

Begin by preparing the stuffing. Fry the onion in the hot butter or oil until soft but not coloured. Stir in the breadcrumbs, parsley and seasoning and allow to go cold. Bind with the beaten egg. If boning your own chicken do so in the following way:

STAGE 1 Place the chicken, breastbone down, on a chopping board. Remove the wing tips and the ankle joints of the legs. Using a sharp knife, cut through the skin along the backbone from neck to tail.

STAGE 2 Using a small boning or vegetable knife with a firm blade, work the flesh away from the bones. Work down one side of the chicken first and then, when the skin and flesh are released from the carcass section, work down the leg and the wing. Use your fingers alternately with the knife to ensure that all the meat comes away from the bones, but make sure that the skin, particularly over the breast area, is not punctured because this acts as the wrapper for the stuffing.

STAGE 3 When removing the wing and leg bones, release both from the carcass at the first joint; then hold the bone in one hand and scrape down the bone. When the flesh is removed from the bones they will pull out quite easily. Again, take care that the skin is not split. Having completed one side of the bird, turn it round and repeat the process on the other side.

STAGE 4 When the leg and wing bones are removed, the only remaining bones are those forming the carcass. Carefully lift the breast meat from the breast bone, using either your fingers or the blade of a small knife. This should almost completely release the carcass section from the bird, but to finish the process hold the carcass in one hand and cut along the breast bone and cartilage to release it finally, once again being particularly careful not to puncture the skin over the breast. Pull the leg and wing pieces to the inside and flatten the bird on the table. It is now ready for stuffing.

With the chicken skin side down on the work surface, place the slices of ham on top of the breast meat, divide the sausage meat in half and spread each piece over the ham. Put the breadcrumb stuffing down the centre of the bird from neck to tail.

Fold the sides of the chicken on top of the stuffing, tucking in the excess skin and flesh at the neck and tail ends. Using a large trussing needle and fine string, stitch the edges together to enclose the stuffing. Do not stretch the skin or pull it too tightly over the stuffing otherwise the breast skin may burst and the finished result will not be so attractive. Transfer the boned, stuffed chicken to a roasting pan, breastside up. Rub with butter. This will help to baste it and keep it moist during the cooking. Pour round the chicken stock and roast in a pre-heated oven for two hours or until the juices run clear when the meat is punctured with a fine skewer.

Serve either hot or cold, cut in slices. If the galantine is being served hot, make a gravy using the roasting juices to go with it.

NOTE Galantine of chicken, either cooked or uncooked, freezes well for several months.

CHICKEN 'FRIGASSE'
Sicín in Anlann Bán

Fricasée or 'frigasse' as it is called in a number of eighteenth century Irish manuscript 'receipt' books, is the word used to describe a method of preparing poultry, generally by stewing or boiling, after which it is served in a sauce made from the cooking liquor thickened with egg yolks and cream. The dish is usually garnished with button onions and mushrooms.

In earlier times the term was used to describe different types of stew made with both white and brown stock, using not only poultry but also stewing lamb, veal, rabbit, fish and vegetables. When cooking chicken for frigasse, it is often boiled in milk rather than water or stock. I use about 600 ml (20 fl oz) milk and 2.25 litres (4 pints) water.

This recipe is an adaptation from an eighteenth-century manuscript in the library of Bishop Story of County Cavan.

SERVES 4
1.5 kg (3½ lb) boiling or roasting chicken
2 blades of mace
½ lemon
1 large onion, peeled and quartered
1 large carrot, peeled and quartered
Sprig of thyme, bay leaf, parsley stalks, tied together
6 peppercorns
600 ml (20 fl oz) milk
2.25 litres (4 pints) water
FOR THE GARNISH
100 g (4 oz) mushrooms, sliced
25 g (1 oz) butter
12 pickling/button onions
4–8 rashers streaky bacon, rind removed
½ lemon, cut into 4 wedges
1 bunch watercress
FOR THE SAUCE
50 g (2 oz) butter
50 g (2 oz) plain flour
600 ml (1 pint) cooking liquor from the chicken
1 egg yolk
65 ml (2½ fl oz) double cream
2 anchovies, finely chopped
1 × 1.25 ml (¼ teaspoon) ground mace
Salt and freshly milled black pepper
1 × 15 ml (1 tablespoon) mushroom ketchup (see page 84)
2 × 5 ml (2 teaspoons) capers

If there are giblets with the bird remove them and wash well, discarding the liver which can be saved for use on another occasion. Wipe the bird inside and out with kitchen paper, removing any lumps of fat from inside the carcass. Put the two blades of mace and the half lemon inside the cavity of the bird and truss to hold it in a neat shape. Set in a large saucepan, breast-side uppermost. Surround by the quartered vegetables and add the bouquet of herbs, peppercorns and giblets. Pour on the milk and water. It should barely cover the bird. Set over a high heat and bring to the boil. Cover and reduce the temperature to simmering. For a boiling fowl cook for 2–3 hours or until tender, or 45–60 minutes for a roasting chicken.

While the chicken is cooking prepare the garnish. Fry the mushrooms in the melted butter until just beginning to colour. Cook the button onions, skins on, in the boiling water for a few minutes to make the skins easy to remove and cook the onions. Drain and peel. Roll the rashers of bacon into neat rolls, lay on a baking tray and grill until cooked and crisp. Keep warm.

When the chicken is cooked remove from the cooking liquor, skin and carve into joints: 2 legs, 2 breast and wing portions and the remaining breast. The legs, if large, can be cut into 2; alternatively the chicken flesh can be removed from the bones and cut into manageable-sized pieces. Keep warm while making the sauce.

Melt the butter in a large saucepan and stir in the flour to blend. Remove from the heat. Strain off 600 ml (20 fl oz) of the cooking liquor and gradually add to the flour and butter mixture, stirring constantly to prevent lumps forming. The sauce should be very smooth. Return to the boil to thicken, stirring continually. Blend the egg yolk with the cream and gradually stir into the sauce. Add the remaining ingredients, stirring to combine and continue cooking for a few minutes. Stir in the chicken portions or pieces along with the mushrooms and onions. Warm thoroughly and adjust the seasoning if necessary.

Serve on a large flat dish, garnished with bacon rolls, lemon wedges and watercress.

CHICKEN and HAM PIE
Piog Sicín agus Bagúin

This is one of the most popular dishes in the country, not only being served in most houses in the land but being made and sold in home bakeries, delicatessens, supermarkets, coffee shops, restaurants and pubs. Today there are a number of companies making chicken and ham pies of excellent quality, but if you prefer to make your own, here is my mother's family recipe. The quantities are for a 25 cm (10 in) double-crust pie or tart.

SERVES 6–8
1 × 368 g (13 oz) packet frozen puff or flaky pastry
FOR THE FILLING
275–350 g (10–12 oz) cooked chicken
150–175 g (5–6 oz) cooked ham, in a piece
1 small onion, finely chopped
175 g (6 oz) mushrooms, wiped and sliced
25 g (1 oz) butter
1 small egg, beaten
FOR THE WHITE SAUCE
50 g (2 oz) butter
50 g (2 oz) plain flour
150 ml (5 fl oz) chicken stock
150 ml (5 fl oz) milk
1 × 5 ml (1 teaspoon) made English mustard
Salt and freshly milled black pepper
1 × 25 cm (10 in) enamel, china or pyrex plate
OVEN TEMPERATURE 220°C (425°F, gas mark 7)
OVEN TIME 25–30 minutes

Begin by preparing the sauce. Melt the butter in a large saucepan, add the flour, stirring to form a paste, and cook gently for a few minutes. Gradually add the milk or milk and stock, stirring constantly to prevent lumps from forming. Cook on a very gentle heat for about 5 minutes. Season with salt, pepper and mustard.

Fry the onion in the 25 g (1 oz) of butter until soft but not coloured. Add the sliced mushrooms and continue to fry until both are cooked. Break the chicken into bite-sized pieces and add to the sauce along with the mushrooms, onion and ham. Check the seasoning and allow to go completely cold before using it to fill the tart.

Divide the prepared pastry in half, use one half to line the pie plate and the other half as the lid to cover the savoury filling. Roll out the pastry for the base into a circle, about 2.5 cm (1 in) larger than the diameter of the plate, and cut a circular strip, about 2.5 cm (1 in) in diameter, from round the outer edge of the pastry circle.

Line the plate with the large circle of pastry, easing it on to the plate without stretching it. Brush the edges with beaten egg and lay the 2.5 cm (1 in) pastry strip on top, both pastry edges meeting. Press the edges together. Pile the cold savoury filling into the centre of the pie leaving 2.5 cm (1 in) of the pastry showing around the plate. Brush this with beaten egg. Roll out the second half of the pastry until just large enough to cover the top of the pie and allow a few trimmings for decoration. Carefully roll the pastry around the rolling pin and unroll over the top of the filling. Seal the pastry top and bottom by pressing the edges together. Trim away the excess pastry using a very sharp knife, then 'knock' the cut edges together using the back of a knife. This will give a well-risen crusty rim to the tart. Decorate the pastry rim as desired. Roll out the pastry scraps and cut leaves or similar shapes for decoration. Brush these and the top of the tart with the beaten egg, arrange the decorations as desired and bake in a very hot oven until well risen and golden brown. Serve with boiled or baked potatoes and a green vegetable or salad.

MICHAELMAS GOOSE
Gé Fhéile Mhíchil

Goose was the bird generally eaten in Ireland on festive occasions, particularly Christmas and Michaelmas on 29 September. It should be well hung before being cooked, anything from five to ten days, depending on the temperature during storage. Traditionally goose was cooked in the pot-oven over the open turf fire where it would have been stuffed with potato and onion and boiled, braised or roasted. Today, it is still stuffed with potato and onion, but also a stuffing made from them or one of sage, onion and breadcrumbs.

Nowadays, we are advised not to stuff the cavity of poultry as it reduces heat penetration and may give rise to the development of food-poisoning bacteria. For this reason I either only stuff the neck/breast area and put an onion and potato in the cavity, or I cook the stuffing separately in a roasting tin in the oven at the same time as the bird for about 45 minutes. The secret of a good goose is long slow cooking after an initial hot blast.

SERVES 8–10
1 × 4.5–5.5 kg (10–12 lb) goose, oven-ready with giblets
FOR THE STOCK
Giblets
1 onion, peeled and cut in half
1 carrot, peeled and quartered
1 stick of celery, quartered
1 bay leaf
Parsley stalks
6 whole black peppercorns
900 ml (1½ pints) water
FOR THE SAGE AND ONION STUFFING
1 onion, finely chopped
2 × 15 ml (2 tablespoons) butter
225 g (8 oz) fresh breadcrumbs
2 × 5 ml (2 teaspoons) dried sage, finely chopped
2.5 ml (½ teaspoon) salt
Freshly milled black pepper
1 egg, size 4, beaten
GARNISH
Watercress
OVEN TEMPERATURE AND TIME
200°C (400°F, gas mark 6) for 30 minutes then reduce to 180°C (350°F, gas mark 4) for 2 hours

Begin by preparing the stock. Wash the giblets and put the neck, heart and gizzard into a saucepan with the wingtips from the bird (cut off at the elbows), vegetables, herbs, seasoning and water. Reserve the liver for the stuffing. Cover the pan, bring to the boil, then reduce the heat and simmer for 1½–2 hours. Strain and reserve for making the gravy.

Next make the stuffing by frying the onion in the hot butter until soft but not coloured. Chop the liver and add to the onion. Continue to fry for a few minutes, then remove from the heat. Stir in the breadcrumbs, herbs and seasoning and mix to blend. Bind with the beaten egg.

Prepare the bird by thoroughly washing both inside and out, making sure the cavity of the bird is absolutely clean. Remove any pieces of

fat from inside the cavity and around the tail. Dry well with absorbent kitchen paper. Place the stuffing in the neck/breast area of the bird. Using string or skewers, truss or secure the upper-arm portions of the wings close to the body of the goose so as to keep it in a neat shape. Tie string around the leg ends.

Set the goose on a wire rack in a roasting pan. This will allow the excess fat to drain off. Do not prick it, baste it or cover it with aluminium foil.

The fat released from the goose during the cooking should be saved, as it stores well in the refrigerator and is excellent for frying and roasting, especially potatoes.

Cook the prepared goose in the pre-heated oven for 30 minutes to begin the cooking, then reduce the temperature and continue to cook until the bird is tender.

Chicken and ham pie.

When the goose is cooked, transfer to a hot serving dish and keep warm while making the gravy. Drain all but 1 × 15 ml (1 tablespoon) of the goose fat from the roasting pan. Sprinkle in 1 × 15 ml (1 tablespoon) plain flour and blend to make a smooth paste. Gradually add about 300 ml (10 fl oz) of the strained goose stock, stirring well to remove the sediment and prevent lumps from forming. Strain into a saucepan and boil for a few minutes to thicken. Adjust the seasoning and serve with the roast goose along with carrots and Brussels sprouts or braised red cabbage (see page 85).

VEGETABLE RECIPES

FROM TOP: *Champ and colcannon (page 82).*

CHAMP, CALLY, POUNDIES, PANDY
Brúitín

All these names are given to very similar versions of one dish, most commonly known all over the world as champ. It is the traditional way of serving mashed potatoes and is perhaps the best-known and most popular potato dish in Ireland.

Champ was a favourite meal on Fridays and fast days particularly during Lent. It is also associated with Hallowe'en, the festival which marks the end of the rural year on All-Hallows Eve, 31 October. At this time, it was the custom to place the first two portions of champ on the top of the flat pier at the farm gate for the fairies.

In the old cottages, where there was a clay floor, there was often a hollow worn where the big iron potato pot sat while the potatoes were being mashed. After the skins had been removed, the dried boiled potatoes were pounded with a large wooden block with a long handle called a beetle. A traditional rhyme helps to set the scene:

> *There was an old woman*
> *who lived in a lamp,*
> *She had no room*
> *to beetle her champ.*
> *She up's with her beetle*
> *And broke the lamp,*
> *And then she had room*
> *To beetle her champ.*

The beetling in large households was generally done by the man because it was heavy work; in those days it was quite usual to cook about 3 kg (7 lb) potatoes for each person. Chopped scallions, including the green part, were simmered in a little milk until well blended and creamy, then poured on to the mashed potatoes. Sometimes the scallions were added without cooking. The potato was seasoned well and then piled on large hot plates or in bowls. A well was made in the middle of each heap of potatoes to hold a large lump of butter. The champ was served piping hot and was eaten from the outside using a spoon or fork. Each mouthful of potato was dipped in the melted butter. A glass of milk or buttermilk completed the meal. Although champ is still served as a meal in itself, it is more frequently served as an accompaniment to grilled sausages or boiled bacon (see page 58).

SERVES 4
1 kg (2 lb) potatoes
Salt
150 ml (5 fl oz) milk
4 spring onions or scallions, finely chopped
Freshly milled black pepper
50–100 g (2–4 oz) butter

Wash the potatoes and boil in their skins in salted water until tender. Drain and dry over a low heat, covered with a cloth. Peel and mash well. Put the milk and chopped onion in a saucepan, bring to the boil and simmer for a few minutes. Gradually add to the mashed potatoes and mix well to form a soft but not sloppy mixture. Divide between four warm plates or bowls, make a well in the centre, add the butter and serve immediately.

NOTE Sometimes a raw beaten egg is added to the centre of the potato along with the butter.

Chives, parsley, young nettle tops, peas and broad beans can be substituted for the scallions; the nettle tops, peas or beans are first cooked in the milk.

COLCANNON
Cál Ceannann

Colcannon is a similar dish to champ and is also made from mashed potatoes. It is flavoured and indeed coloured with shredded kale, a member of the cabbage family, but it is also often made with white cabbage. Traditionally colcannon is served at Hallowe'en, often with a lucky charm, such as a ring, coin, sixpence or button, wrapped up and hidden in the centre. Although it is not eaten as frequently as champ, it is just as well known, which may have something to do with the traditional rhyme:

> *Did you ever eat Colcannon*
> *When 'twas made with yellow cream,*
> *And the kale and praties blended*
> *Like the picture in a dream?*
>
> *Did you ever take a forkful*
> *And dip it in the lake*
> *Of heather flavoured butter*
> *That your mother used to make?*
>
> *Oh you did, yes you did*
> *So did he and so did I,*
> *And the more I think about it*
> *Sure, the more I want to cry*

> *God be with the happy times*
> *When trouble we had not*
> *And our mothers made Colcannon*
> *In the three-legged pot.*

SERVES 4–6
450 g (1 lb) kale or green leaf cabbage
450 g (1 lb) potatoes
6 spring onions, scallions or chives
150 ml (5 fl oz) milk or cream
Salt and freshly milled black pepper
50–100 g (2–4 oz) butter, melted

Remove the tough stalk from the kale or cabbage and shred the leaves very finely. Cook in a little boiling salted water until very tender. The kale will probably take 10–20 minutes. Drain well. Cook the potatoes in their skins until tender, then drain, peel and return to the heat to dry, covered with a cloth. Mash while warm until very smooth.

While the potatoes are cooking, chop the onions and simmer in the milk or cream for about 5 minutes. Gradually add this liquid to the potatoes beating well to give a soft fluffy texture. Beat in the kale or cabbage along with the seasoning. Heat thoroughly over a gentle heat and serve like champ in hot dishes or bowls with a well in the centre for the melted butter.

NOTE Sometimes I blend the kale (not the cabbage) in a food processor with the hot milk and scallions until they are fairly smooth, then beat this into the mashed potatoes. It gives a wonderful all-over green colour as opposed to the traditional method which is more of a speckled green. Do not try to blend the potatoes in the food processor, as it produces an unpleasant glue-like texture.

FRIED ONIONS AND POTATOES
Prátaí agus Oinniúin Friochta

This is a very popular supper dish and is served with buttermilk.

SERVES 2
2 large onions, peeled and thinly sliced
6 large potatoes, peeled, boiled and sliced
Bacon fat, butter or oil for frying
Salt and freshly milled black pepper

Fry the onions in the hot fat over a gentle heat until soft but not coloured. Add the potato slices, increase the heat and continue to fry until both potatoes and onions are beginning to brown. Serve very hot and well seasoned with salt and freshly milled black pepper.

BAKED ONIONS
Oinniúin Bácáilte

Choose large onions of the same size, approximately 250 g (8 oz), wipe them but leave the skins intact. Place in an ovenproof roasting dish with about 1 cm ($\frac{1}{2}$ in) water and bake in a pre-heated oven at 180°C (350°F, gas mark 4) and bake for 1–1$\frac{1}{4}$ hours. Test with a skewer to see if they are tender. Serve on a plate with butter and salt and pepper.

BOILED ONIONS
Oinniúin Bruite

This was a popular dish in my aunt's home in County Cavan. Sometimes a sauce was made out of the cooking liquor and flavoured with lots of chopped parsley.

The onions are peeled very carefully, leaving the root intact. They are then split halfway through their length from the flower end into quarters. The onion is opened out slightly and stuffed with a mixture of butter, finely chopped parsley and salt and pepper. These are then placed in a large saucepan with enough milk and water to cover about a third of the bulb. This is brought to the boil, then the heat is reduced, the pan covered and left to simmer for 30–45 minutes until the onions are tender. Lift them on to a soup plate and serve with a little of the flavoured milk or a parsley sauce (see page 59) made from the cooking liquor. Serve with wheaten bread (see page 132).

PARSNIPS AND CARROTS
Meacan Bhána

Parsnips and carrots have been popular vegetables in Ireland from the earliest times and have been used both separately and together. Generally, they are boiled until tender, as whole vegetables when small, or sliced, diced or cut in strips when larger. They are also mashed separately or together to form either a coarse or fine purée. Prepared this way they are a

Parsnips.

popular accompaniment to roast beef, lamb or pork.

Parsnips are particularly good when cut into finger-sized pieces, boiled for a few minutes, drained, dried and deep-fat fried like chips until golden brown.

They are also excellent cut into large pieces, cooked in boiling water for a few minutes, then drained, dried and roasted around a joint of meat in the oven along with roast potatoes.

PARSNIP CAKES
Cístí Meacan Bán

These make good accompaniments to roast meats, particularly pork and ham or fried sausages and bacon. Parsnip croquettes are made in a similar way, but shaped into small logs and deep-fat fried. This is the recipe my grandmother made with the parsnips from her cottage garden.

SERVES 4
450 g (1 lb) parsnips, cooked and mashed
2 × 15 ml (2 tablespoons) plain flour
Salt and freshly milled black pepper
Pinch of ground mace
1 × 15 ml (1 tablespoon) butter, melted
1 egg, size 2, beaten
8 × 15 ml (8 tablespoons) breadcrumbs
Butter or oil for frying

Combine the mashed parsnips with the flour, seasoning and butter in a large bowl and blend well. Mould into flat round cakes, about 6 cm (2½ in) in diameter and 1–2 cm (½–¾ in) thick. Dip into the beaten egg, toss in breadcrumbs and fry in a frying pan in the hot butter or oil until golden brown on both sides. Drain well before serving.

MUSHROOM KETCHUP
Mushroom ketchup has been a favourite flavouring in Ireland for many centuries. It was commonly eaten with boiled potatoes, like gravy, as well as being added to stews and casseroles. The best-flavoured ketchup is made using dry, open mushrooms, known in Ireland as 'flats'. This recipe is an adaptation from the eighteenth-century manuscript 'recipt' book of the Echlin family from County Down.

MAKES 300 ml (½ pint) mushroon ketchup
1 kg (2 lb) flat open field mushrooms
20–40 g (1–1½ oz) salt
TO EVERY 1.2 LITRES (2 PINTS) LIQUOR
15 g (½ oz) allspice berries
2.5 cm (1 in) piece of root ginger, peeled
2 blades of mace
1 × 50 g (2 oz) onion, chopped

Break up the mushrooms and layer with the salt in a stone or earthenware jar. Leave covered in a cool place for 3–4 days to draw out the juices, stirring and pressing them from time-to-time. Once they have been soaked sufficiently, put in a cool oven for 3–4 hours to further draw the juices. Strain into a saucepan, pushing through as much juice as possible. Tie the allspice berries, ginger, mace and onion in a muslin bag and add to the pan. Bring to the boil and simmer for 2 hours until well reduced. A little red wine and brandy may also be added if liked. Remove the bag of spices and pour the ketchup into small sterilised bottles. Seal and sterilise for 15 minutes.

A MUSHROOM 'FRIGACY'
Beacáin in Anlann Bán
In the eighteenth and nineteenth centuries mushroom frigacy was a very popular dish. Large field mushrooms were flavoured with butter and herbs, stewed gently to draw out the juices which were then thickened with butter or cream. I have come across a number of recipes in eighteenth-century manuscripts which range from the very simple, using just mushrooms, spice and onions, to more elaborate concoctions of orange juice, claret and stock.

This is my adaptation of a mushroom 'frigacy' taken from two County Down manuscript books. The quantities are for 3 main-course servings or 6 first-course portions, as this is the amount a normal-size frying pan will hold.

SERVES 3 as a main course and 6 as a first course
50 g (2 oz) butter
6 large flat field or open mushrooms, approx.
750 g (1¾ lb)
1 small onion, finely chopped
Salt and freshly milled black pepper
Pinch of nutmeg
1 × 5 ml (1 teaspoon) fresh marjoram, chopped
1 × 1.25 ml (¼ teaspoon) fresh thyme, chopped
120 ml (4 fl oz) stock or red wine
TO THICKEN
1 egg yolk
25 g (1 oz) butter, softened
1 × 5 ml (1 teaspoon) cornflour
1 × 15 ml (1 tablespoon) stock, water or wine
TO SERVE
9 slices bread
2 × 15 ml (2 tablespoons) parsley, finely chopped

Wipe the mushrooms, trim away any tough stems and peel if necessary; cut into quarters. Heat the butter in a large shallow frying pan and when foaming add the mushrooms and onions. Season well with salt and pepper and add the nutmeg and herbs. Cook gently over a low heat for about 10 minutes to draw out their juice. Turn and cook for a further 5 minutes until tender. They need to stew rather than fry. Pour on the stock or wine and bring to the boil.

To thicken the sauce, blend the egg yolk with the cornflour and the stock, water or wine. Draw the pan off the heat. Push the mushrooms to one side of the pan, allowing the juices to run. Stir in the egg yolk mixture along with the butter. Return the pan to a gentle heat and cook for about 3 minutes to thicken, taking care not to boil or the egg will scramble.

Toast the slices of bread on both sides, remove the crusts and cut a circle from each slice using a 9 cm (3½ in) cutter. Lay the 3 circles of hot toast, slightly overlapping, in a shamrock shape on warm plates and arrange the mushrooms in their sauce on top. Garnish with chopped parsley and serve immediately.

CABBAGE AND BACON
Cabáiste agus Bagún
Cabbage was traditionally cut into wedges or coarse shreds and cooked in a lot of boiling water for a long time, which generally destroyed its texture, quality and nutritive value. Today, however, more enlightened cooks shred it finely and cook it quickly in only a little water.

A favourite Irish dish combines rashers of crispy fried bacon with cabbage that has been shredded and boiled before being tossed in the hot bacon fat. It can be prepared as follows:

Remove the tough stalk from the cabbage and shred the leaves very finely. Wash well, drain and put in a large saucepan with just enough boiling water to create some steam, about half a cup. Cover with the saucepan lid and boil rapidly for 3–5 minutes until the cabbage is almost tender. The cooking time will vary depending on the type of cabbage used: those with young tender leaves will obviously cook more quickly than the tough, crinkly-leaved winter cabbage. When the cabbage is cooked, drain and dry well over a gentle heat.

Fry some rashers of bacon in a large frying pan until cooked and crisp. Remove from the pan and keep warm. Toss the cooked cabbage in the hot bacon fat for a few minutes then pile on hot plates and top with the bacon rashers.

The cabbage is also often served with fried sausages.

BRAISED RED CABBAGE
Cabáiste Dearg Galstofa

Red cabbage, although readily available in Ireland, is generally pickled rather than boiled. It is, however, an excellent hot vegetable and is delicious with the addition of apple and spices. It is generally served with game, especially venison, and pork and pork sausages. The secret of success in handling this rather tough vegetable is long slow cooking.

SERVES 8–10
750 g–1 kg (1½–2 lb) red cabbage
1 large onion, peeled and sliced
1 clove garlic, chopped
1 × 15 ml (1 tablespoon) butter
450–750 g (1–1½ lb) cooking apples, peeled, cored and sliced
4 × 15 ml (4 tablespoons) red or white wine vinegar
2–3 × 15 ml (2–3 tablespoons) brown sugar
1 × 1.25 ml (¼ teaspoon) ground mace
1 × 1.25 ml (¼ teaspoon) ground nutmeg
1 × 2.5 ml (½ teaspoon) ground allspice
Salt and freshly milled black pepper
150 ml (10 fl oz) vegetable or ham stock
OVEN TEMPERATURE 160°C (325°F, gas mark 3)
OVEN TIME 1–1½ hours

Discard the tough outer leaves of the cabbage, cut into quarters and remove the hard stalk and core. Shred the cabbage very finely. In a large ovenproof casserole or saucepan arrange a layer of cabbage, seasoning with the salt and pepper, then a layer of onion, garlic and apples. Mix the spices together with the sugar and sprinkle on top of the onions and apples. Continue layering the cabbage, onion and apples until everything has been used up. Mix the vinegar with the stock and pour on top of the cabbage mixture. Dot the top with pieces of butter, cover lightly with greaseproof paper and a close-fitting lid. Bring the liquid to the boil on the top heat, then reduce the temperature and cook very slowly for about 1–1½ hours until the cabbage and onions are tender and the liquid has evaporated. Alternatively, the cass-erole or pot can be transferred to the oven after the liquid has been brought to the boil. Stir once or twice during the cooking. Red cabbage re-heats very successfully.

PICKLED RED CABBAGE
Cabáiste Dearg Picilte

Malt vinegar, flavoured with spices, was used to pickle many different types of vegetables such as cauliflower, beetroot, mushrooms, onions and red cabbage. The vegetables were either boiled first or simply laid down in salt before being drained and bottled in the spiced liquid. Such pickled vegetables were very popular in the eighteenth and nineteenth centuries and were served with a wide variety of boiled and roast meats and game. Pickled red cabbage was a particular favourite and was the usual accompaniment to Irish stew; the sharpness of the pickled cabbage counteracting the fattiness of the stew, especially when mutton was used. When pickling vegetables, it is important to use them when they are crisp and fresh.

MAKES 4 × 600 ml (1 pint) jars
1 medium red cabbage, approx. 1.5 kg (3 lb)
4 × 15 ml (4 tablespoons) salt
FOR THE SPICED VINEGAR
5 cm (2 in) cinnamon stick
1 × 5 ml (1 teaspoon) whole cloves
1 × 5 ml (1 teaspoon) whole allspice berries
1 × 5 ml (1 teaspoon) whole black peppercorns
1 piece root ginger, peeled, about the size of a walnut
1 bay leaf
4 blades of mace
1.2 litres (2 pints) distilled vinegar

Discard the outer leaves of the cabbage and divide into five or six sections, removing the tough core. Shred the leaves very finely. Arrange these in a large basin, sprinkling each layer with 1 × 15 ml (1 tablespoon) salt. Cover the bowl with a plate and leave in a cold place for 1–2 days.

While the cabbage is salting prepare the spiced vinegar. Bruise the spices with a heavy weight between two sheets of greaseproof paper or in a pestle and mortar. Tie loosely in a piece of muslin. Place with the vinegar in a saucepan with a lightly fitting lid and slowly bring to the boil. Remove from the heat and leave to infuse for a few hours without taking off the lid. Remove the bag of spice. This liquid can be used wherever a spiced vinegar is required for pickling vegetables such as cauliflower, cucumbers, mushrooms and onions. Once the cabbage has been salted sufficiently, drain well but do not wash. Pack the cabbage into steri-lised glass jars and cover with the spiced vinegar. I generally like to float a few pepper-corns and a blade of mace in each jar which not only helps the flavour but makes some veget-ables look more attractive. Seal carefully, ex-cluding all the air. Store in a cold dry place for 1–2 weeks before eating. After 2–3 months the vegetables lose their crispness.

PICKLED BEETROOT Wash the beetroot and boil for 1½ hours before peeling. Slice and pack loosely into jars, then cover with the cold spiced vinegar and seal.

PICKLED CAULIFLOWER Divide crisp white cauliflower into florets, leaving on a little stalk with each head. Cook in enough boiling water to cover for 5 minutes. Drain and refresh under cold running water until completely cold. Loosely pack into glass jars, pour on the cold spiced vinegar, seal well and store in a cold dry place. They are ready to eat in about 3 days.

PICKLED MUSHROOMS Recipes for pickled mushrooms appear in a number of eighteenth-century manuscript 'receipt' books. This one was written by Lady Caldwell in the 1700s and involves stewing the mushrooms before cover-ing them with spices and vinegar.

To pickle musheroons. Lady Caldwell
Wash the musheroons in a strong pickle of salt and water, then take them out and put into a saucepan, with a good quantity of mace, pepper, cloves and a little ginger, stew all together till the liquor is almost quite consumed, and when they are cold pour cold vinegar over them, rub them clean and put them down to boyle in vinegar with the same spices as above, and when cold put them up, and if there is not enough of pickle to cover them after boil-ing, boil some more vinegar and put about them till they are covered . . .

LIVING OFF THE WATER

Until recently, agriculture and fishing played a dual role in Ireland's coastal areas, complementing and supporting each other in their own seasons. Where agriculture gave poor returns, people had to search for other means to supplement their diet. In this sense their lifestyle was very similar to that carried on by the hunters and gatherers, the very first settlers in Ireland many thousands of years ago. Although these Mesolithic people did not practise agriculture as we understand it today, they did know about edible plants and roots, fruits, nuts and berries and the seasonal movement of wild animals and fish.

In early spring they camped on the coast near the estuaries of the thousands of rivers and tributary streams which flowed through the island, and gathered and ate the mussels, oysters, periwinkles, cockles, limpets and seaweed from the bays. They knew how to catch the cod, mackerel and ling that swam near the shore, using long bone- or wooden-handled harpoons with tiny flint blades, and they were adept at trapping nesting sea birds, such as the puffin and gannet, and gathering their eggs. In summer they caught

ABOVE: *Mussels and bacon (page 108).*

———————————

OPPOSITE: *A selection of Irish shellfish, including oysters, mussels, Dublin Bay prawns, lobsters and scallops.*

salmon in the estuaries and then followed them on their journey up the rivers to the lakes where they would spawn.

Here, inland, there was also a rich harvest of fish. In AD 1166 the writer and historian Giraldus Cambrensis wrote:

> This Ireland is also specially remarkable for a great number of beautiful lakes, abounding in fish and surpassing in size those of other countries I have visited. The rivers and lakes also are plentifully stored with the sorts of fish peculiar to these waters and especially three species – salmon, trout and muddy eels and oily shad.

We also know from Giraldus Cambrensis that 'the Shannon abounds in lamprey', and from later documented accounts that mullet, roach, rud, tench and bream were to be had, along with an abundant supply of freshwater crayfish, from the limestone loughs of Lene, Sheelin and Derravaragh and others in the centre of the country. We know, too, from the archaeological remains of kitchen midden sites by the estuaries, rivers and lakes, that char, pollan, pike, perch and carp were present.

The Brehon Laws, which come to us from pre-Christian times, and which were in operation in all parts of Ireland outside the English Pale up until the time of Henry VIII, emphasised the importance of fish, giving a recognised status to fishermen in early Irish society. The *mur bhreatha*, or sea decisions, also showed the care taken by the Irish law-givers to preserve the rights of each clan to fish in their own rivers. In addition to these, throughout the centuries legendary stories and the lives of the saints have constantly reminded us of the importance and significance of fish in the diet of the people, particularly to the coastal and island dwellers.

INSHORE FISHING

Along the coast and on the islands it has to be remembered that there was a much wider variety of produce from the shore than the land, and at certain times of the year, and in certain areas, a more abundant supply. From the bays the local community gathered molluscs and shellfish, which were eaten in great quantities and provided them with their main source of protein. In 1788 a clergyman, describing the diet of the people in the Rosses, County Donegal, wrote:

> Their shellfish they got in the following manner; the men went to the rocks with a hook tied to the end of a strong rod; and with what they pulled from under the rocks, as many crabs and lobsters as they wanted; the lobsters commonly weighing from five to twelve pounds each: for scollops and oysters, when the tide was out, the younger women waded into the sea where they knew the beds of such fish lay; some of them, naked; others having stripped off their petticoats, went in with their gowns tucked up about their waist; and by armfuls, brought to shore, whatever number of scollops and oysters they thought requisite; the scollops weighing from two to four pounds each.

Lobster was also caught by lowering hand-constructed wicker baskets or pots into the sea at night from the small curraghs. The lobsters crawled into the pots and became trapped. This practice is still carried out all around the coast today, to a lesser or greater degree. At one time lobsters were plentiful and cheap and highly sought after in the major towns. Although they are still greatly in demand, they are no longer cheap or as readily available at the local markets or shops, as most, like the majority of our seafood, is exported to the markets and tables of Europe.

The native oyster (*Ostrea edulis*) was at one time more widely found around the coast than it is today, particularly along the western seaboard where there were great numbers of feeding and breeding beds such as those once at Sligo. In the 1840s Clew Bay in County Mayo was said to abound with oysters taken in large quantities using a dredge rope. The major centre for oysters, however, has always been Galway where they have such a long history and are so inextricably linked to the local economy that an international festival is held at the start of the season in September to celebrate their importance. From then until April, following the age-old adage to 'eat oysters only when there's an ''r'' in the month', oysters are in plentiful supply. The oysters are eaten in the flat part of the shell rather than the cupped and washed down with plenty of stout.

In County Down, along the east coast of the island, a number of oyster farms are now in operation, supplying fine-quality oysters to both the home and overseas market. The best known of these is Cuan Sea Fisheries in Whiterock Bay. In recent years the Pacific oyster (*Crassostrea gigas*), with its frilly pear-shaped shell, has been introduced. This has enabled fresh oysters to be produced all year round as Irish waters are too cool for them to spawn here. Although bigger and less expensive than the native oysters, they are not quite as delicate or flavoursome.

Scallops are dredged for in the same way as for oysters, using small boats and nets. Mussels grow almost everywhere, clinging to the rocks, sheltering in the bays and lying bound up with stones, shingle and seaweed in the mud along the estuaries. When the tide begins its retreat these are exposed, revealing a rich-textured blue mass just ready for picking or dredging with nets. Due to the popularity of mussels today, both at home and overseas, many mussel farms have been established around the coast. Here the shellfish are generally grown on ropes and flat rafts, which results in mussels that are bigger than the truly wild variety, free from an excess of sand and much easier to harvest. The native mussel (*Mulilus edulis*), like its companion the oyster, is noted for its fine delicate flavour and has always been popular with both the locals and those who live further inland in the major towns. Before refrigeration, supplies were moved around the country in barrels, and sold in the towns to the poor for next to nothing. In Dublin, however, they were always highly prized and fetched good prices.

Cockles are also picked by hand from the stretches of sand exposed when the tide goes out. Experienced cockle collectors know exactly which part of the bay to dig and the special markings on the sand to look for. Where the sand curls like a worm is the place to dig, using a spoon, a rake or a spade. To take the cockles alive, which as with any shellfish is the only way to gather them or indeed buy them, it is necessary to dig down into the sand for about 7.5–10 cm (3–4 in). A constant reminder of this is contained in the traditional song:

> In Dublin's fair city,
> Where the girls are so pretty,
> I first set my eyes on sweet Molly
>   Malone.
> She wheeled her wheelbarrow
> through streets broad and narrow,
> Crying, 'Cockles and mussels alive,
>   alive, oh!'

Custom would also have it among the local fisherfolk that cockles should not be picked until they had been covered three times with the April tides – 'had three drinks of April water' – after which the cockle season could begin. During the summer months all along the coast women and children were commonly seen picking cockles off the strand and filling their aprons, tin cans or buckets. They sometimes ate them raw, picking them out of the shells with a pin, but more often they were taken home, washed, boiled over the turf fire and eaten with oatcakes. In many places not only were cockles and mussels gathered for food, they also provided – and sometimes do still provide – the family with a meagre income which could be used to buy other foods such as flour, oats and clothes. Others, like myself, just enjoy the experience of the search and the freshness of the haul. Cockles lying on the surface of the beach are dead and should never be gathered.

Limpets and periwinkles were also gathered off the rocks and shores. Tomás Ó Crohan in his book *The Islandman* has a wonderfully evocative description of the women of the Blasket Islands, skirts gathered together and pulled between their legs, crossing a deep channel in the bay to another island where the limpets and winkles were plentiful. He recounts the rescue of the women after they were cut off by the tide and nearly drowned on their return journey: '. . . the old hag over the way was going under when he (my father) caught her by the hair. I was at my last breath by the time my father landed: the old hag very nearly pulled him under as he tried to save her with her apron full of limpets.' These limpets, Tomás Ó Crohan explains, were very much part of his diet: 'And the food I got was hen's eggs, lumps of butter, and bits of fish, limpets and winkles – a bit of everything going from sea or land.' His mother cooked them on the fire: 'She [his mother] was roasting the limpets,

Oysters and Guinness (page 107).

89

which have a distinctive flat stalk and branch into a round fan shape. Found on stones and rocks all along the Atlantic coast, Carrageen is gathered at low tide in April and May when it is still young. It is then either used immediately or dried and stored for later use. In Donegal and other parts of the west and southern coasts of Ireland, it can still be seen spread on the rocks to dry, occasionally washed by the rain, bleached by the sun and dried by the air before being packed, stored, sold and exported. Carrageen has a gelatinous quality which has been used for years to thicken soups, make drinks and set jellies and milk puddings. In Donegal it was also boiled in water and given to calves to supplement their diet.

Sloke (*Porphyra umbilicalis*), also known as sea spinach or laver, is commonly found on rocks and stones at most levels of the beach all round the Irish coast. Its fronds are thin and a translucent purple-green colour. It is traditionally served as a vegetable with fish or bacon, after being well washed, soaked, and boiled for four to five hours. In the wealthy homes along the coast, such as that of the Nugent family at Portaferry on the County Down coast, sloke was served in a silver bowl, now part of the collection of Georgian silver at the Ulster Museum in Belfast.

Dulse (*Palmaria palmata*), also called 'dillisk' or 'dillesk', is a reddish-brown seaweed found all around the Irish coast. It is usually sold dried in the markets, fish stalls and shops throughout the country, and was often eaten like sweets or with a bowl of willicks, the local name for periwinkles or winkles. At the Lammas Fair in Ballycastle, County Antrim, dulse and yallaman (yellowman) – a bright yellow toffee – were sold from the stalls. Traditionally they were given by a boy to his sweetheart, as is recorded in the following old song:

throwing them to us one by one like a hen with chickens.' They were also very much part of the diet of shore dwellers and were often cooked in the rock pools on the beach. A fire would be lit and stones warmed in it. These were then transferred to the rock pools where they boiled the water and cooked the limpets.

From the sand along the water's edge, razor fish and sand eels were also found. The sand eels, long miniature silvery eels, also called sand-lances, were at one time considered a great delicacy and widely eaten in Ireland. They were easily dug out of the sand with a three-pronged fork, similar to that used for digging out slugs for bait. Digging

for sand eels was a favourite occupation during the summer months when there was an abundant supply ranging from 7.5 to 30 cm (3–12 in) in length. Razor fish, also present in many sandy and shingle shores along the water's edge, particularly during the spring tides, were either enticed out of their holes or dug out from about 60 cm (2 feet) below the surface.

In addition to these shore-line fish, many varieties of edible seaweed and plants, rich in sodium, iodine and magnesium, have been used and eaten by coastal dwellers throughout the centuries. Carrageen (*Chondrus crispus*), also known as Irish moss or sea moss, grows in clusters of purple-brown fronds,

At the auld Lammas Fair, were you
    ever there?
Were you ever at the Fair of
    Ballycastle, oh?
Did you treat your Mary Anne to dulse
    and yallaman?
At the auld Lammas Fair at
    Ballycastle, oh!

Samphire, an asparagus-like sea vegetable, grows on the mud of salt marshes in
some coastal regions, particularly on the east
coast of the island. In fact, the bay near my
cottage in County Down is carpeted with its
tree-like fronds in July, August and September, and when picked young is tender and
succulent with a slightly tart taste. This
fleshy plant can be eaten raw or boiled.

At many places along the coast, and on the
smaller off-shore islands, seabirds and their
eggs also added to the locals' food supply. On
Rathlin Island the cooking of puffins is
vividly remembered by one of the young
islanders:

> They wouldn't gut them or pluck them
> or anything. They would roll them up in
> mud and throw them into the middle of
> the ashes [in the fire] and lay them in
> there for maybe two or three hours. And
> then they would take them out, the mud
> was just like cement on them. They used
> to break it off them, and the feathers
> and skin and all would come off, and
> they were just left with a bird, you
> know, the flesh. They ate them. The guts
> and everything that was inside them
> was in a wee ball inside them. They used
> to just pull that out, and that's how they
> cooked them.

The boats that these coastal dwellers and
islanders originally used to catch fish from
deeper waters were unsophisticated craft,
made either from scooping out a solid log to
make a canoe, or by working branches of

Samphire.

trees or light wood into a simple frame which
they then covered with hide or canvas and
made waterproof with tar. These boats were
called 'curraghs' and ranged in size from the
one-man curragh up to the famous four-man
racing curragh from the Aran Islands. With
or without sails they were characteristic of
the traditional boats used all along the
Atlantic coast up until the end of the seventeenth century. In some areas, in addition to
these curraghs, simple wooden-framed boats,
originally introduced by the Viking invaders
in the eighth and ninth centuries, enabled the
coastal dwellers to fish in the deep waters of
the bay and just off the coast. Here they
could catch the large shoals of herring and
mackerel as they travelled inshore at certain
times of the year to spawn. Look-outs on the
island, usually the women and children,
watched for the shoals of fish as they moved
along the shore, showing up as large dark
patches in the water. The onlookers then
directed the boats to them so that they could
net their catch.

Due to the lack of facilities for keeping the
herrings and the many other varieties of fish
caught off the coast such as mackerel, ling,
cod, haddock, pilchards, hake and dogfish,
they either had to be eaten immediately, or
were dried or salted down for use out of
season when no fresh fish was available. Salt
was imported from the Atlantic coasts of
Europe and English salt mines, or brought
from salt pans in other parts of Ireland. On
the shore, the women gutted and salted the
fish, both for their own use and for sale to the
merchants who took them in barrels to the
villages and towns further inland for re-sale
in the markets and shops. The fish cadgers
took fresh fish into the interior. The merchants usually exported the salted fish, while
dried fish was exported or sold for local
consumption. Barrels of herrings were exported in great quantities from Donegal in the
late eighteenth century. Infact, a fishing
station was built in 1773 on the island of
Rutland, off Burtonport. Unfortunately, the
herring migrated and left it dead by 1793.

The herring-fishing industry today.

kippers. After salting they might also be stuck on a skewer or pole and hung up from the rafters over the open turf fire until they were heavily smoked and became known as 'red herrings'. Nowadays herrings are generally enjoyed in their fresh unsalted state or else lightly smoked. Unfortunately, however, as a result of over-fishing, herring stocks have dramatically decreased and consequently prices have increased.

Ling, a member of the cod family, along with herring was one of the regular catches and staple foods of the coastal population, particularly along the western seaboard. When not eaten fresh, ling was generally dried or salted like the herrings: in July it was a frequent sight to see these now large flat fish, gutted and split, pegged to a line like the washing, impaled on nails or hooks on a long piece or wood, or draped on low hedges or bushes where they looked like white stiffened shirts. At night they were brought inside for protection and after a week or two the fish were well dried out, stiff as a board and ready for storing for up to a year. To speed the process of drying, as well as giving a stronger flavour, the fish were often salted before drying, stacked in piles of about ten in earthenware crocks, flesh side up with salt between each fish and left for about two weeks.

Before cooking, both the salt herring and ling were cut into pieces and soaked overnight, either in water or milk, then boiled in fresh milk the next day until cooked and tender, and served with potatoes. In periods of deep poverty the diet of the majority of the people was confined to a stew of unpeeled potatoes topped with a piece of salt ling or herring, simmered over a low peat fire. This gave a strong flavour of salt and fish to the monotonous flavour of the potatoes.

For many years now salt herring and ling have been out of fashion, with the exception of a few small villages on the south-west

Such activity provided a small income for the coastal families and, along with their meagre produce from the land, enabled them to live, albeit in many cases no more than at subsistence level. The gutting and salting were carried out on the quays in the open air, even after the Congested Districts Boards in the 1890s provided gutting and salting stations for herrings at a number of places along the

west coast and on the larger islands, such as Aran and Tory, in an effort to turn this small fishing activity into a more comfortable, viable and commercial proposition.

Herrings were at the height of their popularity in the eighteenth and nineteenth centuries and were enjoyed fresh, boiled or fried, or hung up by the fire where they developed a smoky taste and were known as coast, and the English market in Cork. However, perhaps with increased travel to Spain, France and Italy, ling, like its European counterpart, salt cod, may once more make its appearance in the fishmongers, this time as an interesting local speciality – like the *bacalao* of Spain, the *baccala* of Italy and the *morue* of France – rather than the food of poverty and famine.

Mackerel, like herring, is found in abundance around the Irish coast. The shoals are so prolific in summer, when the fish are at their best for eating, that they often come right into the harbour, carelessly presenting their beautiful silvery-blue and green skin to both novice and expert fisherman alike. In the summers of my childhood around the County Down coast I often watched these gaudy mackerel being pulled in their dozens over the side of the harbour wall, giving many a young man his first taste of fishing.

This rich oily fish with its firm flesh must be eaten while the skin retains its lustre, as soon after catching as possible, as it deteriorates rapidly because of its oiliness. Fishermen have the right idea, boiling their freshly caught mackerel in seawater for about ten minutes which makes a dish fit for a king. Cooked this way, they are delicious served cold with mayonnaise. Mackerel is often referred to as 'poor man's trout', being very similar in flavour. Mackerel were also salted for use throughout the year.

Other fish like cod, whiting, haddock, halibut, pollock, mullet, sea bream and blochan (coalfish) could also be caught, both by net and with a fixed-line rod cast from the rocks. However, it was not until larger fishing boats appeared that these and other deep-sea fish like sole, plaice, red gurnet, conger eel, skate, ray and dogfish were caught in any significant number.

Two other sea creatures, the seal and the porpoise, were particularly valued by the people who lived on the small islands just off the mainland, such as the Blasket Islands in West Kerry. There, both were highly prized and were a great resource to the people who could get a pack of meal for one of them, or exchange a piece of one for some pork. Tomás Ó Crohan wrote in *The Islandman*, 'We thought more of a seal in those days than of the very best pig'. They were also valued for their skins which made covers for the curraghs and shoes for rock climbers.

Seal hunting was dangerous work, sometimes involving swimming into the underwater caves where the seals breed and then dragging or hauling the catch to the boats. 'Our big boat was loaded down to the gunwale with four cow seals, two bulls, and two two-year-olds – one for each of the crew. Every one of the men had a barrel full of seal meat, and we reckoned in those days that every barrel of seal meat was worth a barrel of pork. The skins fetched eight pounds.' The seal catchers in County Cork wore 'bags quilted with charcoal on their arms for the animals let go their hold when they bit on the crunchy charcoal'. In some places, however, there was a taboo against eating seals because of the belief that members of certain families could change themselves or be changed to seals. Porpoises, often referred to as sea pigs, were slaughtered after being driven ashore by boats. Like the seal their meat was highly valued and was shared with neighbours, and salted down to last through the winter. Neither seals nor porpoises are eaten today.

For two hundred years hunting the basking shark, also known as the sunfish, was very much a way of life off the west coast of Ireland, from Donegal in the north to Cork in the south. In Donegal shark and whale fishing were combined. These fish move down the west coast of Ireland in summer, and in early May they haunt the Sunfish Bank, thirty miles off Achill Island, where they come to the surface in the morning and the evening. Here and elsewhere the sunfish were harpooned from curraghs, small rowing boats and hookers in a most haphazard and dangerous way. The decked vessels, however, had the advantage as they could stand by and wait for the sharks for several days. In the early nineteenth century it was reported that as many as thirty or forty fish were sometimes killed on the Sunfish Bank in one day when the weather was fine. The most intense shark fishing activity took place off the Claddagh and Connemara districts of Galway and the outlying islands such as the Arans, Inishbofin and Inishark.

The basking shark was greatly valued for its liver, and it was said that one fish could yield up to seven to ten barrels of liver and produce 90–450 litres (20–100 gallons) of golden-brown oil. This was in great demand as the fuel for lamps before the advent of paraffin and large quantities were exported in the early nineteenth century to London, where it was used to light the city lamps. The oil was also used by the country people for dressing wool, preserving timber, soothing burnt or bruised skin and for the relief of muscular pain.

Commercial shark fishing on a larger organised scale was only very seldom practised, but in 1947, after the Second World War, Achill Fishery was established to help produce industrial oil which was exported to Britain, Norway, Holland, West Germany, Finland and the USA. Eventually the value of the oil fell and as a result the fishery went into decline.

Such were the hazards of the sea that it was not uncommon for whole families of fathers and sons to set out, never to return. The tragedy of the fisherfolk is encapsulated in John Millington Synge's evocative play *Riders to the Sea*, which tells the story of Maurya who has lost her husband, her father-in-law and her six sons to the water and who echoes the lament of every wife and mother of the fishermen around the coast.

> They are all together this time and the end has come ... Michael has a clean burial in the far north by the grace of the Almighty God. Bartley will have a fine

coffin out of the white boards and a deep grave surely. What more can we want than that? No man at all can be living forever, and we must be satisfied.

It is little wonder therefore that superstition abounds around the activity of fishing. One of these prevents women from having anything to do with the boats or the sea, their fishing activities being confined to the land and the salting of fish, the preparation of bait, the gathering of shellfish and watching and praying for the safe return of their men from the shore side.

Looked on as an industry, Irish fishing has always been a precarious business, changing with the movement and volume of fish and dependent on the political and economic climate of the time. For many centuries a commercial fishing industry in addition to that carried on by the large foreign vessels off the southern and western coasts was of great economic importance, bringing large revenues to the lords of the adjacent coasts in the form of fishing dues, charges for the use of harbours and of drying grounds for nets and for the fish itself. Although these vessels were not Irish it is probable that Irish merchants may have had some involvement in this developing industry. Irish ships owned by entrepreneurs rather than fishermen; also fished the waters and Irish merchant ships were active on the trade routes off north-west Europe. There was a thriving trade with Spain, Portugal, Belgium, France, Holland, England and Scotland. Wine was exchanged for fish and other commodities; salt was imported to preserve the herrings, ling, mackerel, hake and pilchards which became important exports from the major parts of Galway, Cork, Kinsale, Waterford, Arklow, Dublin, Wexford, Drogheda, Dundalk, Dungannon, Ardglass and Carrickfergus.

However, in the seventeenth century, because of the changing habits of the fish and other problems, including the lack of capital, the main industry fell into a state of decay.

Ports remained as dilapidated as ever. Lack of scientific knowledge, an absence of manpower, and the increase and cheapness of other foods militated against the growth and development of the industry.

By 1819 the commercial fishing situation had deteriorated so much that Ireland had actually become a fish-importing rather than a fish-exporting country. This absurd situation stirred the authorities into action and finance was made available for building modern fishing boats and for curing fish, along with grants and incentives for building roads, curing stations, dwellings and facilities for education. This saw the beginning of the boom period in the Irish fishing industry, with herrings and mackerel as the major exports.

From 1886 to 1901 there was a lucrative export trade in mackerel to the United States, and contemporary photographs of Kinsale, Berehaven, Killybegs and other ports, jammed with Irish mackerel boats, testify to the rising tide of confidence on which the industry was floating. At the beginning of the twentieth century, steam trawling was introduced and there was a considerable export trade in shellfish and molluscs. Dunmore East in County Waterford was doing well on herrings, selling to buyers in North Germany and the United States, and generally the industry continued to prosper with the advent of the First World War, and the diversion of the British trawling fleets to war duty. The Irish fleet took their place in the market. The demand for motorised boats soared, loans were made, boats bought and, until 1920 when the British trawling fleet was decommissioned, this new breed of fishermen made a handsome living. However, after the war, with renewed competition from the British trawling fleets who were once again able to supply a wide variety of fish at lower prices, the Irish fleet was left with expensive fish it could not sell and heavy repayment on its boats which it could not pay. Demoralised, they with-

drew from the industry, leaving their boats on the shore to rot.

Since 1923, when a separate Irish state was formed, the commercial fishing industries in the north and the rest of Ireland once more began to move forward but at a slightly different pace. Northern Ireland was quicker to develop its major ports of Portavogie and Kilkeel at County Down. More modern, powerful, economical and better-equipped boats, with the latest technology, were introduced. Younger men were attracted to the industry, most buying their own boats. Research stations were also set up. Education for fishermen was introduced along with fish processing and fish farming, until, in 1941, the value of fish landed in the north of Ireland was almost as much as in the whole of the rest of Ireland. Similar developments to those in the northern counties were also underway and considerable growth was made in the export of lobsters and prawns; the Connemara oyster stock flourished; a sophisticated fishing fleet was commissioned; the largest port in Ireland at Killybegs in Donegal was inaugurated, along with fish processing and canning plants; a training college at Greencastle, County Londonderry, was established and other ports were modernised.

The entire industry throughout Ireland is still in a period of growth, but as always also has its problems: over-fishing, dwindling stocks, disputes over fishing grounds and European Community policy. Fish exports continue to thrive and demand on the home market has increased in both quantity and variety, indeed to such an extent that it is not always easy to get what you want – so much is being exported! Promotion, marketing and advertising by the Seafish Industry Authority in the north, and An Bord Iascaigh Mhàra in the rest of Ireland, along with the current advice from the medical profession to eat more fish as part of a healthier diet, has focused attention on the benefits and rich rewards to be had from fish, one of the country's greatest assets. The association of fish with penance, poverty and famine are thus slowly being eroded and its pleasures appreciated.

INLAND FISHING

Ireland's unpolluted waterways have always been noted for the quality and abundance of their fish. Indeed, it was the fish around the coast and in the rivers and lakes that brought the first settlers to Ireland. Today, anglers and tourists from all over the world come to Ireland to fish the famous salmon rivers of the west, innumerable brown trout lakes of the mountains, as well as to sample those from the now well-established rainbow trout fisheries.

Of all the fish caught in these inland waters, the most noted and sought after is the salmon, which is caught in the estuaries and the rivers as it leaves the sea to begin the journey inland to spawn. From February to mid-September, salmon are to be found in almost every stream or brook, being at their most plentiful from May until the end of July. On many occasions I have watched them in their hundreds dancing and leaping below the bridge beside my cottage in County Down just where the river meets the sea, and from the Salmon Weir Bridge in Galway. Arthur Young also enjoyed a similar sight at Ballyshannon, and described it in *A Tour in Ireland* (1776–9): '. . . was delighted to see the salmon jump, to me an unusual sight: the water was perfectly alive with them.'

Not only has the salmon fascinated and satisfied people through the centuries, it also has a long and honoured history and features in many of the heroic tales and legends of the past. In the Irish sagas a king called Fintan is said to have escaped the flood by being changed into a salmon. It is said that as he was swimming under a hazel tree, considered

Fishing for salmon, Dundrum, County Down.

to be the Tree of Knowledge, some nuts fell and hit him on the back, imparting to him the tree's knowledge. Ever after, this fish was known as the 'Salmon of Knowledge'.

Legend also has it that Fionn MacCumaill (Finn MacCool), the leader of a band of heroic warriors called the Fianna, acquired the gift of knowledge from the salmon while cooking it for his poet friend and master. Forbidden to taste it, he watched hungrily as it cooked. As the fish roasted over the fire, a blister arose on its skin and he pressed it with his finger to burst it. He burnt his thumb and stuck it in his mouth to cool it and unwittingly had the first taste of the salmon. The salmon's knowledge immediately passed on to Finn, making him the wisest of men and causing him to be elected leader of the Fianna.

In ancient Ireland, salmon was the main dish served at the lavish banquets given by the kings. At this time the whole salmon was rubbed with salt and impaled on a stick before being cooked over an open fire and basted with butter and honey.

Salmon is also often cooked and enjoyed beside the rivers where it is wrapped in several layers of wet newspaper, laid in the ashes of an open fire and then covered with more hot ashes and embers. When the paper has dried, the salmon is cooked. Many eighteenth- and nineteenth-century manuscripts also refer to pickling salmon, a practice which is seldom carried out today, although at this time Irish salt-salmon was exported in large quantities to America.

The commercial salmon fishery is a very important and valuable industry in Ireland today, as is the smoking of sides of salmon for both overseas and home consumption. Sea trout, also called white trout in Ireland, is also of considerable commercial value and can be found all around the coast and particularly in the lakes and rivers of the west of Ireland during the summer.

Many other fish from the sea, rivers and lakes were also enjoyed by the Irish. The household accounts of Holy Trinity Priory, Dublin, in the late thirteenth century show just how varied the selection was: 'In Lent and on Fridays, plenty of fish was available: salmon, oysters, salted fish and herring were most common, less rarely [perhaps means more] for special guests, trout, eels, turbot, plaice, gurnard and salted eels were on the menu.'

The brown trout, another indigenous fish, is also found in large quantities in almost every river and lake throughout the country. One of the traditional methods of cooking it is described in an account of a fishing trip to Innisfallen in County Kerry by A. Cosmopolite in *The Sportsman in Ireland* (1897):

> But from his boat was produced a fine lake trout of five pounds, which he had taken by trailing. The lads were active, and in a few minutes an excellent turf fire was blazing; three sticks, gipsy fashion, were stuck up, the tea kettle was boiling, the cloth laid on the velvet green and the trout suspended for roasting. The major had not forgotten a good dried salmon, which broiled with some of the smaller trout, furnished forth a noble breakfast.

Eels were originally caught using a variety of pronged spear, which was still widely used until quite recently, or with baited lines and long conical nets, almost identical to those used today on the River Bann and Lough Neagh. However, the eels were more frequently caught in riverine weirs, specially designed to catch eels, salmon and trout and attached to religious houses and those of the wealthy landowners. Today, the eel fisheries on the River Bann and Lough Neagh are the most important in Western Europe.

Originally eels were eaten fresh, beheaded, skinned and cleaned, and if young or small mature fish, were boiled and then quickly fried. Older, tougher eels were also boiled, and sometimes served with a white sauce. Eels were also salted and stored like herrings for winter use and in Athlone were presented with an onion stuck in their mouths. In the eighteenth century, in the larger houses, they were often potted, like herrings, in wine vinegar and seasoning.

Pollan, another species of freshwater fish, is found in Lough Neagh and in some of the other inland waters in Ireland, such as Lough Ree. They are often described as freshwater herrings and are believed to have been one of the few indigenous fish present in Ireland during the last Ice Age. At one time the fish-sellers' cry was 'Pollan alive and kicking in the cart': they are generally served fresh from the lough, gutted, rolled in seasoned flour and fried.

Perch is also found in Lough Neagh and the many other freshwater loughs and rivers throughout the country. They are generally poached or baked and served with a parsley sauce. In the north of Ireland, the young perch are called grunts and are delicious, skinned and fried like eels or pollan, or made into soup.

Pike are also widely found in the rivers and lakes and at one time were a popular fish, particularly in the large country houses where they were generally stuffed and roasted or stewed and served with a rich sauce. Although no longer so popular in Ireland, they are still highly sought after by visiting anglers. They are best simply baked in the oven with plenty of butter, seasoning and lemon juice, or barbecued straight from the water.

Crayfish, which are small freshwater lobsters, are slightly smaller than American crayfish. They are found in the limestone lakes in the centre of the country, like Loughs Sheelkin, Lene and Derravaragh, and only need to be lightly steamed or boiled before eating.

Although the variety of fish found in Ireland's inland waters is limited, stocks are good and the quality excellent.

A market display of Irish fish.

FISH AND SHELLFISH RECIPES

*There is an abundant supply of seafood
around Ireland's coastline.*

WHOLE POACHED SALMON
Bradán Scallta

Whole salmon fish, from three years old, vary in weight from 3.5 to 7.25 kg (8–16 lb) and are generally cooked in a flavoured liquid (court-bouillon) in a fish kettle, which should be able to accommodate its length, on top of the cooker. If a fish kettle is not available, a double thickness of aluminium foil can be folded around the salmon to make a container for both fish and cooking liquor. A whole salmon is cooked for about 8 minutes to the pound when the fish is over 2.75 kg (6 lb) in weight.

In one eighteenth-century manuscript the whole fish was seasoned, both inside and out, with a mixture of salt and pepper, finely shredded horseradish, capers, two minced anchovies and some grated bread and a little butter. The poaching liquor was made from a mixture of claret and water or white wine, cider and water. The salmon was served with pickles.

SERVES 12

1 × 3.5 kg (8 lb) whole fresh salmon, gutted
FOR THE COOKING LIQUOR
1.2 litres (2 pints) cold water
1 × 15 ml (1 tablespoon) salt
150 ml (5 fl oz) malt vinegar
1 carrot, peeled and sliced
1 onion, peeled and sliced
1 stick celery
Sprig of thyme, 2 bay leaves, bunch of parsley,
tied together
10 peppercorns
FOR THE GARNISH
1 bunch watercress

Wash the salmon under cold running water, then dry well and trim off the fins. Combine all the ingredients for the cooking liquor in a saucepan, bring to the boil and simmer for 15–20 minutes. Put into the fish kettle along with the salmon. Cover with the lid and cook gently, never allowing the liquid to boil as the quality of the fish will be destroyed. Poach until the salmon is tender. This will take about 1 hour. Alternatively, fold a double thickness of foil around the salmon, set it in a roasting tin and cook in the oven at 150°C (300°F, gas mark 2) for the same length of time. When cooked, the fish should feel firm to the touch and a skewer should easily pierce its flesh. Remove carefully from the kettle or foil, drain well and set on a hot serving dish. Skin, cut into pieces and serve with plain boiled potatoes, fresh new peas and garnished with watercress.

COLD POACHED SALMON If the salmon is to be served cold, leave it to cool in its cooking liquor before skinning and transferring to a serving plate. Decorate with alternate, overlapping layers of very thinly sliced cucumber and garnish with lemon wedges and watercress. Serve with mayonnaise and cucumber salad.

POACHED SALMON STEAKS
Stéigeacha Bradáin Scallta

Individual salmon steaks can be poached in a frying pan either in fish stock, flavoured or plain water or wine seasoned with lemon juice, peppercorns and herbs. They can also be cooked in a microwave oven.

SERVES 1

1 × salmon steak about 2–2.5 cm (¾–1 in) thick,
approx. 250 g (9 oz)
65–150 ml (2½–5 fl oz) liquid
2 × 15 ml (2 tablespoons) lemon juice
4–6 peppercorns
Sprig of thyme, small bay leaf, parsley stalks, tied
together
Pinch of salt
2 × 15 ml (2 tablespoons) onion, finely chopped

Set the salmon steak in a small frying pan, pour on the liquid and add the rest of the ingredients. Bring the liquid to the boil, then cover, reduce the heat and simmer for 8 minutes until the flesh is pale pink with milky curds on its surface. The fresher the salmon, the thicker the curd will be.

If cooking in a microwave, use a suitable container and cover with a domed lid. Cook on full power for 3–3½ minutes.

Remove from the cooking liquor and discard the skin and bone. Serve with new boiled potatoes, garden peas, lightly steamed cucumber, courgettes or asparagus and melted butter. The cooking liquid can also be made into a sauce by reducing it and then finishing with butter or cream and some freshly chopped herbs like parsley, tarragon, fennel, chervil and chives.

GRILLED SALMON STEAKS
Stéigeacha Bradáin Griosctha

Grilled and fried salmon steaks have a completely different taste and texture to poached salmon steaks, but are equally delicious. They are also very quick to prepare and take about 4 minutes on each side to cook.

SERVES 1

1 salmon steak, about 2–2.5 cm (¾–1 in) thick
approx. 250 g (9 oz)
Salt and freshly milled black pepper
25 g (1 oz) butter

Lay the steak on an oiled grill rack or foil-lined baking tray. Season with the salt and pepper and dot with the butter. Cook under a pre-heated high grill for 4 minutes on each side. On turning the steak, brush with a little melted butter and season again. Serve with a crisp green salad or freshly boiled vegetables.

TROUT WITH HAZELNUTS
Breac le Búiste Collchnó

This dish combines two traditional Irish ingredients, trout and hazelnuts, both freely available from the countryside. Hazelnuts have been valued for centuries for their flavour as has the abundant supply of freshwater trout from the lakes and rivers throughout Ireland.

SERVES 4

4 brown or rainbow trout, approx. 1 kg (2 lb) each
Salt and freshly milled black pepper
50 g (2 oz) plain flour
50 g (2 oz) butter
100 g (4 oz) hazelnuts, roughly chopped
2 × 15 ml (2 tablespoons) parsley, finely chopped
1 lemon, cut in wedges
OVEN TEMPERATURE 180°C (350°F, gas mark 4)
OVEN TIME 25–30 minutes

Clean the trout well, removing any blood from the backbone. Remove the gills but leave the head intact. Wash and dry. Make a few incisions along the sides of the fish. Season with salt and freshly milled black pepper inside and out and dust in the flour. Heat half the butter in a roasting dish or pan, lay the fish in it and cook for a minute on each side, until the flesh is set and lightly coloured. Transfer to a pre-heated oven and cook for 25–30 minutes. Remove from the oven, sprinkle with the chopped hazelnuts and flash under a hot grill for 30 seconds to toast lightly. Make sure the nuts do not burn, as they will taste bitter. Transfer to a hot serving dish, sprinkle with finely chopped parsley and garnish with the lemon wedges.

MIXED SEAFOOD WITH CHEESE SAUCE
Bia Na Mara le hAnlann Cáise

Cod is one of the main fish caught off the Irish coast and is widely used in Irish kitchens. It is most frequently baked, dipped in batter and fried, poached or made into cakes, pies and other savoury dishes. In this recipe, strips of cod are combined with prawns and mushrooms and coated in a cheese sauce. Any other firm-fleshed fish and shellfish can also be used. This makes an excellent savoury dish for either a first or main course.

SERVES 4 as a main course or 6–8 as a first course
450g (1 lb) cod fillets
15 g (½ oz) butter
50 g (2 oz) button mushrooms, chopped and thinly diced
100 g (4 oz) cooked prawns
FOR THE CHEESE SAUCE
450 ml (15 fl oz) milk
Piece of onion
6 peppercorns
Blade of mace
Bay leaf
40 g (1½ oz) butter
40 g (1½ oz) plain flour
Salt and freshly milled black pepper
1 × 15 ml (1 tablespoon) lemon juice
100 g (4 oz) cheddar cheese, grated
4 individual ovenproof dishes to hold approx. 300 ml (10 fl oz)
OVEN TEMPERATURE 180°C (350°F, gas mark 4)
OVEN TIME 20–25 minutes

Begin the preparations for the sauce. Put the milk into a saucepan along with the onion, peppercorns, mace and bay leaf. Bring to the boil, then remove from the heat and leave to infuse for about 15 minutes. Melt the 15 g (½ oz) butter and lightly grease 4 individual ovenproof dishes. Remove the skin and any

Cod's roe ramekins.

bones from the fish and discard, then cut the fillets into finger-size strips. Divide the fish between the dishes and scatter the mushrooms and prawns on top.

Complete the sauce by melting the butter in a saucepan and stirring in the flour to make a smooth paste. Cook gently for a few minutes, stirring all the time. Strain the infused milk and gradually add to the flour and butter mixture, stirring all the time to prevent lumps from forming. When all the milk has been added, return the saucepan to the heat, season with salt and freshly milled black pepper and cook for a few minutes to thicken the sauce. Add the lemon juice and two-thirds of the cheddar cheese and stir until melted. Pour over the fish and sprinkle with the remaining cheese. Set on a baking tray and bake in the pre-heated oven for 20–25 minutes until golden brown. Serve with wheaten bread (see page 132) and salad.

COD'S ROE RAMEKINS
Raimicíní Eochraí Throisc

Cod's roe was a frequent addition to the Irish diet in coastal areas, particularly when food was scarce. The roe was tied loosely in muslin, then cooked in boiling salted water for 30–40 minutes depending on its thickness. It was then lightly pressed between two plates so that it could be cut into compact pieces for frying. When fried it was cut in slices about 2 cm (¾ in) thick, dipped in beaten egg and dusted in fine breadcrumbs. It was fried in bacon fat until golden brown on both sides. Frequently it was served with a rasher of bacon and slices of fried potato. Another way of using the cod's roe was to mix it with breadcrumbs, soak it in egg and milk and bake it in the oven, either in one large dish or individual ramekins. This makes an excellent first course/light supper dish, served with wheaten bread.

MAKES 8 × 120 ml (4 fl oz) ramekins
225 g (8 oz) cod's roe, skinned, or 2 × 200 g (8 oz) tins of pressed cod's roe
100 g (4 oz) fine breadcrumbs
A generous pinch of ground mace
Pinch of paprika pepper
Salt and freshly milled black pepper
2 × 15 ml (2 tablespoons) parsley, finely chopped
3 × 15 ml (3 tablespoons) lemon juice
1 egg, separated
150 ml (5 fl oz) milk or cream
OVEN TEMPERATURE 200°C (400°F, gas mark 6)
OVEN TIME 15–20 minutes

Lightly butter eight small ramekin dishes. Chop the roe and put into a large bowl with the breadcrumbs, seasonings, parsley and lemon juice. Beat the egg yolk with the milk or cream and pour over the cod's roe mixture. Leave for about 10 minutes to allow the breadcrumbs to soak up all the liquid. Beat the egg white until stiff and fold into the soaked mixture. Use this to almost fill each of the ramekins. Set on a baking tray and bake in the oven until they are puffed up and golden brown. This will take about 15 minutes. Serve with wheaten bread (see page 132).

FRIED HERRINGS IN OATMEAL
Scadáin Friochta i Min Choirce

Frying is perhaps the most popular way of cooking fresh herrings, and also one of the quickest. There are a variety of ways both to prepare and fry the herring, but whichever you choose, it first needs to be gutted and cleaned, its head, tail and fins removed and its body well washed and dried. It can then be left as it is,

tossed in seasoned flour or oatmeal and fried in bacon fat, butter or oil. Alternatively, it can be split, boned and opened out before frying in the same way. It can also be brushed with mustard and/or dipped in beaten egg before being coated in the flour or oatmeal. The oatmeal itself can range from fine to coarse, depending on what is available and the finished texture required.

SERVES 4
4 herrings, approx. 100 g (4 oz) each, prepared
1 egg, beaten
75 g (3 oz) medium-fine oatmeal, or plain flour
Salt and freshly milled black pepper
Bacon fat, butter or oil for frying

Either leave the herrings whole or open them out. Dip each in the beaten egg, then roll it in the seasoned oatmeal or flour. I have found that both the oatmeal and flour stick to the herrings better when they are opened out, and as a result look better for presentation.

Heat the fat in a large frying pan and when hot put in the fish, flesh side down so that it cooks first. Reduce the heat and cook until golden brown. This will take about 4 minutes on each side. Drain on kitchen paper before serving with lemon wedges and mustard sauce. If the herrings are small allow two per person.

MUSTARD SAUCE
Anlann Mustaird
This is a delicious spicy sauce to serve with herrings (see above) and fish cakes (see page 104).

MAKES 300 ml (10 fl oz) of sauce
25 g (1 oz) butter
25 g (1 oz) plain flour
300 ml (10 fl oz) milk
Squeeze of lemon juice
1 × 5 ml (1 teaspoon) vinegar
1 × 15 ml (1 tablespoon) made English mustard
Salt and freshly milled black pepper

FROM TOP: *Potted herrings, fried herrings in oatmeal and marinated herrings.*

Melt the butter in a small saucepan and stir in the flour, gradually add the milk, stirring all the time to prevent lumps from forming. Still stirring, continue to cook for about 5 minutes until the sauce is thick and the flour is cooked. Add the lemon juice, vinegar, mustard and seasoning.

MARINATED HERRINGS
Scadáin Spíosraithe
This was one of my grandmother's favourite recipes. She made it frequently in the summer when the herrings were in season and were brought to her house by the fishman in his horse and cart. She served it with home-made wheaten bread and butter and a salad of crisp leaves from her vegetable garden. Nowadays, I serve it as a first course in exactly the same way but in smaller quantities, cutting the rolled herring in slices and serving it in rings.

8 large herrings, heads and tails removed, split and boned
2 × 15 ml (2 tablespoons) salt
4 large dill pickles
1 large onion, cut in short slices
1 × 15 ml (1 tablespoon) made English mustard
8 wooden cocktail sticks
FOR THE MARINADE
600 ml (1 pint) white wine vinegar
150 ml (5 fl oz) cold water
6 peppercorns
1 × 5 ml (1 teaspoon) whole allspice berries
1 × 5 ml (1 teaspoon) whole coriander seeds
1 × 2.5 ml (½ teaspoon) mustard seeds
2 blades of mace
1 dried chilli
2 bay leaves
1 × 15 ml (1 tablespoon) soft brown sugar
12 fennel stalks

Place the prepared herrings in a colander and sprinkle with the salt. Allow them to drain for about 3 hours.

Meanwhile make the marinade. Combine all the ingredients for the marinade in a saucepan except for the fennel. Bring to the boil, then simmer gently for 5–10 minutes. Remove from the heat and leave until cold. Rinse the herrings to remove the salt and dry off any excess moisture using kitchen paper. Cut each dill

pickle in half lengthwise. Lay the herrings, skin side down, on a board and spread a thin layer of mustard over the flesh. Place a piece of dill pickle and some pieces of onion at what was the head end of the herring and roll up from top to tail. Secure each roll with a cocktail stick (the skin should be on the outside). Lay the fennel stalks in the bottom of a glass or porcelain casserole dish and pack the herrings tightly on top. Cover with the remaining pieces of onion. Pour over the marinade, cover with a glass or aluminium foil lid and keep in the refrigerator for 48 hours before eating. Once marinated, the herrings will keep for 7–10 days.

POTTED HERRINGS
Scadáin Potáin
Today, potted herrings are generally prepared by the fishmonger or bought from the supermarket in convenient packages. However, the home-made variety still has the edge and is worth the very little effort required.

SERVES 4
8 herrings, approx. 100–150 g (4–5 oz) each
Salt and freshly milled black pepper
350 ml (12 fl oz) vinegar
120 ml (4 fl oz) cold water
6 whole cloves
150 g (5 oz) onion, sliced
2 bay leaves
10 peppercorns
OVEN TEMPERATURE 160°C (325°F, gas mark 3)
OVEN TIME 40–45 minutes

Gut the herrings and remove the heads and tails. (Your fishmonger will do this for you.) Scrape off the loose scales and wash well under cold running water, split and lay flat. Season well with salt and black pepper and roll up, from head to tail, flesh side inside. Secure with a wooden cocktail stick and pack tightly in an ovenproof dish.

Combine the vinegar, water, cloves, onion, bay leaves and peppercorns in a saucepan and bring to the boil. Pour over the herrings, cover tightly with foil and cook in the pre-heated oven for 40–45 minutes until the flesh is tender. Leave to go cold in the cooking liquor and serve with salad, brown bread and butter and a glass of Guinness.

CLOCKWISE, FROM TOP LEFT: *Fisherman's pie (page 105), mixed seafood with cheese sauce (page 101) and fish cakes (page 104).*

FRIED MACKEREL WITH GOOSEBERRY SAUCE
Ronnaigh Friochta le hAnlann Spionáin
The combination of mackerel – fried, grilled or baked – and gooseberry sauce is said to have been introduced to Ireland by the Normans. Its sharpness is excellent with the rich oily fish.

SERVES 4
4 mackerel
50 g (2 oz) seasoned flour
75 g (3 oz) bacon fat or butter
FOR THE GOOSEBERRY SAUCE
MAKES approx. 400 ml (14 fl oz)
450 g (1 lb) gooseberries
175 ml (6 fl oz) cold water
2 × 15 ml (2 tablespoons) granulated sugar
25 g (1 oz) butter
2 × 15 ml (2 tablespoons) fennel leaves, chopped

Begin by preparing the gooseberry sauce. Put the topped-and-tailed fruit in a saucepan with the water. Bring to the boil then add the sugar, butter and half the fennel. Cook gently for 6–7 minutes, until the berries split and burst open. They should still show texture rather than be cooked to a purée. Stir in the remaining fennel.

Gut the mackerel, cut off the fins, remove the head and tail and cut into fillets, removing the backbone. Roll the fillets in seasoned flour and fry in hot bacon fat or butter until lightly cooked. Arrange the fillets on each plate and serve with the hot sauce and new potatoes.

RHUBARB SAUCE Wash, trim and cut 275 g (10 oz) of rhubarb into 1 cm ($\frac{1}{2}$ in) pieces. Bring gently to the boil with 85 ml (3 fl oz) of cold water, then simmer until pulpy. Stir in 1–2 × 15 ml (1–2 tablespoons) of granulated sugar and 25 g (1 oz) of butter and serve hot. Makes approx. 400 ml (14 fl oz) of sauce.

FISH CAKES
Iascmheallta
At one time fish cakes were an excellent way of including fish in the diet of those who were not keen to eat it, particularly children. Today, with the advent of so many breaded-fish items in the supermarket, home-made fish cakes are almost a thing of the past. However, when made with smoked fish or a combination of smoked and fresh fish, they are exceedingly good.

SERVES 4
450 g (1 lb) smoked haddock, cut thickly
50 g (2 oz) butter
Squeeze of lemon juice
450 g (1 lb) potatoes, cooked and mashed
Salt and freshly milled black pepper
2 × 15 ml (2 tablespoons) parsley, finely chopped
Pinch of mace
Grated rind of $\frac{1}{2}$ lemon
1 egg, size 3, beaten
TO FINISH
25 g (1 oz) plain flour
Salt and freshly milled black pepper
1 egg, size 3, beaten
50 g (2 oz) breadcrumbs
2 × 15 ml (2 tablespoons) oil for frying
OVEN TEMPERATURE 180 °C (350°F, gas mark 4)
OVEN TIME 15–20 minutes

Butter an ovenproof dish with half of the butter

and lay the fish on top. Sprinkle with the lemon juice, cover with lightly buttered foil and bake in a pre-heated oven for 15–20 minutes. Remove the fish from the baking dish, discard any bones and put the flesh in a large mixing bowl along with the potatoes and remaining butter. Break up the fish and mix well with the potatoes. Season with the salt and pepper and stir in the parsley, mace and lemon rind. Leave to go cold, then mix in the beaten egg.

Divide the mixture into eight pieces, each approximately 75 g (3 oz) in weight. Shape into flat cakes, approximately 1 cm ($\frac{1}{2}$ in) deep. Mix the flour on a plate with salt and pepper and lightly coat each cake. Dip in the lightly beaten egg and then in the breadcrumbs to give an even covering. Dust off the excess crumbs and fry in the hot oil until golden brown in colour and very hot all the way through. This will take approximately 6 minutes on each side. Remove from the pan and drain on absorbent kitchen paper. Serve very warm with a spicy sauce such as mustard (see page 103) or tomato.

FISHERMAN'S PIE
Pióg Éisc

This simple but tasty dish is a favourite in many Irish homes on Friday where the tradition of not eating meat on this day is still carried on. Plain white or smoked fish such as haddock, cod or whiting is generally used with perhaps the addition of a few prawns or oysters where they are inexpensive and readily available. I add a few sliced mushrooms and sometimes a finely chopped onion and gherkin, particularly when using unsmoked fish. These additions give the pie a little extra flavour.

SERVES 4–6
450 g (1 lb) smoked haddock
2 × 15 ml (2 tablespoons) lemon juice
100 g (4 oz) mushrooms, sliced
25 g (1 oz) butter
2 eggs, hard boiled
FOR THE WHITE SAUCE
250 ml (8 fl oz) milk, infused with piece of onion, 2 cloves, 6 peppercorns, blade of mace, bay leaf and parsley stalks
25 g (1 oz) butter
25 g (1 oz) plain flour
150 ml (5 fl oz) liquor from cooking the fish
1 × 5 ml (1 teaspoon) mustard
Salt and freshly milled black pepper
1 × 15 ml (1 tablespoon) parsley, finely chopped
FOR THE POTATO TOPPING
750 ml (1$\frac{3}{4}$ lb) potatoes
25 g (1 oz) butter
3–4 × 15 ml (3–4 tablespoons) milk
Salt and pepper
25–50 g (1–2 oz) Cheddar cheese, grated
OVEN TEMPERATURE
For the fish: 180°C (350°F, gas mark 4)
For the pie: 190°C (375°F, gas mark 5)
OVEN TIME
For the fish: 15–20 minutes
For the pie: 30 minutes

Place the fish in a buttered ovenproof dish, sprinkle with the lemon juice, cover with buttered greaseproof paper and cook in the pre-heated oven for 15–20 minutes. Reserve the cooking liquor from the fish to add to the milk for the sauce. Fry the mushrooms in the butter until just beginning to colour.

Prepare the white sauce by infusing the milk with the flavouring ingredients for 15–30 minutes, then melt the butter in a saucepan and stir in the flour. Strain the infused milk into a measuring jug and add enough of the cooking liquor from the fish to give 375 ml (13 fl oz). Gradually add this to the flour and butter mixture to make a smooth paste. Cook over a gentle heat to thicken the sauce, stirring all the time. Stir in the mustard, seasoning and parsley.

Remove the bones from the fish and put the flakes in a bowl along with the mushrooms and hard-boiled eggs, roughly chopped. Pour on the white sauce and mix to combine without breaking up the ingredients too much. Put into a deep ovenproof pie dish.

Mash the boiled potatoes until free from lumps and beat in the butter, milk and seasoning to give a light consistency. Pile on top of the fish mixture, covering it evenly. Sprinkle with the grated cheese and bake in the pre-heated oven until piping hot and brown and crispy on top.

LOBSTER WITH HERB MAYONNAISE
Gliomach le Maonáis Luibheanna

In many Irish homes, which had easy access to

Dublin lawyer (page 106).

the sea and a fresh supply of lobsters, a favourite summer lunch or supper dish was cold boiled lobster with a plain or herb mayonnaise. This dish was often served in my grandmother's home in County Down for Sunday tea.

When cooking lobster the timing is generally 12 minutes for the first 450 g (1 lb), 10 minutes for the next 450 g (1 lb) and 5 minutes for each additional 450 g (1 lb).

SERVES 2
1 lobster, about 1 kg (2$\frac{1}{4}$ lb)
1 hard-boiled egg, sieved
3 × 15 ml (3 tablespoons) parsley, finely chopped
1 × 15 ml (1 tablespoon) chives, finely chopped
1 × 15 ml (1 tablespoon) capers, finely chopped
150 ml (5 fl oz) thick mayonnaise
Lemon juice
Watercress and lemon wedges, to garnish

Plunge the lobster, head first, into fast boiling water, return to the boil and cook uncovered for 18–22 minutes. Drain the lobster and remove the claws. Place the lobster on a chopping board, with its tail extended, and cut in half through its length. Discard the stomach sack in the head and the dark intestinal vein running down through the centre of the tail meat. Rub the greyish-green liver and the pink roe (if any) through a sieve into a mixing bowl. Beat in the sieved hard-boiled egg, parsley, chives and capers. Stir in the mayonnaise and a little lemon juice to taste.

Carefully lift out the flesh from the tail shells and cut in slanting slices. Put into a bowl and add enough mayonnaise to moisten. Return to the shell halves. Moisten the flesh in the head shells with a little of the mayonnaise.

Arrange the two lobster halves on a plate and garnish with the cracked claws, watercress leaves and lemon wedges. Serve chilled with the remaining mayonnaise and a mixed-leaf salad.

DUBLIN LAWYER
Gliomach Bhá Bhaile Átha Cliath

At one time lobster would have been eaten more frequently and widely than it is today, mainly because it was less expensive and more readily available. Now it is regarded as a luxury item, commanding premium prices in both shops and restaurants. Dublin lawyer is one of the traditional ways of serving lobster and is delicious in its simplicity. For the best results it is necessary to use a live lobster.

SERVES 2
1 lobster, about 1 kg (2¼ lb)
50 g (2 oz) butter
4 × 15 ml (4 tablespoons) Irish whiskey
150 ml (5 fl oz) double cream
1 × 5 ml (1 teaspoon) mustard
1 × 5 ml (1 teaspoon) lemon juice
Salt and freshly milled black pepper

Plunge the lobster, head first, into fast boiling water for 2 minutes. Remove and refresh under cold water to stop the cooking. Cut the lobster lengthwise through the centre, dividing it in two. Remove the grit bag near the head and discard. Remove the soft greyish-green liver and coral and reserve for the sauce. Remove the meat from the shells and cut into chunks. Reserve the shells for serving. Break the claws and remove the meat. Heat the butter in a large frying pan and quickly fry the pieces of lobster

flesh until just cooked, but not coloured. Add the coral. Warm the whiskey slightly, pour over the lobster and flame it. When the flames have died down, add the cream, mustard, lemon juice and seasoning. Mix with the pan juices and bring to the boil. Remove the lobster meat from the pan and transfer to warm shells. Boil the cream rapidly to reduce slightly and concentrate the flavours. Pour over the lobster meat in the half-shells and serve immediately.

Oysters with cheese sauce.

DUBLIN BAY PRAWNS
Piardáin Bhá Bhaile Átha Cliath

*Dublin Bay prawns are not in fact prawns at all, but are members of the lobster family, hence their correct name Norwegian lobster (*Nephrops norvegicus*). As their Latin name indicates, they were first identified in Norway, but they can be found along the entire Atlantic coast from the North Cape to Morocco, as well as* in the western Mediterranean and the Adriatic. *Irish Nephrops are highly prized for their fine delicate flavour.*

Dublin Bay prawns are best when simply prepared in their shells. You can either steam them for about 3 minutes, toss them in butter for 3–4 minutes or grill them for the same length of time. They are served hot with butter and lemon juice, or cold with mayonnaise and salad, and are absolutely delicious.

OYSTERS AND GUINNESS
Oisrí agus Leann Dubh

The most popular way of eating oysters has always been in their raw state, fresh from the shell; sometimes with a squeeze of lemon, sometimes with a little cayenne pepper, but always washed down with a glass of creamy Guinness.

Oysters should only be bought fresh and alive, or in commercially prepared and frozen dishes. The shells of fresh oysters should be tightly closed and if storing for several days or up to a week, should be packed in ice or held in the coldest part of the refrigerator. Before using, oysters should be washed and scrubbed well to remove dirt, sand and grit. They should only be opened just before serving.

To open an oyster, hold it in a thick cloth firmly in one hand. Insert a strong sharp knife, an old-fashioned pointed can opener, or a screwdriver, into the hinge of the shell. Give a sharp twist upwards and prize off the shell. If you have difficulty opening the oysters from the hinge, try to prize the shells open by inserting the knife at the side of the shell. Take care not to lose the oyster juices. There is a knack to opening oysters and once it has been learnt you will have no hesitation in buying them.

When oysters are served as a snack, first course or light lunch, 6–12 are arranged on a plate in their half-shells with cracked ice, garnished with lemon wedges and accompanied by wheaten bread (see page 132) and butter.

Fresh oysters are generally served in the deep half of the shell which retains their juices. In Galway, however, they are traditionally eaten from the flat half of the shell, which I feel is a pity as the precious juice is lost.

OYSTERS WITH BACON
Oisrí le Bagún

Here fresh oysters are wrapped in rashers of bacon, threaded on to small cocktail sticks or skewers, grilled and served with lemon and wheaten bread. Other shellfish such as mussels, scallops and clams can be cooked in the same way and make an excellent first course or canapé.

SERVES 1
6–8 oysters
3–4 thin rashers bacon

Open the oysters, remove the rind from the bacon, cut each rasher in half across its width, and flatten out. Lay an oyster on each piece of bacon and roll up neatly. Thread on to a skewer and lay on buttered aluminium foil on a grill rack and cook for 4–5 minutes under a pre-heated grill until the bacon is beginning to colour and the oysters are lightly cooked. Serve with lemon wedges and wheaten bread (see page 132).

OYSTERS WITH CHEESE SAUCE
Oisrí le hAnlann Cáise

Here oysters are served in their half-shells, coated in a light cheese sauce and cooked under the grill. Mussels, clams and scallops can also be cooked in the same way and make a delicious first course.

SERVES 1
6 fresh oysters
FOR THE CHEESE SAUCE
15 g ($\frac{1}{2}$ oz) butter
20 g ($\frac{3}{4}$ oz) plain flour
150 ml (5 fl oz) milk
25–50 g (1–2 oz) cheese, grated
Pinch of salt and freshly milled black pepper
Squeeze of lemon juice
TO SERVE
Lemon wedge
Wheaten bread

Wash and scrub the oyster shells thoroughly and open carefully. Remove the oyster flesh from the shells and pour the liquid into a small pan. Add the oysters to the pan and simmer gently for about 30 seconds. This will extract the moisture from the oysters and prevent the sauce from becoming too runny during the cooking. The juice is reserved for the sauce.

Clean the bottom half of the shells, set an oyster on each and arrange on a bed of salt in a dish suitable for grilling.

Make the sauce by melting the butter in a saucepan, stirring in the flour and gradually adding the milk and oyster juice to form a smooth mixture. Return the pan to the heat and cook gently until the liquid thickens and forms a smooth sauce. Stir in half the cheese and the seasoning and cook for a further few minutes. Spoon a little sauce over each oyster, sprinkle with the remaining cheese and cook under a pre-heated grill for 5–6 minutes until the oysters are lightly cooked and the cheese golden brown. Serve with a lemon wedge and wheaten bread (see page 132) and butter.

OYSTER SAUCE
Anlann Oisrí

This is a delicious sauce adapted from the eighteenth-century Echlin manuscript from County Down. It makes an excellent accompaniment to any poached or roasted fish, particularly firm-fleshed white fish such as monkfish.

SERVES 4–6
1 small onion, finely chopped
50 g (2 oz) butter
100 g (4 oz) mushrooms, sliced
2 anchovies, chopped
1 × 5 ml (1 teaspoon) capers
10 fresh oysters
450 ml (15 fl oz) stock, composed of oyster juice
and fish stock (see page 109)
1 × 15 ml (1 tablespoon) cornflour
3 egg yolks
1 × 15 ml (1 tablespoon) vinegar
1 × 15 ml (1 tablespoon) parsley, finely chopped

Fry the onion in the melted butter until soft but not coloured, then stir in the mushrooms and continue to fry over a high heat for a few minutes. Add the anchovies and capers. Wash and scrub the oysters, open and strain the juice into a measuring jug and make up to 450 ml (15 fl oz) with fish stock. Add to the pan along with the oysters, each cut into three pieces. Bring to the boil and simmer for a few minutes. Mix the cornflour, egg yolks and vinegar, and add a little warm, but not boiling, stock from the pan, stirring to blend. Add to the pan and heat gently to thicken the sauce. Stir in the parsley and serve hot.

MUSSELS IN WINE SAUCE
Diúilicíní in Anlann Fíona

Mussels were once regarded as the poor-man's oysters. Where oysters were either too expensive or unavailable and a good supply of mussels was free for the picking along the local shore, they were eaten in abundance. One of the easiest and most common ways to prepare them was in a simple stew with onion, leek, garlic and parsley. Allow about 12 mussels per person.

SERVES 2
24 fresh mussels
50 g (2 oz) butter
1 large onion, finely chopped
1–2 cloves garlic, crushed
1 small leek, white and green finely sliced
300 ml (10 fl oz) dry white wine
150 ml (5 fl oz) water or fish stock (see page 109)
TO THICKEN THE COOKING LIQUID
25 g (1 oz) butter
25 g (1 oz) plain flour
Salt and freshly milled black pepper
2 × 15 ml (2 tablespoons) parsley, finely chopped

Wash and scrub the mussels, removing the beard and discarding any that are open. Drain. Melt the butter in a large frying pan and gently fry the onion, garlic and leek until soft but not coloured. Add the mussels, white wine and water or fish stock. Bring the liquid to the boil, then cover the pan and cook for 5–8 minutes until the mussels are open, shaking the pan several times during the cooking. Arrange the mussels in soup plates and keep warm.

Mix the butter and flour together to form a paste and little by little add to the juices in the pan, stirring to thicken. Season with salt and freshly milled black pepper. Sprinkle with parsley and pour over the mussels. There should be about 900 ml (1½ pints) of sauce. Serve with wheaten bread (see page 132).

MUSSELS AND BACON
Diúilicíní agus Bagún

The estuary beside my house is filled with beds of mussels which were the main source of food for the locals during times of shortage. Nowadays they hardly ever eat them, considering them a famine food and remembering the hard times. Others, however, including myself, regard them more highly and come in search of these delicacies when the tide is low. One of the most popular dishes of the area is mussels and bacon. The mussels are first steamed, then removed from their shells and fried in the pan with rashers of best bacon and served with boiled potatoes.

SERVES 4
48 fresh mussels
150 ml (5 fl oz) water
8 rashers bacon
50 g (2 oz) bacon fat or butter
2 × 15 ml (2 tablespoons) parsley, finely chopped

Wash and scrub the mussels, removing the beard. Put in a large frying pan or saucepan, add the water, bring to the boil, cover and steam for 5–8 minutes, shaking the pan occasionally until the shells open. Remove the mussels from the shells. Remove the rind from the bacon and cut each rasher in half. Roll each piece neatly and secure with a cocktail stick or skewer. Put into a pan of boiling water and cook for a few minutes. This helps to remove the excess salt and helps to prevent the rolls from opening. Lift from the pan, drain and dry well. Remove the skewers and fry in the bacon fat or butter until cooked and beginning to colour and crispen. Add the mussels, tossing them in the fat over a high heat for a few minutes. Sprinkle with the parsley and serve with boiled potatoes.

STUFFED MUSSELS
Diúilicíní le Búiste

This simple dish of mussels in half-shells, topped with garlic-flavoured breadcrumbs and grilled, makes an appetising first course. This is a favourite recipe of my neighbour, Delia McGowan, who has been gathering and using mussels from her local bay for over forty years.

SERVES 1–2
12 fresh mussels
65 ml (2½ fl oz) water
50 g (2 oz) butter
2 large cloves garlic
6 × 15 ml (6 tablespoons) fine white breadcrumbs
Squeeze of lemon juice
Freshly milled black pepper
2 × 15 ml (2 tablespoons) parsley, finely chopped

Wash and scrape the mussels thoroughly, removing the beard and discarding any open shells. Put into a large frying pan or saucepan with the water. Bring to the boil, cover and steam for 6–8 minutes until the shells open. Remove the upper half of the shells, leaving the mussels in the lower shell. Set these in a shallow ovenproof dish.

Beat the butter and garlic together until soft, then stir in the breadcrumbs. Add a squeeze of lemon juice to taste, with salt and freshly milled black pepper and parsley. Divide this mixture between the mussels covering the surface of each. Place under a pre-heated grill and cook until golden brown. Serve immediately with extra lemon if desired.

COCKLES
Ruacain

Cockles were traditionally gathered with an iron spoon as the tide receded. Little mounds on the sand show where they lie. Those lying on the surface are dead and should never be gathered.

Cockles are prepared by washing and scrubbing them under cold running water and discarding any whose shells are open. They are generally cooked by steaming them in a little water in a large, covered frying pan or saucepan. Sometimes a few chopped and fried vegetables such as onion, carrot and leek are added for extra flavour and the cockles cooked for 3–5 minutes until the shells have opened. They are eaten straight from the shells with a little melted butter, pepper and salt.

COCKLES AND BACON RASHERS
Ruacain agus Bagún

Cockles, like mussels, are delicious served with bacon.

SERVES 1
8–12 cockles
2 rashers bacon
50 g (2 oz) butter or bacon fat
Freshly milled black pepper
1 × 15 ml (1 tablespoon) parsley, finely chopped

Prepare and cook the cockles as above and remove from their shells. Cut the rind from the bacon and fry in half the fat until cooked and crisp. Remove from the pan and keep warm. Add the rest of the butter to the pan and add the cockles. Fry for a few minutes to warm thoroughly. Sprinkle with black pepper and parsley and serve on a hot plate with the bacon. Serve with Guinness and oatcakes (see page 136).

SCALLOPS
Muiríní

Scallops are also widely found around the coast of Ireland and are highly prized for their delicate flavour and texture. They are used for starters, savouries and main course dishes.

Scallops must be alive and absolutely fresh for use, or else frozen. If they are alive, it is important to prepare them properly before cooking so that they expel the sand which they take in with their food. To do this, scrub the shells thoroughly, then put them in a basin of salted water for several hours before using.

To open the scallops, hold them firmly in your left hand in a tea towel, flat side uppermost. Slide a short, strong pointed knife between the shells and cut through the muscle on the inside of the flat half. Lift off the upper shell. Hold the lower half in your left hand, loosen around the grey edge of the scallop with the knife and lift out of the shell. Pull the grey edge away from the white meat and orange roe. Carefully separate the white meat, known as the nut, from the roe or coral. Discard the grey edge or use in fish stock.

The scallops can be grilled on skewers, the white meat threaded alternately with the corals, brushed with butter and grilled for about 4 minutes; fried lightly with butter, garlic and parsley for about 5 minutes; or left in their shells with a layer of breadcrumbs and butter above and below, and cooked in the oven

for about 20 minutes. Sometimes a few fresh mushrooms are also added. In Ireland the combination of bacon and shellfish is a common one and scallops are often fried with small pieces of bacon; a light sauce made from the cooking juices and a little white wine is served over the mixture.

BAKED SCALLOPS
Muiríní Bácáilte

Like most shellfish, scallops benefit from being lightly cooked and simply served.

SERVES 1
2–4 prepared scallops depending on size
1 scallop shell
15 g (½ oz) butter
2–4 × 15 ml (2–4 tablespoons) fine breadcrumbs
1 clove garlic, finely chopped
1 × 15 ml (1 tablespoon) parsley, finely chopped
Salt and freshly milled black pepper
OVEN TEMPERATURE 200°C (400°F, gas mark 6)
OVEN TIME 5–7 minutes

Prepare the scallops by trimming off the muscle, a small pale coloured attachment which pulls off easily. Rinse the scallop quickly under cold running water and drain. Scrub the shell and dry. Butter with half the butter. Mix the breadcrumbs with the garlic and parsley and sprinkle a thin layer over the shells, about half of the total quantity. If the scallops are large, slice into three diagonally or leave whole and lay in the shells on top of the crumbs. Season with salt and pepper and cover with the remaining crumbs. Cut the rest of the butter into very small pieces and set on top of the crumbs. Put the shell on a baking tray and bake in the pre-heated oven for 5–7 minutes until the scallops are cooked and the crumbs golden.

PERIWINKLES
Faochain

These tiny little shellfish, usually known as 'winkles' or 'willocks' in the north of Ireland, are tasty little fish, and were traditionally sold at most seaside resorts along with dulse.

They are cooked by boiling them in salt water for about 5 minutes. Having been drained and cooled, they are eaten by removing the small

black shield covering the opening to the shell and picking out the fish with a pin. They are delicious as they are, or dipped in oatmeal. When they are shelled they can be added to other dishes or used to make soup.

FISH STOCK
Stoc Éisc

A well-flavoured stock is, without doubt, the basis of good cooking. It is the foundation of soups, sauces and gravies as well as braised and stewed dishes. Without it they would lack flavour and substance and our cooking would be insipid and uninteresting. This fish stock, like any stock, is easy and inexpensive to make; it just requires a little time and the desire to have a well-flavoured end product.

MAKES 2 litres (3½ pints)
1 kg (2¼ lb) fish bones and heads from sole, turbot, whiting, or any white fleshed fish
100 g (4 oz) onions, chopped
1 leek, white part, sliced
1 stick of celery, sliced
50 g (2 oz) mushrooms, sliced
50 g (2 oz) butter
120 ml (4 fl oz) dry white wine
Sprig of thyme, blade of mace, parsley stalks and a bay leaf, tied together
2 litres (3½ pints) cold water
Squeeze of lemon juice to sharpen

Remove the gills from the fish heads and discard. Soak the heads and bones in cold salted water for about 3–4 hours. (I sometimes leave these to soak in a cold place overnight.) Wash and prepare the vegetables, then sweat gently in the butter in a large pan until soft but not coloured. Add the soaked, washed, rinsed and roughly chopped bones and heads. Cook gently for a few minutes. Pour on the water, bring to the boil, skimming the surface frequently. After 5 minutes add the bouquet garni, reduce the heat and simmer uncovered for 25 minutes.

Strain the stock carefully, letting it run through a muslin-lined sieve. Do not force the liquid through; let it drip like jelly. Add the squeeze of lemon juice, cover and leave to cool before storing in the refrigerator, where it will keep for a few days or in the deep freeze where it will keep for several months.

LIVING OFF THE WILD

In rural Ireland, from earliest times, foods which could be obtained free from the country as well as the sea have played a vital part in the lives of the people. We know from archaeological remains that the first settlers in Ireland lived on the natural resources around them: wild boar, hare and dog; salmon, trout, eels, sea bass and flounder; pigeon, duck, grouse and capercaillie; wild fruits, nuts, berries and plants.

It would appear that in the spring these hunters and gatherers lived on the coast near the estuaries of rivers where they could gather shellfish, edible seaweeds and other sea vegetables. Here they also caught sea birds, took their eggs, and followed the salmon up rivers to the lakes where a variety of freshwater fish were abundantly available (see pp. 87–88). In the winter they moved their camps to the forests where they could hunt and trap game and wild birds and collect berries, fruits, nuts and plants.

From early written sources it would appear that a large number of wild plants have been used in Ireland since prehistoric times. One which is frequently mentioned is water-

ABOVE: *Pheasants should be hung for a week to ten days before cooking.*

___

OPPOSITE: *Roast pheasant (page 120), served with traditional accompaniments.*

cress, *biolar*. 'Dray [dry] bread and cresses are pure foods for sages,' observed one writer. Another suggests it was used at feasts as a salad with meat. It was also boiled to produce a broth or soup. Watercress still grows in rivers and streams all over Ireland and is available for picking as long as the water is unpolluted.

Sorrel, *samhadh*, was mentioned, along with watercress, in the life of St Kevin as one of the 'curious sallads' of the Irish. It is widespread in grasslands, particularly on acid soils, and is one of the first green plants to appear in the spring when other greens are scarce. It has a cool sharp astringent taste when raw and was often eaten by the workers in the fields to quench their thirst during haymaking. Sorrel is cooked in much the same way as cabbage and eaten as a vegetable on its own. Like watercress, it is also used for soups and sauces.

Shamrock was also eaten as a salad and to relieve hunger during times of want and famine (people were even known to eat grass during times of extreme hardship). Edmond Campion, an Elizabethan orator, wrote of the Irish in 1571, 'Shamrotes, watercresses, rootes, and other hearbes the feed upon,' and Feynes Moryson, the sixteenth-century traveller notes in his *Itinerary*, 'The Irish willingly eat the herb shamrock . . . which as they run and are chased to and fro they snatch out of the ditches.' John Dunton also commented nearly a century later: 'They feed upon shamrock, watercress, roots and other herbs. Oatmeal and buttermilk they mix together. They drink whey, milk, beef broth and eat meat without bread.' It is not, however, widely eaten today.

Two plants common in all parts of the country are nettles and charlock. Charlock, *praiseach bhui*, is known as the weed of cornland and grows to 0.6 metres (2 feet) in height, has a bright yellow flower and belongs to the cabbage family. When boiled it resembles leafy brown kale and in Counties Antrim, Armagh, Monaghan, Waterford and Galway it is known as 'wild kale'. In England it is known as 'wild mustard' or 'cornweed'. In the twelfth-century poem *The Vision of MacConglinne*, it is described as 'the priest's fancy, juicy kale'. In 1757, in *Burdy's Life of Skelton*, when Mr Skelton visited Ireland to see the state of the poor, it was recorded that 'In a cabin he found the people eating boiled prushia [sharlock] by itself for their breakfast'.

Nettles were equally widespread and abundant. It is thought that they first made their appearance almost 6000 years ago when the first farmers cut down the trees in the forest to clear the ground for crop cultivation. They were generally used to make soup and pottage, a thick broth usually of meat and herbs. In the Life of Saint Colmcille (Columba) from the *Lismore Lives of the Saints*, a story is told concerning nettles:

Once when Saint Columba was walking near the monastery [in Iona] he saw an old woman cutting nettles. He asked her what she wanted them for. She replied: 'I have but one cow and I am expecting to calve soon; until that happens I live

on nettle pottage which I have eaten for a long time back.' He was much impressed with this and said, 'This poor woman eats nettles, and endures hunger, waiting for an uncertain event – the calving of her cow; why should I not live on the same pottage too, since the thing I look for is very certain – namely, heaven?' Whereupon he ordered his cook to give him for supper henceforth nettle pottage without milk or butter. But as time went on the brethren, who had heard with dismay of the change for the worse in his diet, were rather surprised that he still continued in excellent condition. The saint soon began to suspect some fraud on the part of his cook, so he sent for him and asked him 'What do you put in my pottage every day?' The cook replied: 'I know nothing that goes in your pottage unless it could come out of the iron pot or out of the pot-stick.' The saint examined the pot-stick and found the cook had made it hollow like a reed and thus contrived to pour milk into the pottage.

Nettles were used not only for making soup but also as medicine for all types of sores and swellings and in particular were used as a cure for measles and shingles. Rich in vitamins and minerals they were thought to purify the blood and, to this day, many country people believe that during the spring, between April and May when they are young and tender, they should be served at least three times to prevent sickness during the rest of the year. In County Galway it was said that, 'The man of the house went out on May Eve and cut a handful of nettles. He boiled them and everyone in the house drank some of the juice so that they would enjoy good health during the whole year.'

My grandmother made such a drink by covering the tender nettle tops with boiling water, boiling them for fifteen minutes before straining and serving the liquid on its own, or

with milk and sugar. I can remember drinking it a few times, but generally made myself scarce when it was being administered. However, I do still make nettle soup every spring and thoroughly enjoy it.

In the eighteenth and nineteenth centuries nettles and charlock were mentioned repeatedly in the writings of the time, both as the food of the poor and as food used during periods of local or general famine as well as during the seasonal scarcity of food. This generally occurred during the summer months, between the time when supplies of the old crop of potatoes were exhausted and the new potatoes were ready for digging, a situation which arose out of the almost total dependence on the potato.

Early Irish literature contains references to a plant called *cainnenn*, variously translated as leek, onion and garlic, which was found throughout the countryside in woods and damp shady places. These were known to have been used as a relish, seasoning, preservative and flavouring, being specifically used to flavour the butter stored in the peat bogs during the spring and summer. In later times, leeks and onions are frequently mentioned in the Anglo-Norman documents, and in 1591 leek and onion seed is recorded as coming into Clonmel in County Tipperary.

From the eighteenth- and nineteenth-century 'receipt' manuscript books, it is also clear that many types of wild herbs were also used in the Irish country kitchen, both for medicinal and culinary purposes. Wild mint and thyme, chives, borage, chamomile, rosemary and bay are frequently mentioned.

Mushrooms, too, have been used since the earliest times and many different varieties still grow abundantly in fields and moist dark places. Just outside my cottage, at varying times of the year, I gather large flat field mushrooms, shaggy ink caps, chanterelles, parasol mushrooms and giant puff balls. Traditionally, freshly gathered mushrooms were simply fried on the pan, over an open fire, in butter or bacon fat, cut into slices if

Nettle Broth (page 52).

large or left whole if small. Sometimes the small whole mushrooms were stewed in milk and the sauce thickened with flour or cornflour. Cooked mushrooms were either served on their own, with bread or potatoes, or combined with other ingredients and stewed. Mushroom ketchup was a favourite relish certainly in the eighteenth and nineteenth centuries for flavouring sauces, stews, soups and stuffings, and for using as a condiment with cooked meats. Although not particularly popular in modern Irish cookery, I find it invaluable for adding flavour and spice to many savoury dishes and make it every season. Button and oyster mushrooms are now being cultivated commercially in Ireland and ensure a regular supply throughout the year.

Fruits, nuts and berries were not only important foods for the early hunters and gatherers on the island, but have supplemented and enhanced the diet of country people throughout the centuries. All the wild fruits like the raspberry, strawberry, blackberry, blaeberry and cranberry were eaten, including the sloe – the fruit of the blackthorn – one of the tartest, most acid tasting of all the wild fruits. Wild strawberries are quite common on heaths, woodlands and grassy places and produce a delicious, small, sweet and fragrant berry from June until late August. Wild raspberries are also found in woods and heaths from July to September, and the wild cherry is found in woods and hedges from early July and can be substituted for cultivated cherries in any recipe, but needs extra sugar as it is generally very sour. Similarly, the crab apple is also found in woods, hedges and scrub land, the fruit best picked from August to October. Since it is such an ancient fruit – its burnt remains have been found on prehistoric sites – there is much folklore associated with it, such as the need to pick it before 31 October, the night when the *puca* (a dangerous spirit) is likely to spit on it and

blight it. The crab apple is used mainly for jelly and wine, and a thick set purée which is excellent with pork, duck or goose.

The berry of the wild rose, known as the rosehip, is found in woods, hedges and scrub, and brightens the countryside with its vivid colour. It is high in vitamin C and for this reason has been used for generations for making syrup to prevent colds and to promote a feeling of well being. It is also used to flavour fruit syrups and sauce for ice-cream, and for making wine.

The brilliant orange clusters of rowan berries, fruit of the mountain ash, are used for making jelly; and the tiny black berries of

the elder tree for generations have been made into preserves and drinks. Elderflowers, too, are used both for medical purposes and for flavouring syrups, cordials and drinks, particularly sparkling wine. The two most popular ways I was taught to use elderflowers was in conjunction with gooseberries for jam, and dipped in light batter for elderflower fritters. I use four good-sized flower heads, dusted but not washed, for each 450 g (1 lb) of gooseberries, and make a thin batter of 100 g (4 oz) plain flour, one egg and tepid water. The flower heads are dipped in the batter and then deep-fat fried until a pale golden colour.

Of all the berries, however, my favourite

has always been the bilberry (blueberry, blaeberry, fraughans, whortleberry), gathered in late summer and autumn from the mountains and hedgerows throughout the country. I have vivid childhood memories of the berrying expeditions in Armagh: walking through endless meadows, clambering over moss- and bracken-covered stone walls and paddling through clear sparkling rivers and streams, billy-can in one hand and skirt tails bundled in the other, on the journey to the heather-covered mountain. Under the hot sun we picked and ate the juicy berries, hands, face and clothes stained purple with their glorious nectar. On the way home we always swam in the flooded peat bog, cooling our bodies and, in a fashion, correcting our appearance. The berries, or what was left of them, were eaten with sugar and fresh cream from the dairy, or made into jelly and jam, or baked into pies sometimes with blackberries. Although these trips were spontaneous, when both the weather and the mood were right it was traditional to go bilberry picking on the last Sunday of July or the first Sunday of August, to mark the Feast of Lughnasa – the end of summer and the beginning of autumn in the rural calendar. This day was officially known as 'Bilberry' or 'Garland' Sunday, and the custom of climbing the heights to pick bilberries in some parts of the country still survives. Although Lughnasa was originally a pagan festival, in some places it assumed the character of a religious pilgrimage (a fixed annual event which celebrated the day of the local patron saint and provided the opportunity to associate worship with pleasure). There were market stalls, music, singing, dancing, and general merry-making. People feasted on bacon, cabbage and potatoes, followed by bilberries and cream. In some places the young girls involved in the picking made their berries into a cake, which was eaten later that night at the dance.

Blackberries, although less significant, were nonetheless popular and much easier to find and gather. Widespread and abundant in woods, hedges, waste places and heathland, their fruit, when ready for picking, turns a wonderful deep purple-black and lasts from late August to October. In Ireland it has always been important that all the fruit required for making pies, jams, jellies and cordials is gathered before Hallowe'en so that the *puca* cannot ruin them. In the Glens of Antrim it is also said that the devil shook his club and his blanket at the fruits.

Nuts, also regarded as fruit, were certainly eaten from 7000 to 6000 BC, but it would appear, from both legend and fact, that only the indigenous hazelnut was picked from the wild. Other nuts, such as walnuts and almonds, mentioned in the eighteenth- and nineteenth-century 'receipt' manuscript books, were either imported or taken from trees introduced to Ireland, and were generally only used in the large houses of the wealthy. Hazelnuts are mentioned in the twelfth-century poem *The Vision of MacConglinne*, and walnuts and filberts in the eighteenth-century writings of Mrs Delaney, a well-known socialite: 'I have just been gleaning my autumn fruits, melon, figs, Beury pears, grapes, filberts and walnuts'.

Filberts, along with acorns, were eaten whole or crushed to form a kind of meal, known as *maothal*. In early Christian times, those devoted to a religious life built their cells in remote woody districts and waste lands, which seem to have been generally covered with a scrub of hazel, judging from the quantity of hazel twigs found in turf bogs. Nut meal was naturally a valuable food to these early monks and, mixed with milk, became the meal eaten on fast days. Nuts were also a popular ingredient in the dishes of the upper classes. From the manuscript 'receipt' books of the eighteenth century onwards, it is known that they were used in stews, as stuffings for fish, poultry, meat and game, and combined with local, fresh and imported dried fruits to make puddings, cakes, pies and biscuits.

A land of milk and honey is how many poets, writers and commentators have described Ireland throughout history. Freely available from the countryside, honey was highly valued, both as a flavouring with heather or clover, and as a sweetener, certainly up until the introduction of sugar by a Norman baron shortly after the arrival of Strongbow at the end of the twelfth century. Honey was frequently added to bread dough, milk and ale; was used to make mead, one of the most important alcoholic beverages drunk by the Irish; to baste meat and fish during cooking; mixed with lard; or served on its own as a condiment, in which portions of meat, fowl, game or fish were dipped.

The wilds of Nephin Beg, County Mayo.

In the legend of Bricrius' Feast, one of the most famous stories of the Ulster Cycle, honey cakes and mead were included in the banquet along with beef broth, roast boar and salmon. In *The Vison of MacConglinne*, the gluttonous poet's description of roasting a piece of meat illustrates one of the many uses of honey:

And he called for juicy old bacon, and tender corned-beef, and full-fleshed wether, and honey in the comb, and English salt on a beautiful polished dish of white silver, along with four perfectly straight white hazel spits to support the joints. The viands which he enumerated were procured for him, and he fixed unspeakable, huge pieces on the spits. Then putting a linen apron about him below, and placing a flat linen cup on the crown of his head, he lighted a fair four-ridged, four-apertured, four-cleft fire of ash-wood, without smoke, without fume, without sparks. He stuck a spit into each of the portions, and as quick was he about the spits and fire as a hind about her first fawn, or as a roe, or a swallow, or a bare spring wind in the flank of March. He rubbed the honey and the salt into one piece after another. And big as the pieces were that were before the fire, there dropped not to the ground out of these four pieces as much as would quench a spark of a candle; but what there was of relish in them went into their very centre.

When the meat was cooked, MacConglinne sat himself down on his seat with his two legs crossed, 'Then taking his knife out of his girdle, he cut a bit off the piece that was nearest to him and dipped it in the honey that was on the aforesaid dish of white silver.'

So important was honey in early Ireland that a special section of the Brehon Laws was

devoted to bees and bee keeping, including the problem relating to the ownership of both the bees and the honey itself. In this matter a clear distinction was made between domesticated and wild bees, and by law any man who found a swarm of bees was only entitled to a portion of the honey, the rest having to be shared with his neighbours from whose lands the bees had gathered the nectar. Provision of ownership was also made for every possible type of swarming, whether it be in rocky crevices, trees, woods, lakes, other wild places, or within an enclosure, a green, or in a herb garden.

There was even a penalty laid down for the owner of a hive if one of the bees stung a passer-by: if the victim could prove that he had not killed the bee after the attack, his recompense was a full meal of honey. Similarly, when a woman separated from a man, she had to get either the makings of a hive of honey or the swarm of bees.

In the section on fosterage in the Laws, it was also laid down that the sons of kings and chieftains were to be fed on stirabout, made from wheaten meal and new milk and eaten with honey. For this reason, rents and tributes had to be paid in honey. Although much of this was obviously used to sweeten and flavour foods, the large quantities supplied as rents and tributes suggest that the greater part of the honey produced in ancient times was fermented into mead. It was probably originally made by simply dissolving honey in water as the Romans did, but in medieval times aromatic plants also seem to have been added. When matured, it was a very potent drink and as highly thought of as wine, particularly by women. According to legend, the great banqueting hall of Tara, the seat of kings and princes, was called the 'mead circling house'; here feasts were held and copious amounts of mead drunk. Mead, flavoured with hazelnuts, was said to be one of the joys of a hermit's life.

A display of game.

The countryside has also always provided a wide variety of edible animals and birds for all those skilled enough to catch them. Trapping and snaring has been practised in Ireland for thousands of years, with many simple but ingenious devices being employed both to catch food to eat and to cull predators. We know from the lives of the saints and illuminated manuscripts, such as The Book of Kells, that a great variety of birds, such as the lark, thrush, blackbird, nightingale, eagle, wild peacock and goose, snipe, partridge, plover, woodcock, pheasant and swan, were common in Ireland, many of them finding their way to the table. Blackbirds were of particular importance to the ordinary people of Ireland, not only adding variety to the otherwise monotonous diet of praties and salt herrings, but supplementing it during hard times, right up to this century. In the big houses and Norman castles, blackbirds were sometimes cooked in a pie, as the well-known nursery rhyme tells us. Swans were served at banquets in medieval times, and snipe, woodcock, grouse, plover, pigeon and pheasant are still enjoyed to this day.

In the twelfth and thirteenth centuries the Normans introduced fish to freshwater ponds and started breeding pigeons, in great numbers, in large dovecots. These were cooked in a great variety of ways, from pot-roasting to stewing, and were then baked in pies, often with other game birds and meat. At one time the larger birds were either impaled on a hazel stick or meat spit and roasted over the open fire, while the smaller birds, particularly sea birds like puffins and guillemots, were completely coated, feathers and all, with a layer of mud several inches thick. They were then put into the ashes of a hot fire, just like baking a potato, and cooked until the mud was very hard. When this was broken the skin and feathers came away with it, revealing a succulent, skinless bird which had completely cooked in its own juices. This method was also found useful for cooking hedgehog, another wild creature much en-

joyed by country dwellers, the prickles being conveniently removed with the hardened clay. Today, wild game birds are mostly braised, pot-roasted, oven-roasted or stewed, with the more tender parts, such as the breast, being fried in the pan. Indeed, many a hunter and sportsman will frequently use only the breast portion of a small bird, such as the pigeon and blackbird, cutting it free from the bird and removing feathers and skin in one quick operation.

The Normans also introduced rabbits to Ireland, and fallow deer to supplement the dwindling stocks of native red deer. Tomás Ó Crohan in *The Islandman* tells us not only of the number of rabbits taken but how they were often caught by his dog Oscar who sometimes had to be dug out of the rabbit hole along with his catch:

> He'd [his father] just got Oscar out, with five huge rabbits, pulled out of the hole along with the pup. My father was cleverer than I was, for he'd made a channel at the end of the stone, in the place where he guessed the end of the hole would be, and when he thrust his hand in, he found a rabbit, and then two, till he had five of the finest rabbits that were ever taken out of a single hole. He flung them over his shoulder and went off home.

Rabbits, when skinned and prepared, were either roasted or braised as whole joints, or cut into pieces and stewed before being included in pies and terrines.

The red deer, roe deer and the imported fallow deer, along with the wild boar, were collectively referred to as venison. Wolves, badgers, foxes, squirrels, otters and wild cats at one time were also hunted, for food and, with the arrival of the Normans and the Tudors after them, for sport, as they were passionately fond of the chase. In many of the large country estates, hunting and shooting parties are still very much part of the countryman's way of life.

GAME RECIPES

LEFT TO RIGHT: *Steak and pigeon pie (page 121) and rabbit and mustard stew (page 122).*

ROAST PHEASANT
Piasún Rósta

Pheasants have been eaten in Ireland for a very long time and are still plentiful, being the only game bird bred for shooting. Feynes Moryson in his Itinerary *of 1605 wrote: 'Ireland hath pleanty of pheasants, as I have known sixtie served at one feast . . .'.*

They are in season from October to February and are not only enjoyed by sportsmen, but by all who appreciate their strong flavour. In country areas they are generally available in local butchers' shops, or in the cities in 'high-class' butchers. They are sold, like most game birds, by the brace – a cock and a hen – and should have been hung for a week to ten days before cooking. Hen birds, as a rule, are more tender and succulent than cocks. Young birds and hens can be roasted if well hung, but cocks and older birds should be pot-roasted or braised to keep them moist and make them tender. A good-sized bird will serve 2 people.

SERVES 2

1 plump oven-ready pheasant, approx. 750 g
(1¾ lb)

25 g (1 oz) butter

2 slices fat bacon

65 ml (2½ fl oz) red wine or stock

2 × 15 ml (2 tablespoons) plain flour

200 ml (7 fl oz) pheasant stock

Salt and freshly milled black pepper

1 bunch watercress

PHEASANT STOCK

25 g (1 oz) butter or fat

Pheasant giblets (heart, gizzard, neck and liver)

1 small onion, peeled and quartered

1 small carrot, peeled and sliced

500 ml (20 fl oz) water

1 bay leaf

6 whole peppercorns

OVEN TEMPERATURE 220°C (425°F, gas mark 7)

OVEN TIME 45–60 minutes

Begin by preparing the pheasant stock. Wash the giblets, dry them and fry in the butter in a saucepan along with the onion and carrot until they begin to brown. Pour on the water and add the bay leaf and peppercorns. Bring to the boil, then reduce the heat and simmer for an hour. Strain and remove the fat before use. Truss the bird so that it remains in a neat shape. Spread the butter over the breast and legs of the bird and cover with the bacon rashers to prevent the flesh from drying out during the cooking. Set in a shallow roasting dish and roast in the pre-heated oven for approximately 45 minutes, basting frequently with the hot fat and juices during the cooking. Pour on the glass of wine or stock.

When the bird is cooked, transfer to a serving dish and keep warm while making the sauce. Drain off all but 1 × 15 ml (1 tablespoon) of the cooking fat, add the flour to the roasting dish and stir to blend with the remaining fat and sediment. Add the stock, a little at a time, to make a smooth liquid. Strain into a saucepan, bring to the boil to thicken, and season with salt and freshly milled black pepper.

Remove the bacon and trussing string from the bird. Keep the bacon warm. Cut the pheasant in half through the breast and back bone or remove the legs, cut the breast in half and take each piece off the bone. Serve with the sauce and traditional accompaniments: sprouts; braised celery; chestnuts; fried or browned crumbs; bread sauce and game chips (very thinly sliced potato rings deep-fat fried). The flavour of pheasant also combines well with slightly acid fruit such as apples, grapes, oranges and lemons.

POT ROAST PHEASANT
Piasún Potrósta

This is one of the best ways to cook pheasant and other older game birds as it helps to keep them moist during the cooking. Serve with braised celery, Brussels sprouts and chestnuts or braised red cabbage.

SERVES 2

1 plump oven-ready pheasant, trussed, approx.
750 g (1¾ lb)

50 g (2 oz) butter

1 medium onion, sliced

1 medium carrot, sliced

Sprig of thyme, bay leaf, parsley stalks, tied
together

Freshly milled black pepper

2 slices fat bacon

150 ml (5 fl oz) pheasant stock (see above)

150 ml (5 fl oz) red wine

Wipe the bird and brown it on all sides in the hot butter in a large saucepan. Remove from the pot. Add the vegetables and cook for a few minutes in the remaining fat. Set the browned pheasant on top of the vegetables, add the bunch of herbs and season lightly with the pepper. Cover the breast and legs of the bird with the bacon and add 65 ml (2½ fl oz) pheasant stock. Put on the lid and cook gently for 45–60 minutes.

Transfer the pheasant from the pot to a serving dish, remove the bacon and trussing string and keep warm. Add the remaining pheasant stock and red wine to the pot and stir to remove any sediment which may have formed. There should be about 200 ml (7 fl oz) of liquid. Blend 1 × 15 ml (1 tablespoon) cornflour with a little of this to form a smooth paste, then add to the pot. Stir well to blend. Bring to the boil and cook for a few minutes to thicken, stirring constantly. Season well, then strain, discarding the cooking vegetables. Return the sauce to the pot and keep warm while carving the bird. This can be done by either cutting it in half through the breast and back bone or by removing the legs and cutting the breast in half, taking each half off the bone. The half-bird is served in its entirety, the leg and breast pieces arranged together on the plate. The sectioned bird looks more attractive on the plate and is easier to eat. Cover each portion with the cooked bacon and serve with the sauce.

ROAST STUFFED PIGEON
Colúr Rósta le Búiste

Pigeons are at their best from March to October. This dish is a family favourite and is perhaps the nicest way of serving tender young birds. When they are young the breast will be fat, the beak flexible, the neck thick, the breast bone supple, the skin rosy and the flesh red. Any stuffing suitable for duck or poultry can be used. Allow a bird per person.

SERVES 2

2 plump young pigeons, oven-ready, approx.
250 g (9 oz) each

50 g (2 oz) butter

Freshly milled black pepper

1½ × 15 ml (1½ tablespoons) plain flour

200 ml (7 fl oz) game stock, water or wine

1 bunch watercress

FOR THE STUFFING

50 g (2 oz) onion, finely chopped

25 g (1 oz) butter

50 g (2 oz) fresh breadcrumbs

1 × 15 ml (1 tablespoon) raisins, chopped

1 × 15 ml (1 tablespoon) hazelnuts, chopped

1 × 15 ml (1 tablespoon) parsley, finely chopped

Salt and freshly milled black pepper

1 egg yolk

OVEN TEMPERATURE 220°C (425°F, gas mark 7)

OVEN TIME 35–40 minutes

Begin by making the stuffing. Soften the onion in the butter without colouring, then stir in the rest of the ingredients. Use to fill the cavity of the pigeons. Truss into a neat shape. Heat the 50 g (2 oz) butter in a roasting dish and brown the birds evenly on all sides. Set breast-side up and season with milled black pepper. Cook in the pre-heated oven for 30 minutes. then remove the birds from the oven and dust with $\frac{1}{2}$ tablespoon flour. Return to the oven and cook for a further 10 minutes. When cooked, transfer to a serving dish and keep warm while making the sauce.

Pour off all but approximately 1 × 15 ml (1 tablespoon) of the fat in the roasting pan. Stir in the remaining 1 × 15 ml (1 tablespoon) flour, mixing it with the sediment. Pour on the liquid, stirring to blend. Bring to the boil and cook for a few minutes to thicken. Strain and return to a clean saucepan to keep warm while cutting the birds in half through the breast and trimming away the back bone. Serve the two halves, resting on a pool of sauce, on the plate. Garnish with watercress and serve with game chips, cranberry sauce and seasonal vegetables.

STEAK AND PIGEON PIE
Pióg Stéige agus Colúir

Steak and pigeon pie was at one time a very popular dish in the large country houses throughout Ireland and is still made in homes where pigeons are a frequent addition to the larder after shooting expeditions.

SERVES 4

FOR THE STEW

50 g (2 oz) butter

2 plump young pigeons, prepared

Pigeon and Guinness stew (page 122).

750 g (1½ lb) chuck steak, cut into 2.5 cm (1 in) squares

1 large onion, finely chopped

75 g (6 oz) mushrooms, sliced

40 g (1½ oz) plain flour

450 ml (15 fl oz) game or chicken stock

Salt and freshly milled black pepper

1 bay leaf

Parsley stalks

FOR THE PASTRY

370 g (13 oz) flaky or puff pastry

1 small egg, beaten

1 × oval pie dish with rim, 10 × 16 cm (9½ × 6½ in), 1.2 litres (40 fl oz) capacity and 4 cm (1½ in) deep

OVEN TEMPERATURE Pastry 220°C (425°F, gas mark 7)

OVEN TIME 20–25 minutes

Melt the butter in a large saucepan or flame-proof casserole and brown the pigeons all over. Remove from the pot and divide in half through the breast. Fry the meat in the remaining butter until brown, then add the onion and mushrooms and cook for a few minutes. Stir in the flour and gradually add the stock continuing to stir to combine. Season with salt and freshly milled black pepper and add the bay leaf and parsley stalks tied together. Return the pigeons to the pot, bring to the boil, then reduce the heat and simmer for 1½ hours until the meat is tender.

When the stew is cooked, remove the herbs and discard. Transfer the pigeons to a chopping board, remove the meat from the bones and return to the pot, mix well and pour into the pie dish with a pie funnel in the centre. Leave to go cold.

Roll the pastry to an oval shape, about 5 cm (2 in) larger than the top of the pie dish. If using frozen pastry, this is not always easy and the edges will probably have to be trimmed to create the oval. These trimmings can be used to make leaves or other decorations for the top of the pie. Cut a 2.5 cm (1 in) wide strip from round the edge of the pastry. Divide in two. Cut one strip in half lengthwise. Moisten the rim of the pie dish with a little beaten egg or water and set these two narrow pastry strips on top, pressing them firmly into position. Brush with egg or water. Use the remaining pastry strip to cut leaves or other shapes to decorate the top of the pie.

Roll the pastry oval around the rolling pin and unfold on top of the pie dish, taking care not to stretch it. Trim and press the pastry layers together, flaking the edges with the back of a knife to seal.

Brush the top of the pie with the beaten egg and decorate with the pastry leaves or shapes; also brush with egg. Make a hole in the centre of the pie to let the steam escape during the cooking and set on a baking sheet. Bake in the pre-heated oven until the pastry is crisp, risen and golden brown. This will take about 20–25 minutes. Serve hot.

PIGEON AND GUINNESS STEW
Stobhach Colúr agus Leann Dubh

This is one of the many ways in which pigeons and other game can be cooked with flavouring vegetables and liquid in a casserole. The vegetables can be varied according to their availability.

SERVES 2
2 pigeons, approx. 250 g (9 oz) each
75 g (3 oz) butter
1 large onion, halved and sliced
450 g (1 lb) small carrots, thinly sliced
50 g (2 oz) plain flour
300 ml (10 fl oz) Guinness
300 ml (10 fl oz) game stock or water
1 bay leaf, sprig of thyme, parsley stalks, tied together
Freshly milled black pepper
225 g (8 oz) small mushrooms
2 × 15 ml (2 tablespoons) parsley, finely chopped

Divide each pigeon in half by cutting down either side of the breast bone, removing the flesh from the carcass and freeing the leg from the back at the leg joint. Heat 50 g (2 oz) of the butter in a large frying pan and fry the pigeon halves until brown on all sides. Transfer to a pot or fireproof casserole dish. Fry the onions and carrot for a few minutes to colour slightly, then add the flour, stirring to combine. Pour on the Guinness and water or stock, stirring to blend. Bring to the boil and pour over the pigeons in the pot. Add the bay leaf, thyme and parsley stalks, tied together, and season with freshly milled black pepper. Cover and cook on a gentle heat for 15 minutes. While the pigeons are cooking, fry the mushrooms in the remaining 25 g (1 oz) butter until browning, then drain and add to the stew. Continue to cook for a further 30–40 minutes until the pigeons are tender. Adjust the seasoning, adding salt if necessary, and sprinkle with parsley. Serve with mashed, boiled or jacket potatoes.

RABBIT
Coinín

In the twelfth and thirteenth centuries the Normans introduced rabbits to Ireland and they were widely used and much appreciated by the country people. Today they are still hunted by sportsmen and are at their best between October and February. A good-sized wild rabbit will weigh approximately 1.25 kg (2½ lb) and will feed 2–4 people. Rabbits are also commercially farmed for the table and are available in many butchers and poultry shops throughout Ireland. Tame rabbits can weigh between 2.25 and 2.75 kg (5 and 6 lb) and have much more meat on them. The saddle of rabbit makes an excellent roasting joint if wrapped in bacon. The rest, i.e. the legs, shoulders and ribs or middle neck, is only suitable for stewing or braising.

TO JOINT A RABBIT FOR STEWING OR BRAISING Remove the ribs, shoulder and neck by cutting from the body of the rabbit just below the ribs. This is cooked with the stew or braised for flavour, but discarded before serving as there is very little meat on it.

The saddle and legs are divided just above the top of the legs. After removing the membrane and flap, the saddle is cut in half.

The legs are divided in two lengthwise along the leg bone.

RABBIT AND MUSTARD STEW
Stobhach Coinín agus Mustaird

Rabbit meat is improved by soaking it for 12 hours in a mixture of water and vinegar. This will help to whiten the flesh and to make it more digestible. Begin preparations a day in advance.

SERVES 4
1 large rabbit
100 g (4 oz) bacon in a piece
25 g (1 oz) butter or bacon fat
1 large onion, sliced
2 × 15 ml (2 tablespoons) plain flour
750 ml (1¼ pints) chicken or game stock
Salt and freshly milled black pepper
1 × 15 ml (1 tablespoon) made English mustard
Sprig of thyme, bay leaf, parsley stalks, tied together
65 ml (2½ fl oz) double cream
1 × 15 ml (1 tablespoon) parsley, finely chopped

Joint the rabbit by removing the legs and cutting the back into three or four pieces. (The head and neck are used for stock.) Put the rabbit pieces into a large bowl and cover with water, adding some salt and a teaspoon of vinegar to 600 ml (20 fl oz) water. Leave to soak overnight in the refrigerator. Drain and dry thoroughly. Remove the rind and fat from the bacon and cut into 1 cm (½ in) cubes. Cover with cold water, bring to the boil, then drain. Melt the butter or bacon fat in a large pot or flameproof casserole and fry the onion until soft but not coloured. Add the rabbit pieces to the bacon and fry quickly over a high heat to colour. Stir in the flour and continue to cook, colouring the flour slightly. Pour on the stock stirring well to blend. Add the salt and pepper, mustard and herbs tied together with string. Bring to the boil then reduce the heat, cover and cook gently for 50 minutes–1¼ hours until the rabbit is tender. Stir in the cream, return to the boil, correct the seasoning, stir in the parsley and serve.

RABBIT PIE
Píóg Coinín

Rabbit stewed in this way and the meat left on or taken off the bones after cooking makes an excellent base for a rabbit pie. This can be made in the same way as for the chicken and ham pie on page 78.

FRIGACY OF RABBIT
Coinín in Anlann Bán

Frigacy of rabbit was a very popular dish in eighteenth- and nineteenth-century Ireland in the large country houses. Chicken can also be prepared in the same way.

SERVES 4

1 rabbit, approx. 1.25 kg (2½ lb), prepared and jointed and soaked overnight in water, vinegar and salt

600 ml (20 fl oz) chicken stock or water

2 onions, cut in half and sliced

Bay leaf, sprig of thyme, parsley stalks, tied together

65 g (2½ oz) butter

40 g (1½ oz) plain flour

150 ml (5 fl oz) cream or milk

100 g (4 oz) button mushrooms, wiped

Salt and freshly milled black pepper

2 × 15 ml (2 tablespoons) parsley, finely chopped

Remove the rabbit pieces from the soaking water and put in a large saucepan. Cover with fresh cold water and bring to the boil. Throw off this initial boiling water. Neaten the joints, trimming away excess skin, fat and gristle. Return to the pan and add the stock or water. Add the onions and herbs, tied together with string, bring to the boil, then reduce the heat, cover and cook for 1–2 hours until the rabbit is tender. Rabbits bred for the table will take less time to cook than wild rabbit. Drain off the cooking liquor into a measuring jug; there should be about 600 ml (20 fl oz) which is required for the sauce. Remove the bunch of herbs from the pot and discard.

Melt 40 g (1½ oz) butter in a saucepan and stir in the flour to make a thick paste. Remove from the heat and gradually stir in the strained liquid, stirring constantly to blend and prevent lumps from forming. Return to the heat, bring to the boil and continue to stir until the sauce is of a smooth creamy consistency. Add the cream or milk and cook very gently while preparing the mushrooms.

Fry the mushrooms in the remaining 25 g (1 oz) of butter over a high heat until just beginning to colour. Add to the sauce and season with salt and freshly milled black pepper. Pour over the rabbit, warm over a gentle heat for 5–10 minutes to combine the flavours before transferring to a serving dish and sprinkling with parsley.

MARINADE FOR VENISON

Venison has been eaten in Ireland from the earliest times, but bone remains found at prehistoric sites show that it was less significant than other meats and fish and was generally eaten by kings and lords rather than the common people. In the early sagas there are many mouthwatering descriptions of great feasts where venison frequently featured. It was not until Norman times, however, that deer became more widely eaten.

Today venison is enjoyed for its low-fat and high-lean content. Farmed venison is beginning to appear in specialist shops and is more tender than its wild equivalent. Both are improved by marinating them for a day or two before cooking.

FOR a 1.5–1.75 kg (3½–4 lb) joint

100 g (4 oz) onion, sliced

100 g (4 oz) carrot, sliced

50 g (2 oz) celery, sliced

85 ml (3 fl oz) oil

150 ml (3 fl oz) wine vinegar

6 black peppercorns, crushed

6 juniper berries, crushed

1 clove garlic, crushed

Parsley stalks, bay leaf, sprig of thyme, tied together

450 ml (15 fl oz) red wine

450 ml (15 fl oz) water

Brown the vegetables in the oil, then add the remaining ingredients. Bring to the boil and simmer for 30 minutes. Leave to go cold before using to cover the meat in a deep china or glass dish. Marinate for 1–3 days. The marinade can also be used as part of the cooking liquor, generally in the proportions $\frac{1}{4}$–$\frac{1}{2}$ the quantity of the stock. More than this produces a very sharp sauce.

ROAST VENISON
Fiafheoil Rósta

The best cuts of meat for roasting are the saddle, loin or haunch. An average size of roast is about 1.5 kg (3½ lb) and will serve 10–12. Both wild and farmed venison improve with being marinated and also need to be larded with fat or covered with bacon rashers during the cooking to prevent them from drying out as their flesh is so lean.

SERVES 10–12

1 × 1.5 kg (3½ lb) joint of venison on the bone, marinated for 1–3 days (see previous recipe)

4–5 rashers fat bacon

50 g (2 oz) butter or dripping

2 × 15 ml (2 tablespoons) water

FOR THE GRAVY

2 × 15 ml (2 tablespoons) plain flour

300 ml (10 fl oz) game stock

150 ml (5 fl oz) strained marinade

1–2 × 15 ml (1–2 tablespoons) redcurrant jelly or quince jelly

Salt and freshly milled black pepper

OVEN TEMPERATURE AND TIME

220°C (425°F, gas mark 7) for 30 minutes, then reduce to 190°C (375°F, gas mark 5) for a further 1½ hours.

Dry the marinated joint and wrap well in the bacon, tying it in place. Heat the butter or dripping in a roasting dish, add the meat and roast in the pre-heated oven for 30 minutes. Add 2 × 15 ml (2 tablespoons) water to the roasting dish to prevent the sediment from burning. Reduce the oven temperature and cook for a further 1½ hours, basting frequently and adding a little extra water if necessary.

When the meat is cooked, transfer to a hot serving dish and leave to rest for 15–20 minutes in a warm place before carving. During this time, make the gravy by draining off all but 2 × 15 ml (2 tablespoons) fat from the roasting dish. Sprinkle on the flour, stirring to combine it with the sediment. Gradually stir in the game stock and strained marinade. Bring to the boil and cook for a few minutes. Strain into a clean saucepan, stir in the redcurrant or quince jelly and correct the seasoning. Serve in a sauce boat with the meat carved in thin slices.

THE BAKING TRADITION

Corn was another staple food of the Irish people. Oats and barley were mainly grown in the north and west, and wheat in the south and east due to the more favourable weather conditions in these areas. A small amount of rye was also grown.

These crops were eaten mainly as bread and porridge. Indeed, at one time most country people ate more cereals in the form of porridge than in any form of bread. There were many different types of porridge: porridge made from wheat, oats and barley, either mixed with water, 'new' milk, sour milk or buttermilk. It could be eaten hot or cold, cooked or uncooked, fresh or fermented and either thick or thin. It could also be flavoured with salt, sugar, butter, honey, herbs and spices, and was not just served at breakfast time but was eaten in large quantities at midday and in the evening.

Sowans, another oatmeal concoction, was made by steeping the husks of oats, sometimes known as 'sids' (the residue left after the oatmeal was ground in the mill) in either hot or cold water for anything from four days to three weeks. The soaking time generally depended on the time of year and the degree

ABOVE: *Soda bread can be cut into 'farls', as here, and cooked on a griddle (page 133).*

OPPOSITE: *Scones (pages 133–4) are served for morning coffee and afternoon tea.*

of acidity required. When fermentation was complete the mixture was sieved and the semi-white liquid used as a drink, a substitute for milk in tea, or as an alternative to buttermilk for making bread. In some parts of Ireland this drink was known as bull's milk. When this liquid was boiled until it thickened and put into glasses or dishes to set before being turned out like jelly or a blancmange it was known as flummery and served as a dessert. Sometimes sugar and cream were added to the thickened liquid before being set.

In bread-making, the type of grain used was dependent on that most widely produced in the area and the purpose for which the bread was required. Wheaten bread, for example, which was not produced in any great quantity, was rated more highly than oaten or barley bread, and was used almost exclusively by the higher social classes, or for feast days and important social gatherings; it was known as the bread of chieftains and kings. Barley bread formed part of the diet of holy men: in the life of St Finian of Clonard we learn that on weekdays he lived on 'woody bread of barley', and a drink of

muddy water, but that on Sundays he ate wheaten bread and broiled salmon, washed down with a cup of ale. Rye was also popular for making bread, right up to the nineteenth century. In Kildare, Wexford, Dublin and Meath it was mixed with wheat to form a bread known as 'meslin' or 'maslin' bread, a bread probably of Anglo-Norman invention. The most common type of bread was probably that made from oatmeal but, according to this popular rhyme, each type had its merits:

Rye bread will do you good;
Barley bread will do you no harm.
Wheaten bread will sweeten your
    blood;
Oaten bread will strengthen your arm.

In medieval times several kinds of bread were made, and were generally referred to as cakes. The usual word for a cake was *bairgen*, a name preserved in the *bairín breac*, a cake speckled with currants or raisins and now often called bairm brack. These cakes came in different sizes. The early laws mention three: the *bairgin banfuine*, 'cake of woman-baking' (woman's cake), which was 'two fists in breadth and a fist in thickness'; the *bairgin ferfuine*, 'cake of man-baking' (man's cake), which was twice the size of the first; and the *bairgin indriub*, a large cake kept whole by the mistress of the house for guests, before whom no cut loaf could be placed.

A bread made from Indian or 'yalla male' (yellow meal) was introduced to relieve the famines of the nineteenth century. This maize flour, brought from America, was mixed with white flour in varying proportions to produce a palatable bread. Maura Laverty in her book *Never No More* describes how her grandmother in the 1920s made ash cakes of yellow meal, in her house on the edge of the Bog of Allen in County Kildare:

Currant soda (page 132).

126

She scalded the Indian meal with salted boiling water, made it into a dough, rolled it out thinly and cut it into little scones. A bed was made on the hearth by raking amongst the ashes on all sides. Each scone was rolled in a cabbage leaf and placed on the bed with hot ashes piled on top and left until cooked. The scorched leaf was then turned back to disclose fragrant little cakes which were delivered with rashers, gravy and egg yolk.

The grain of whatever kind, having been harvested and threshed, was then dried in a kiln before being ground. Though flails for threshing were well known in medieval Ireland, the Irish did not thresh their oats but burned the whole oat sheaf, thus combining the process of threshing, winnowing and drying all in one simple operation. The grain was then cleaned from the ashes and was ready for grinding in a quern. This 'burning in the sheaf', as it was referred to, was so common at times and so wasteful to the straw that several laws were made to stop it.

Generally the corn was ground in mills driven either by water or in some places by wind. Every parish had its own mill and some houses had their own quern or grinding stones. After being ground into meal, the corn was often sifted to produce a finer flour for bread-making. The flour was usually mixed with water to form the dough, but bread made of flour and milk was also quite common. The bread was kneaded in a wooden trough called a losset, and for festive and special occasions honey was kneaded into the dough to make a sweet cake. Other flavourings such as salmon roe and herbs were occasionally added to give a tart flavour.

The character of the traditional breads was influenced by a number of factors. First and foremost, the bread grains that were available; secondly, the facilities available for cooking the bread – an open hearth set at floor level meant that it could be baked on a stone, or wrapped in a large cabbage leaf and put directly on the hot turves, or on an iron griddle; and thirdly, there was a basic need in Ireland for fresh bread baked every day or every couple of days, so that the hard bread that would keep for several months had no place here. As the old Irish proverb says, '*Nva gacha bidh agns sean gacha dighe*' ('Food should be eaten as fresh as possible while drink should be well matured').

Over the centuries, from the time of these first simple cakes, the baking of bread has become one of the great traditions of the Irish kitchen. To this day, the evocative aroma of warm baking bread never fails to transport me back to the summers of my childhood which I spent with my country cousins on their farm in Newtownhamilton in County Armagh. What memories I have of that big homely kitchen, with its floor of large stone flags, its tiny windows letting in only the smallest shaft of light and the big warm hearth with its crackling flames and glowing turf. My cousins and I washed and dressed beside the fire on cold mornings when the ice was thick in our water jugs; it was here that we watched as great rashers of home-cured bacon sizzled on the black iron pan and eggs spluttered in the hot bacon fat; and it was here that I first saw Ireland's traditional breads produced.

When I first began to visit my aunt's home I remember her baking bread on the large smooth flagstone set on the floor immediately in front of the fire, referred to as the 'flag of the hearth'. Every morning before breakfast, when the fire had been coaxed back to life and was glowing hot, she raked some of it out on to this flagstone and allowed it to burn there for some time until the stone was well heated. She then moved this small fire to another part of the flagstone to warm it; the original position was then wiped clean and the bread laid directly on to this clean, warm spot to bake. When it was time to turn the bread, the fire was moved from its second position, that spot was then also wiped clean, and the bread turned on to it, with a great flourish, to finish cooking. These cakes, about 30–38 centimetres (12–15 inches) across and 1.25 centimetres ($\frac{1}{2}$ inch) thick, were very similar to the griddle bread she made in later years, bread that is still made in farmhouses throughout the country, albeit today, in many cases, in an electric frying pan.

The traditional griddle is a flat circular iron plate, usually about 45 centimetres (18 inches) across. In Ireland most griddles have two lugs, or ears, except in some parts of the east, such as County Wicklow, where one-eared griddles used to be common. Sometimes hung over the fire, the griddle was more often rested on a trivet – a rectangular or circular stand on three legs – raising it about 13 centimetres (5 inches) over the hearth, with a pile of glowing turf beneath. Usually the bread was cut into four triangular 'farls' before baking. Sometimes a metal dish or pan was inverted over the cake to retain the heat and give a more even baking. Hot turves were laid on top of this dish, thus providing heat from above and below.

The refinement of this was the pot, or bastable, oven in which my aunt produced her best bread, the traditional 'soda bread' made of whole or white wheat flour and leavened with sour milk or buttermilk and bread soda (bicarbonate of soda). The bread, kneaded lightly into a round shape on her baking board on the kitchen table, was set in the bottom of the flat three-legged iron pot, which was about 38 centimetres (15 inches) in diameter and 10 centimetres (4 inches) deep. The pot was then lightly covered with its flat lid and set in front of the fire. Hot turves were raked underneath it and also set on top of the lid to provide heat from both the top and bottom and to ensure an even cooking. The bastable oven was also turned during the process so that the direct heat from the fire would be evenly distributed around the pot. It was a wonderful sight and smell, only bettered by that of the deep crusty bread that eventually emerged to be cut into thick slices and spread with freshly made butter and jam. This bread, like many of the Irish breads, has its variations and was often mixed with treacle to produce a dark sweet soda bread, or with dried fruit to be called fruit soda, or sometimes in the north of Ireland, 'fruit bannock'.

The dough used to make this white or brown soda bread was also used for bread cooked on the griddle. In this case it was rolled out to about 1.25 centimetres ($\frac{1}{2}$ inch) thick and cut into four triangular farls, sometimes referred to as 'pointers in the north', before being set on the hot, lightly floured iron plate. The farls were cooked gently on both sides then turned up on their ends to complete the cooking. Soda farls are more traditional in the northern counties of Ireland, where they are eaten split in half and buttered, or split in half and fried on the pan in hot bacon fat as an essential part of an Ulster fry, along with bacon, eggs, sausages, black pudding and potato bread. When cut into small farls or rounds they are referred to as griddle scones and, like the white or brown soda, could have fruit, sugar, treacle or even cheese added to them for additional flavour. When the basic ingredients of flour and bread soda had an egg added and were mixed to a smooth batter with milk and dropped onto a hot griddle, the result was 'drop' or 'dropped' scones, wonderfully light puffy little cakes served straight from the griddle with butter and honey or sprinkled with sugar. When my aunt made these over the turf fire we all stood round waiting for the next batch to come off.

When the potato came into common use during the seventeenth century, it was used to make a number of different types of bread. The most well known, particularly in the north of Ireland, is potato bread, often referred to as 'fadge', sometimes more generally as potato cakes or potato farls. Another potato bread, traditional to the northern counties of Cavan and Donegal, is boxty.

In the early days of bread-making the most widely used corn was oats, which were ground into flour and used to make oatmeal bread of varying thicknesses which was cooked on the griddle or hearthstone. Thin oatmeal cakes were also made on the griddle or hearthstone and then rested against a stand to dry out. One traveller in Ireland describes the making of such cakes in a poor farmhouse, near Galway in 1699: 'When she had ground her oats upon the querns or hand mill-stones, with a little water she made a triangular cake which she reared up before the fire against a little wood stool made like a tripod.' Information on making traditional Irish oatcakes would suggest that they could either have been cooked on the griddle and dried out against a wooden stone or wrought-iron stand, or cooked completely by resting them against one of these stands in front of the fire. They were certainly easy to make, but difficult to handle. In the north of Ireland, elaborately designed support stands, or 'fenders', were also used to support four large farls of oatcake while drying out. These stands were made by the blacksmith and were hinged in the middle so that the cakes on either side could be easily moved to or from the fire as required. It was certainly a most ingenious contraption and one of the many pieces of hearth equipment which not only required skill, but strength and alacrity to use – as I discovered when making oat-cakes in this traditional way. These oatcakes, along with the potato bread and many of the other early breads baked on the griddle, were unleavened breads.

Several kinds of bread leaven have been known through the centuries. In early Christian times bread was leavened with barm, a liquid yeast obtained from beer brewing; or from 'souring' ground grain, usually oats in water; or from the water in which buttermilk plant was grown (see page 38). The other leaven used to raise and lighten bread was sodium bicarbonate, in combination with sour milk. This was the most widely used of all the leavens, and soda bread is the best known and most commonly made bread in farmhouses throughout Ireland. One of the oldest of all the leavens was 'sour dough'; this was a piece of fermenting dough left over from a previous baking, which when added to the new dough caused it to rise.

Yeast or barm as a raising agent, along with sour dough, was used mainly in monastic houses, in some very 'strong' farms, the manor houses of the gentry, and in the large inns and town bakeries. Here it was used to make plain and fruit breads, such as bairm brack, and the rich fruit loaf – breads still popular today. The typical built-in oven of the south-east was a cavity in the wall, lined with bricks and sealed by a heavy cast-iron door. A very hot fire was lit inside the oven using sticks, turf and gorse bushes and kept burning until the bricks were very hot and the fire dying down. Its remains were then brushed out and the bread put in to bake in the retained heat. Today, in Schull in County Cork, one of the oldest wall ovens still being commercially used is in operation in Quinlan's Courtyard Bakery. It is a brick oven, installed in 1919, which is heated today by coal, but which probably could also have burned turf or wood. It is believed that the only other similar oven remaining in Ireland is at the Cistercian Monastery in Roscrea in County Tipperary; it burns turf. Every day at the Courtyard Bakery a selection of the typical breads of the area are made by owner Denis Quinlan and master baker Jack Bennett, now in his eighties, who worked for over forty years at the bakery in its heyday and came out of retirement to bring it back to life.

Although bread in all its many guises is the cornerstone of the Irish baking tradition, it does not stand alone, and today the full range of baking skills are still predominantly on display. These can be seen not only on the afternoon tea tables, renowned throughout the world for their range and quality, but in the many bakeries and coffee shops, particularly in the north of Ireland. Here you will find every kind of cake, from the simplest sponge as light as air to the close-textured, butter sandwich cakes in all shapes, sizes and flavours. Rich cakes, too, of fruit, cherries, dates and nuts are firm favourites for keeping, cutting and celebrating. There are tea cakes, chocolate cakes, ginger cakes, boiled cakes, both little and large, and indeed in some places the old-fashioned saffron and seed cakes. There are also oatcakes and biscuits, and sweet fancies referred to as tray bakes – tasty little combinations of pastry, cake, chocolate, fruits, nuts or whatever is available. Then, of course, there are the pastry tarts made from the cultivated or wild fruit in season – rhubarb, gooseberries or blackberries – but none so famous and delicious as the Bramley apple tart, the jewel of the Irish tea table, served with lashings of thick cream.

These baked goods, whether bread or cakes, were not only a feature of afternoon tea but appeared on many meal tables throughout the day. In the morning, griddle, oven or dropped scones would be served sometime between breakfast and lunch along with the ubiquitous cup of tea; in the evening, a full range of baked goods, including pastry tarts, scones, biscuits, bread and cakes, would be served as part of the high-tea table, the main evening meal, and then later on at supper. At harvest time, too, many of the less decorative and perishable of these would have been wrapped in cloths, packed into a basket and carried to the field along with billy-cans of tea and milk. It was part of the summer ritual of bringing in the crops and known as 'taking tea to the field'. Many a time I helped carry one of these laden baskets along country roads, and across meadows and fields and spread the bleached-white flour bag or gingham cloth below a hay stack, in readiness for this homely meal.

Irish baking is very much part of the Irish tradition of hospitality and it is a very poor home that cannot offer some little treat to a friend or passing stranger.

'Taking tea to the field.'

BREAD, CAKE AND BISCUIT RECIPES

Over the centuries, the baking of bread has become one of the great traditions of the Irish kitchen.

SODA BREAD
Arán Sóide

In Ireland the traditional breads were designed to suit both the ingredients and the cooking facilities which were available. Owing to the country's climatic conditions, a soft wheat was grown, which was not suitable for making the yeast breads so popular in other countries. As a result Irish breads developed from using a soft-wheat flour and the popular milk of the time, buttermilk, which raised or leavened the dough along with bicarbonate of soda (often referred to as baking or bread soda). The soda, when mixed with the acids in the buttermilk, acts as a raising agent. Cream of tartar, another acid, is also sometimes added to produce twice as much acid as alkali in the dough and to ensure a very good rise.

Soda bread is a bread of great versatility and appears in many guises. In its most basic form, it looks like a round cake, and can be made of white flour, when it is known as white soda, or brown flour, when it is known as brown soda or, in most parts of the north of Ireland, 'wheaten' bread. These cakes of bread were traditionally cooked in the pot-oven at the side of the fire (see page 127).

The art of making soda bread is to handle the dough quickly and gently and to cook it at a high temperature. In fact the less you do to it, the better the bread.

450 g (1 lb) plain flour
1 × 5 ml (1 heaped teaspoon) bicarbonate of soda
1 × 5 ml (1 teaspoon) salt
25–50 g (1–2 oz) caster sugar
35–50 g (1–2 oz) butter
400–475 ml (14–16 fl oz) buttermilk
1 × 18 cm (7 in) round or 15 cm (6 in) square tin,
between 4–7 cm (1½–2¾ in) deep
OVEN TEMPERATURE AND TIME
220°C (425°F, gas mark 7) for 10 minutes, then
reduce to 200°C (400°F, gas mark 6) for 40–45
minutes

Sieve the dry ingredients into a large mixing bowl, add the sugar and rub in the butter until well dispersed through the flour. Make a well in the centre and pour in almost all the milk at once. Mix with a broad-bladed knife, working very quickly and gently until all the dry flour has been drawn together to form a spongy dough, a bit like a thick porridge.

Turn into the lightly greased tin, leaving the surface rough but level. Sprinkle generously with wholemeal flour, set on a hot baking tray and bake in the pre-heated oven for 10 minutes before reducing the temperature and cooking for a further 40–45 minutes. The bread is cooked when it is well risen, golden brown and feels firm to the touch. Remove from the oven and cover the top with a clean cloth. Leave in the tin until cool before turning out and completely wrapping in the cloth to store. This helps to soften the crust and keeps the bread moist.

The dough can also be shaped into a round cake and cooked on a floured baking sheet without the cake tin. In this case the dough needs to be slightly stiffer, so that it can be worked by hand and cooked without losing its shape.

BROWN SODA OR WHEATEN BREAD
Arán Cruithneachta

The proportions of wholemeal and white flour used to produce this type of soda bread greatly depends on individual taste and whether or not a very light or rough texture is required. I prefer to use stoneground wholemeal flour with a little extra bran and germ added to raise the fibre content as well as to enrich the bread. The quantity of sugar added also varies depending on whether a savoury or sweet bread is required.

350 g (12 oz) wholemeal flour, stoneground,
medium or coarse
100 g (4 oz) plain flour
1 × 5 ml (1 teaspoon) salt
1 × 5 ml (1 heaped teaspoon) bicarbonate of soda
1 × 15 ml (1 tablespoon) wheat or oat bran
1 × 15 ml (1 tablespoon) wheat or oat germ
25–50 g (1–2 oz) caster sugar
25–50 g (1–2 oz) butter
400–475 ml (14–16 fl oz) buttermilk
1 × 18 cm (7 in) round cake tin or 15 cm (6 in)
square tin, between 4–7 cm (1½–2¾ in) deep
OVEN TEMPERATURE AND TIME
220°C (425°F, gas mark 7), for 10 minutes, then
reduce to 200°C (400°F, gas mark 6) for 40–45
minutes

Put the wholemeal flour into a large mixing bowl and sieve in the plain flour, salt and bicarbonate of soda. Stir in the bran, germ and caster sugar, mixing thoroughly to combine all the ingredients. Cut the butter into small pieces and rub into the flour mixture until well dispersed. Make a well in the centre of the dry ingredients, and pour in all the milk. Mix with a broad-bladed knife, working very quickly and gently until all the dry ingredients have been drawn together to form a loose dough, a bit like thick porridge. It is important not to overwork the dough, otherwise it will become tough.

Lightly grease the cake tin and turn the dough into it, leaving the surface rough. Sprinkle with wholemeal flour and bran to give a nutty surface. Set on a hot baking tray and bake in the pre-heated oven for 10 minutes, then reduce the heat and cook for a further 40–45 minutes until the bread is well risen, brown and firm to the touch. When the bread is cooked, a skewer inserted into the centre of it should come out clean. The bread should also sound hollow when tapped. Remove from the oven and cover with a clean cloth. When cool, remove from the tin and wrap in the cloth to go cold. Wholemeal bread, like all the soda breads, is better eaten on the day of baking. However it is good toasted the following day – if there is any left!

CURRANT SODA
Arán Cuiríní

Currant soda, also referred to as fruit soda, curranty cake or fruit bannock, is one of Ireland's most popular soda breads, the basic soda bread recipe being enriched with fruit. This dough can also be rolled out thinly, cut into farls and cooked on the griddle, to produce griddle scones. The dough needs to be slightly stiffer than for bread baked in the oven.

450 g (1 lb) plain flour
1 × 5 ml (1 heaped teaspoon) bicarbonate of soda
1 × 5 ml (1 teaspoon) salt
50 g (2 oz) caster sugar
25–50 g (1–2 oz) butter
100 g (4 oz) dried fruit, sultanas or raisins
400–475 ml (14–16 fl oz) buttermilk
1 × 18 cm (7 in) round cake tin, between 4–7 cm
(1½–2¾ in) deep

OVEN TEMPERATURE AND TIME
220°C (425°F, gas mark 7) for 40 minutes, then reduce to 200°C (400°F, gas mark 6) for 40 minutes

Sieve the flour, bicarbonate of soda and salt into a large mixing bowl. Stir in the caster sugar and rub in the butter until as fine as breadcrumbs. Stir in the dried fruit and make a well in the centre. Pour in all the buttermilk and mix with a broad-bladed knife to draw all the dry ingredients into the liquid, forming a loose dough resembling thick porridge. Lightly grease the cake tin and turn the dough into it, leaving the surface rough. Sprinkle with a little flour, set on a hot baking tray and bake in the pre-heated oven for 10 minutes, then reduce the heat and cook for a further 40–45 minutes until the bread is well risen, brown and firm to the touch. When the bread is cooked, it will feel firm to the touch and a skewer inserted into the centre should come out clean. Remove from the oven and cover with a clean cloth. When cool remove from the tin and wrap in the cloth to go cold. Currant soda is served in slices with butter and jam. It is also excellent toasted the second day.

GRIDDLE SCONES This dough can be divided into two and rolled out to 5 mm ($\frac{1}{4}$ in) thick, then cut into eight farls and cooked on a moderate griddle for 10–15 minutes on each side. These griddle scones are then split in half and served hot or cold with butter and jam.

SODA FARLS
Farlaí Sóide

Each farl of soda bread is cut in half and generously buttered to be eaten hot or cold. It is also fried as an important element in an Irish fry and is often used as the perfect package to hold a fried egg, bacon, sausage and potato bread: a quick snack called an egg or sausage soda. This recipe can be cooked either on the griddle, electric frying pan or in the oven.

MAKES 4 farls
350 g (12 oz) plain flour
1 × 5 ml (1 teaspoon) salt
1 × 5 ml (1 heaped teaspoon) baking soda
250–325 ml (8–11 fl oz) buttermilk

Sieve the dry ingredients into a large mixing bowl. Make a well in the centre and pour in all the milk at once. Mix with a broad-bladed knife working very quickly and gently until all the dry flour has been drawn together to form a firm dough. It is important not to overwork the dough, otherwise it will become tough.

Turn on to a floured work surface and knead lightly until the top of the bread is smooth and a circle is formed. Roll or pat out with a rolling pin. If cooking on the griddle, it should be no more than 1 cm ($\frac{1}{2}$ in) thick. If being cooked in the oven, roll it out to 2–2.5 cm ($\frac{3}{4}$–1 in) thick. Cut into 4 farls.

TO BAKE ON A GRIDDLE While making the soda bread, have the griddle, heavy cast-iron frying pan, or electric frying pan heating on a low heat. The temperature of the pan can be tested before baking by sprinkling a light dusting of flour on to it. The temperature is correct when the flour turns from white to off white in a few minutes.

The farls are then set on the hot griddle or pan and cooked at this constant temperature until they are risen and a firm skin has formed on their surface. This usually takes about 6–10 minutes. Turn the farls and cook for a further 6–10 minutes to cook and colour the second side.

The farls are cooked when they are a light beige colour with a floury surface. They should sound hollow when tapped, and be dry when split along the edge.

TO BAKE IN THE OVEN Pre-heat the oven to 190°C (375°F, gas mark 5). Heat a baking sheet and dredge with flour before setting the farls on top. Bake until well risen and golden brown. This will take about 40–45 minutes.

When the bread is cooked it can be left to cool, each farl standing on its end, leaning against the next, on a wire cooling rack. Alternatively, it can be wrapped while still hot in the folds of a clean linen cloth, which will give it a softer crust.

BUTTERMILK SCONES
Bonnóga Bláthaí

Scones are very much part of the soda bread tradition in Ireland and are served for morning coffee and afternoon tea. They are one of the many bake products made with buttermilk, the liquid left behind in butter-making when the liquid separates from the butter solids. The raising agents used with the buttermilk are bicarbonate of soda and cream of tartar. These react with the acid in the buttermilk, causing the dough to rise. Sour milk or yoghurt also give excellent results. Buttermilk scones are always much lighter and more spongy than those made with plain flour and baking powder, or self raising flour and fresh milk.

The secret of making good scones is light quick mixing and a hot oven.

MAKES 8–12 scones
225 g (8 oz) plain flour
1 × 5 ml (1 teaspoon) bicarbonate of soda
1 × 5 ml (1 teaspoon) cream of tartar
Pinch of salt
25 g (1 oz) butter or block margarine
200 ml (7 fl oz) buttermilk, approx.
Beaten egg or milk to glaze (optional)
OVEN TEMPERATURE 220°C (425°F, gas mark 7)
OVEN TIME 15–20 minutes

Sieve the flour, baking soda and cream of tartar into a large bowl. Stir in the salt. Cut and rub in the butter or margarine until as fine as breadcrumbs. Make a well in the centre of the flour and pour in almost all the milk. Using a broad-bladed knife, stir the milk into the flour as quickly as possible to form a soft dough. Turn on to a lightly floured work surface and roll out to about 2 cm ($\frac{3}{4}$ in) thick. Cut into scones using a 5–6 cm (2–2$\frac{1}{2}$ in) cutter. Alternatively, the scone dough can be divided in two and each piece rolled to a circle, 2 cm ($\frac{3}{4}$ in) thick, and cut into 6 triangles. The scones, whether triangles or circles, are now placed on a lightly floured baking sheet and brushed with beaten egg or milk to glaze. Bake in the pre-heated oven for 15–20 minutes until well risen and light golden-brown in colour. Serve straight from the oven with butter and jam. Scones should be eaten on the day of making, or toasted the following day.

FRUIT SCONES Add 25–50 g (1–2 oz) chopped dates, sultanas, currants or cherries and 25–50 g (1–2 oz) caster sugar before adding the milk.

TREACLE SCONES Add 1–2 × 15 ml (1–2 table-spoons) treacle blended with the milk.

CHEESE SCONES Add 50 g (2 oz) grated cheese before pouring in the milk. After brushing the scones with egg or milk, sprinkle with a little extra cheese.

WHEATEN SCONES Use all wholemeal or half wholemeal and half white flour.

SAVOURY LEEK SCONES Leeks and chives, or spring onions, are favourite vegetables in Ireland and when combined with the basic buttermilk scone mix, produce delicious savoury scones which are excellent served as a cocktail savoury or with soups and starters. To the 225 g (8 oz) scone dough (see page 133), I add 25 g (1 oz) white of leek, very finely chopped, 2 × 15 ml (2 tablespoons) snipped chives, 2 × 15 ml (2 tablespoons) parsley, finely chopped, plenty of milled black pepper and a pinch of cayenne pepper to the dry ingredients. I roll the scones to 1 cm (½ in) thick and cut with a 5 cm (2 in) cutter to get 15 small scones. They are baked in the usual way, but for slightly less time.

NOTE If buttermilk is not available, use 2½–3 × 5 ml (2½–3 teaspoons) baking powder to 225 g (8 oz) plain flour and 200 ml (7 fl oz) milk, or 225 g (8 oz) self-raising flour with the same quantity of milk.

GRIDDLE SCONES
Bonnóga Gridille

In Ireland, before ranges or ovens were common place in most kitchens, many of the traditional breads and scones were baked on the griddle over the burning turf fire. Nowadays, griddles are used less and less, and if one is not available an electric frying pan, a multi-cooker or even a large heavy cast-iron pan can be used instead.

The griddle scones, themselves, use basically the same recipe as for buttermilk scones (see page 133), but with less liquid added to the dough to make it stiffer, about 150 ml (5 fl oz). The dough is divided in two and each piece rolled out to a circle, 5 mm (¼ in) thick. Cut into 6 or 8 triangles and lightly dust with flour.

Heat the griddle or frying pan until it feels comfortably warm to the hand when it is held about 1 cm (½ in) above it, and when a light dusting of flour turns a pale golden colour. Place the scones on the dry hot surface and cook them for 7–8 minutes on each side. When ready they should be golden brown on both sides and slightly springy to the touch. Serve hot with butter.

Griddle scones are particularly good with a little sugar and 50 g (2 oz) dried fruit added to the dough.

DROPPED SCONES
Pancóga

These puffy little scones are really thick pan-cakes, which are made with a very light batter raised with baking soda, cream of tartar and buttermilk. They are much thicker and smaller than the French crêpe, but are also cooked on a griddle or cast-iron pan. In Ireland they are traditionally served for afternoon or high tea with butter and homemade jam.

MAKES 14 drop scones, approx. 6 cm (2½ in) in
diameter
100 g (4 oz) plain flour
1 × 5 ml (1 teaspoon) bicarbonate of soda
1 × 5 ml (1 teaspoon) cream of tartar
25 g (1 oz) caster sugar or 1–2 × 5 ml (1–2
teaspoons) golden syrup
1 egg, size 4
150 ml (5 fl oz) buttermilk

Sieve the flour, bicarbonate of soda and cream of tartar into a large bowl. Stir in the sugar. If using syrup beat with the egg. Make a well in the centre of the flour and pour in the egg and milk. Beat well to make a thick smooth batter.

Have the griddle, heavy cast-iron pan or electric frying pan heated. The electric frying pan should register approximately 160°C (325°F). Drop the mixture from the point of a tablespoon on to the hot griddle. Some people like to lightly grease the surface with a piece of bacon fat. I personally prefer to cook the pancakes on a dry pan. The batter will immediately begin to rise and when a few bubbles begin to break on the surface the scones are ready for turning. Use a palette knife and flick them over gently, so that an even browning can be

obtained on the second side. When cooked, the scones should be golden brown in colour and light and spongy in texture. Keep warm in a clean tea-cloth until all are cooked.

BOXTY
Bacstaí

Boxty is a traditional potato dish found in the northern counties, such as Cavan, Leitrim, Donegal and Monaghan, and is particularly associated with Hallowe'en.

It appears in the form of bread, griddle cakes, dumplings, pancakes and puddings, which all have one thing in common – they use grated raw potatoes. Boxty is also sometimes called 'stampy' and, when served with milk and salt instead of oat bread, is known as 'dippity'. Like many of the Irish potato dishes there are many different versions and as many rhymes and songs written about them, like these:

> *Boxty on the griddle*
> *Boxty in the pan*
> *If you don't eat your boxty*
> *You'll never get a man.*
>
> *Boxty on the griddle*
> *Boxty in the pan,*
> *The wee one in the middle*
> *It is for Mary Anne.*
>
> *I'll have none of your boxty,*
> *I'll have none of your blarney;*
> *But I'll whirl my petticoats over my head*
> *And be off with my Royal Charlie.*

The two main types of boxty are boxty on the griddle, a form of potato bread, and boxty on the pan, a type of potato pancake. Although both of these are well known in Ireland, today they are not frequently made and are very much an acquired taste, the pancakes being more accept-able than the bread or the dumplings.

BOXTY BREAD – BOXTY ON THE GRIDDLE
Bacstaí Gridille

MAKES 8 farls
225 g (8 oz) raw potatoes
225 g (8 oz) cooked potatoes, mashed
50 g (2 oz) plain flour
Pinch of salt

Wash and peel the raw potatoes. Grate them on to a clean cloth. Place the cloth over a bowl and twist the ends to wring out the starchy liquid from the potatoes into the bowl. Place the grated potatoes into another bowl and cover with the mashed potatoes. This will help prevent the grated potatoes from discolouring. Allow the liquid from the grated potatoes to settle until the starch drops to the bottom of the bowl. Pour off the clear liquid and scrape the starch on top of the mashed potatoes. Add the salt and mix well to combine all the ingredients. Stir in the flour to make a pliable dough in the same way as making potato cakes (see page 135). Turn the dough on to a lightly floured work-surface and roll into a circle, about 6 mm ($\frac{1}{4}$ in) thick and 20 cm (8 in) in diameter, and cut into 8 farls. Bake on a hot griddle or a heavy-bottomed frying pan like potato cake until lightly browned on both sides. This will take about 30 minutes. The griddle is not oiled, but sprinkled with a little flour. The thickness of boxty bread can vary a lot, from being quite thin and eaten directly from the griddle with butter, to being thick enough to slice in two the next day and fried in the frying pan with bacon for breakfast.

BOXTY PANCAKES – BOXTY IN THE PAN
Pancóga Bacstaí

MAKES approx. 11 pancakes, 6 cm × 5 mm ($2\frac{1}{2}$ × $\frac{1}{4}$ in)
450 g (1 lb) potatoes, 4 large
2 × 15 ml (2 tablespoons) plain flour
1 × 5 ml (1 teaspoon) baking powder
1 × 2.5 ml ($\frac{1}{2}$ teaspoon) salt
150 ml (5 fl oz) milk

Peel and grate the raw potatoes into a clean cloth. Place the cloth over a bowl and twist the ends to wring out the starchy liquid from the potatoes into the bowl. Keep the potatoes wrapped in the cloth until the liquid from the grated potatoes has settled and the starch has dropped to the bottom of the bowl; this will take a few hours. The potatoes may discolour slightly. When you are ready to make the pancakes, put the grated potato into a bowl and add the flour sieved with the baking

powder and salt. Pour off the clear liquid in the other bowl and scrape the starchy sediment on top of the potato and flour mixture. Mix to a fairly soft batter, of dropping consistency, with the milk. Drop the mixture in tablespoonfuls on to a hot, lightly-greased griddle or frying pan. Cook for 5 minutes on each side until golden brown. Serve hot with butter and sugar, or with fried bacon.

NOTE A friend from County Kerry also makes boxty pancakes from an old family recipe, which includes a beaten egg and a little finely chopped onion. These boxty pancakes were served as a main dish.

BOXTY DUMPLINGS
Domplagáin Bacstaí

MAKES 16 dumplings

Use the same ingredients as for boxty bread (see page 134), but instead of rolling out the dough after kneading, form it into small balls, about the size of a golf ball. Flatten them slightly, then drop them into a pan of boiling salted water and boil for about 45 minutes. Drain well and serve with a sweet cornflour sauce.

Currants or raisins are sometimes added to the raw dough, and occasionally after boiling and draining they are fried in butter or bacon fat in the pan.

POTATO CAKES
Arán Prátaí

Potato cake or potato bread, in the northern counties referred to as 'fadge', is a type of bread or scone made from mashed potatoes. There are several regional variations, but the main difference is in the texture. This is controlled by the amount of flour used, and the shape in which the potato cakes are cut. More flour gives a firmer cake and helps it to keep longer, but it is not quite as light. Potato bread is cooked on the griddle or frying pan and is served hot with butter or sugar. Alternatively, after it is cooked it is fried and eaten with bacon, sausages and egg as part of a dish served for breakfast, lunch or tea called an Ulster fry (see page 60).

Potato bread is best made while the potatoes are still hot. If using leftover potato, heat it for

30 seconds in the microwave, before mixing it with the rest of the ingredients.

MAKES 6–8 farls, or 10 cakes cut with a 7.5 cm (3 in) cutter
225 g (8 oz) potatoes, cooked
1 × 2.5 ml ($\frac{1}{2}$ teaspoon) salt
25 g (1 oz) butter, melted
50 g (2 oz) plain flour

Put the potatoes through a potato ricer or mash well until smooth and free from lumps. Add the salt and melted butter, then work in enough flour to make a pliable dough. Turn on to a lightly floured surface and roll into a circular shape, about 6 mm ($\frac{1}{4}$ in) thick and 22.5 cm (9 in) in diameter. Cut into 6 or 8 farls (triangular shapes) and bake on a hot griddle or frying pan until lightly browned on both sides. This will take about 5 minutes. Do not use oil in the griddle pan, but test to see if it is hot enough by sprinkling a little flour over its surface. When it turns pale golden, the pan is at the correct temperature. Alternatively, potato cakes can be cut into circles with a plain cutter.

POTATO–APPLE CAKE
Císte Prátaí agus Úll

Potato-apple cake is the highlight of the farm-house tea-table in the apple season and on Hallowe'en night when a ring is hidden in the filling for luck. It is made from a top and bottom layer of potato bread filled with apples.

SERVES 2–4

The basic potato bread dough (see above) is divided into two, and each piece is rolled into a circle, about 20 cm (8 in) in diameter. Then 275 g (10 oz) peeled, cored and thinly-sliced Bramley apples are piled on half of each circle. The uncovered half of the potato bread is folded on top of the apples and the edges carefully sealed to prevent the juices from running out during the cooking. They take about 15 minutes on each side.

Traditionally, these would have been baked slowly on the griddle until the potato bread was brown and the apples cooked. Nowadays, however, they are more likely to be cooked on a heavy cast-iron frying pan. Cook for 20 minutes on each side on a low heat.

The success of potato-apple cake depends entirely on its serving. When each cake is cooked, it is carefully split along the curved side and the top carefully turned back. The apples are then covered with thin slices of butter and sprinkled with sugar to sweeten. The top is then folded back on top of the apples and put in the oven to allow the sugar and butter to melt and to form a rich syrupy sauce. Originally this would have been set on the hearth in front of the fire.

POTATO OATEN CAKE
Prátaí Coirce

These flat griddle cakes, or farls, are similar to potato bread, except that the mashed potato is bound with oatmeal rather than flour. They are eaten hot or cold with butter, or fried in bacon fat in the pan, and are often served with bacon and eggs for breakfast. They are deliciously oaty in flavour.

MAKES 12 farls
375 g (13 oz) warm cooked mashed potatoes
100 g (4 oz) fine oatmeal (approx.)
Pinch of salt
50 g (2 oz) butter, melted

Add enough of the fine oatmeal to the mashed potatoes to form a fairly soft dough. Add salt to season, along with the melted butter to bind. Roll out the dough, on a table or board scattered with oatmeal, to a circle approximately 16 cm (6½ in) in diameter and 5 mm (¼ in) deep. Cut into 12 farls and bake on both sides on a hot lightly greased griddle or frying pan until lightly brown on each side.

OATCAKES
Bonnóga Arán Coirce

These simple flat cakes were made from a mixture of oatmeal, water and sometimes lard, and baked on the griddle over a turf fire or on a warmed hearthstone. They were then transferred to a wood or metal stand called a 'hardening' or 'harnen' stand, resting in front of the fire, where they dried out. They were traditionally eaten with butter and a cup of buttermilk. Today they are baked either on the griddle or in the oven and eaten with cheese.

Oatcakes.

MAKES 8 farls/12 biscuits
225 g (8 oz) medium or fine oatmeal
50 g (2 oz) plain flour
1 × 2.5 ml (½ teaspoon) bicarbonate of soda
1 × 1.25 ml (¼ teaspoon) cream of tartar
1 × 2.5 ml (½ teaspoon) salt
50 ml (2 fl oz) water
50 g (2 oz) butter, margarine, lard or bacon dripping
Extra oatmeal for working the cake

Put the oatmeal into a large bowl and sieve in the plain flour with the bicarbonate of soda, cream of tartar and salt. Make a well in the centre of the mixture. Heat the water in a small saucepan and add the fat. Bring to boiling point and quickly pour into the well in the dry ingredients and work together, using a spoon, until the mixture holds together. Sprinkle a board or work surface with a little extra oatmeal and set the spongy mixture on top, scatter with more oatmeal, then roll into a round cake about 23 cm (9 in) in diameter and 3 mm (⅛ in) thick, making sure that the dough is not sticking to the surface. Scatter some oatmeal on top of the cake and rub it in with the palm of the hand. Cut into 8 farls.

If using a griddle, have it pre-heated to temperature and place the farls on top. Bake over a moderate heat until the oatcakes have completely dried out and are a pale golden colour. An electric frying pan can also be used, but the temperature should be set to low.

Oatcakes can also be baked on a floured baking sheet in the oven at 180°C (350°F, gas mark 4) for about 40 minutes. They can also be cut into 7.5 cm (3 in) rounds to make biscuits.

136

BAIRM BRACK
Bairín Breac

Brack is the traditional bread eaten at Hallowe'en (All Hallows Eve, 31 October), or on the evening of All Saints' Day (1 November) in the Christian calendar. The Irish word breac *means speckled and refers to the fruit used in the dough.* Bairm, *which is yeast, was used to leaven the cake. This Hallowe'en bread is sometimes referred to as barm or barn brack. Traditionally, there are two versions of this cake: one, as the name implies, uses yeast as its raising agent; the other uses baking powder and is often referred to as tea brack. When traditionally eaten at Hallowe'en, both the bairm brack and the tea brack had rings hidden in the dough, which signified marriage before Easter to whoever was lucky enough to find one in their slice. Brack is also popular throughout the year as a tea-time cake.*

500 g (1¼ lb) strong plain flour

1 × 1.25 ml (¼ teaspoon) salt

1 × 5 ml (1 teaspoon) mixed spice

50 g (2 oz) butter

175 g (6 oz) sultanas

50 g (2 oz) mixed peel

50 g (2 oz) caster sugar

2 eggs, size 3

20 g (¾ oz) fresh yeast

300 ml (10 fl oz) tepid water

FOR THE GLAZE

2 × 15 ml (2 tablespoons) granulated sugar

2 × 15 ml (2 tablespoons) water

OVEN TEMPERATURE 200°C (400°F, gas mark 6)

OVEN TIME 30–35 minutes

Sieve the flour, salt and spice into a large mixing bowl. Rub in the butter until the mixture resembles fine breadcrumbs. Wash and dry the sultanas well and mix into the flour, along with the mixed peel and sugar. Dissolve the yeast in the tepid water. Make a well in the centre of the flour and add the beaten eggs, together with the water and yeast mixture. Mix to a dough, starting off with a wooden spoon and using your hand in the final stages of mixing. Put the dough on to a floured surface and knead for about 10 minutes until it feels springy and elastic, then put the dough back in the bowl and cover with a cloth. Leave in a warm place to rise until it has doubled in size. This will take about 1 hour.

Divide the dough in half and knead each piece for a few minutes until smooth and in a circle, about 20 cm (8 in) in diameter. Set on a lightly greased baking sheet and leave in a warm place for a further 45–60 minutes until well risen. Bake in the pre-heated oven for 30–35 minutes.

Meanwhile dissolve the sugar in the water over a gentle heat and brush the bracks with it as soon as they come out of the oven. When cooked, the bracks should be a rich-brown colour, firm to the touch and should sound hollow when the bottom is tapped.

TEA BRACK
Bairín Tae

Tea brack is a rich moist cake, dark in colour and heavy with fruit. It is usually brushed with a sticky glaze just before the end of the cooking time to give it a shine. It keeps well in an airtight tin for about a week.

225 g (8 oz) sultanas

225 g (8 oz) raisins

50 g (2 oz) mixed peel

225 g (8 oz) soft dark brown sugar

475 ml (16 fl oz) strong black tea

350 g (12 oz) plain flour

2 × 5 ml (2 teaspoons) baking powder

2 × 5 ml (2 teaspoons) mixed spice

2 eggs, size 2, beaten

1–2 × 15 ml (1–2 tablespoons) liquid honey, to glaze

1 baking tin, 20 × 7.5 cm (8 × 3 in) round, or

18 × 7.5 cm (7 × 3 in) square

OVEN TEMPERATURE 160°C (325°F, gas mark 3)

OVEN TIME 1½ hours

Line the bottom and sides of the cake tin with greaseproof paper and grease lightly with a little melted butter.

Put the sultanas, raisins, peel and sugar in a large bowl and pour on the hot tea. Stir to dissolve the sugar. Soak the fruit overnight to allow the fruit to swell and plump.

Sieve together the flour, baking powder and spice. Mix the beaten egg and the flour into the fruit mixture alternately, beating well between each addition until all the ingredients are well blended. Pour into the prepared cake tin, smooth the top and bake in the pre-heated oven for approximately 1½ hours.

Ten minutes before the end of the cooking time, heat the honey in a small saucepan and brush on top of the cake to give a glaze. Return to the oven to finish the cooking. Leave to cool in the tin for about 15 minutes before turning out on to a wire rack. When cold, store in an airtight tin.

RICH FRUIT LOAF
Bairín Torthaí

One of the few yeasted breads popular in Ireland is the rich fruit loaf. It is available from bakeries throughout the year, but is traditionally served at Hallowe'en, when 'charms' are often buried among the fruit, and at Christmas as one of the special teatime treats. The quality of the loaf is largely dependent on the amount of fruit used and this will vary from bakery to bakery. Making yeast bread is not one of the skills of the traditional Irish kitchen, so fruit loaves are generally bought rather than homemade. However, with a good recipe the skill is easy to acquire and the results are most satisfying. This recipe was kindly given to me by Keith and June Henning of June's Home Bakery in Belfast, one of the best home bakeries in Ireland.

MAKES 3 × 450 g (1 lb) loaves

450 g (1 lb) strong plain flour

1 × 5 ml (1 teaspoon) salt

50 g (2 oz) butter

50 g (2 oz) caster sugar

2 eggs, size 3, beaten

250 ml (9 fl oz) tepid water

35 g (1¼ oz) fresh yeast

1 kg (2 lb) sultanas

100 g (4 oz) cherries

50 g (2 oz) walnuts

25 g (1 oz) ginger slivers

50 ml (2 fl oz) glycerine

3 × 450 g (1 lb) loaf tins

OVEN TEMPERATURE 180°C (350°F, gas mark 4)

OVEN TIME 35–40 minutes

Line the bottom of the loaf tin with greaseproof paper and grease well with a little white fat. Sieve the flour and salt into a large mixing

Chocolate whiskey cake.

few minutes on a lightly-floured work surface, folding the sides and then the ends to the centre, until the dough is smooth. Turn over and drop into the lightly greased tins. Leave in a warm place for 1–1½ hours until the loaf is well risen. Brush lightly with a little beaten egg mixed with some water and a pinch of salt, then bake in the pre-heated oven until a rich deep-brown colour and firm to the touch. When the loaf is cooked it will also have slightly shrunk from the sides of the tin and sound hollow when tapped. Leave to cool before turning out of the tins, then leave to go cold on a wire cooling rack.

BOILED FRUIT CAKE
Císte Torthaí Bruite

This rich moist fruit cake is a teatime favourite and much less expensive than the more traditional rich fruit cake. It is also very quick and easy to make and keeps well.

300 ml (10 fl oz) water
100 g (4 oz) butter or margarine
225 g (8 oz) soft brown sugar
225 g (8 oz) currants
225 g (8 oz) sultanas
3 × 5 ml (3 teaspoons) mixed spice
350 g (12 oz) plain flour
1 × 5 ml (1 teaspoon) bicarbonate of soda
1 egg, size 2, beaten
1 × 20 cm (8 in) round deep cake tin
OVEN TEMPERATURE AND TIME
180°C (350°F, gas mark 4) for 10–15 minutes,
then lower to 160°C (325°F, gas mark 3) for 1¼
hours

Line both the sides and bottom of the cake tin with greaseproof paper. Brush lightly with melted butter or oil. Put the water, butter or margarine, sugar, fruit and spice into a large saucepan. Bring very gently to simmering point and simmer for 20 minutes. Remove from the heat and leave until cold.

Sieve the flour and baking soda together and stir into the fruit mixture along with the beaten egg. Mix thoroughly and turn into the prepared cake tin. Smooth the top and bake in the pre-heated oven for 10–15 minutes, then reduce the heat and continue the cooking for 1¼ hours, or until a skewer when inserted in the centre of the

bowl, then rub in the butter until the mixture resembles fine breadcrumbs. Stir in the sugar and dissolve the yeast in the tepid water. Make a well in the centre of the flour and add the beaten eggs along with the water and yeast mixture. Beat vigorously for about 15 minutes. I do this using the dough hook of my electric mixer. Cover the dough with a damp cloth and rest it for about 20 minutes in a warm place.

When the dough feels like elastic, it is ready for the next stage.

Wash the fruit, dry it well on kitchen paper and then toss in the glycerine. This will help to keep the loaf moist. Scrape the dough, which is sticky in texture, on top of the fruit and mix thoroughly. Cover again and rest for a further 45 minutes in a warm place. The dough should be at a temperature of approximately 27°C (81°F). Push the dough down into the bowl and divide into three pieces. Knead each piece for a cake comes out clean. Leave to cool in the tin for 10 minutes before turning out on to a cake rack.

Wrap well in greaseproof paper or foil and store in an airtight tin.

PORTER CAKE
Císte Pórtair
This is a classic Irish cake which has many variations. Traditionally, porter – a weak form of stout – would have been used, but nowadays Guinness is more readily available. This recipe is my grandmother's version and is a great favourite in my own house. It needs a week to mature before cutting.

450 g (1 lb) plain flour
2 × 15 ml (2 tablespoons) mixed spice
225 g (8 oz) butter or block margarine
225 g (8 oz) currants
225 g (8 oz) raisins or sultanas
100 g (4 oz) mixed peel, chopped
Grated rind of 1 lemon
350 g (12 oz) soft brown sugar
1 × 5 ml (1 teaspoon) baking soda
150 ml (5 fl oz) Guinness or stout
4 eggs, beaten
1 × 23 cm (9 in) round or 20 cm (8 in) square cake
tin, approx. 9 cm (3½ in) deep
OVEN TEMPERATURE AND TIME
160°C (325°F, gas mark 3) for 1 hour, then reduce
to 150°C (300°F, gas mark 2) for 1½–2 hours

Line the bottom and sides of the cake tin with greaseproof paper. Brush with a little melted butter or margarine. Sieve the flour, spices and baking soda into a large bowl. Cut the butter into pieces and rub into the flour until the mixture resembles breadcrumbs. Stir in the fruit, mixed peel, lemon rind and sugar, mixing well to combine. Add the beaten egg. Dissolve the soda in the Guinness, make a well in the centre of the flour and fruit mixture, and gradually work in the Guinness and soda. Mix thoroughly. Pour into the prepared tin, smooth the top and bake in the pre-heated oven for 1 hour, then reduce the temperature, cover the top of the cake loosely with a sheet of grease-proof paper and bake for a further 1½–2 hours.

The cake should be a deep brown colour and firm to the touch when cooked. Leave to cool in

the tin before turning out and removing the paper. This cake stores well in an airtight tin.

CHOCOLATE WHISKEY CAKE
Císte Uisce Beatha agus Seacláide
Until quite recently baking was an important part of the weekly housekeeping procedure in most houses in Ireland. However, today, particularly in the cities, with more women working and having much less time available to spend in the kitchen, baking is generally reserved for special occasions and celebrations. There is one cake which almost always features at such times – the chocolate cake. As with most cakes, there are many different recipes for it. This one is my mother's recipe and is always greatly enjoyed.

SERVES 8–12
3 eggs, size 4
100 g (4 oz) caster sugar
75 g (3 oz) self raising flour
50 g (2 oz) cocoa powder
2 × 15 ml (2 tablespoons) warm water
FOR THE FILLING
3 × 15 ml (3 tablespoons) apricot jam
2 × 15 ml (2 tablespoons) whiskey
300 ml (10 fl oz) double cream, lightly whipped
FOR THE CHOCOLATE COVERING
225 g (8 oz) dark chocolate
1 × 15 ml (1 tablespoon) whiskey
15 g (½ oz) butter
1 egg, size 4
1 × 15 ml (1 tablespoon) double cream
FOR THE DECORATION
150–300 ml (5–10 fl oz) double cream
Chocolate leaves, flakes or grated chocolate
1 × 20 cm (8 in) cake tin at least 4 cm (2 in) deep
OVEN TEMPERATURE 190°C (375°F, gas mark 5)
OVEN TIME 25–30 minutes

Line the base of the cake tin with greaseproof paper. Lightly oil both the paper and the sides of the tin. Beat the eggs and the sugar until very thick and pale. The mixture has been whisked enough when it holds the shape of a figure '8' on the surface for a few seconds. Sieve the flour and cocoa powder on to a plate to make sure they are well mixed. Then sieve again on top of the cake mixture, one third at a time. Fold gently into the egg mixture, using a large metal spoon; make sure the mixture is not

overworked. With the last third of the flour, add the water. Spoon the sponge mixture into the prepared tin and bake in the pre-heated oven 25–30 minutes until the cake shows slight shrinkage at the sides. Remove from the oven and allow to cool for a few minutes before removing from the tin. Transfer to a cooling rack to cool completely.

When the cake is cold, cut into three sections. Place one layer of cake on a serving plate, spread with some apricot jam, sprinkle with 1 × 15 ml (1 tablespoon) whiskey and cover with half of the cream. Place the middle layer of sponge on top and cover it with the remaining apricot jam, whiskey and cream. Cover with the last layer of sponge.

Prepare the chocolate covering by breaking the chocolate into a mixing bowl over a sauce-pan of hot water. Add the whiskey and butter and stir until melted. Beat the egg, and add with the cream to the melted chocolate, stirring well to combine. The heat of the mixture will slightly cook the egg. Use this chocolate cream to cover the sides and top of the cake. Leave until set before decorating.

Whip the double cream for the decoration until it holds its own shape. Use to fill a piping bag with a star nozzle, and pipe rosettes of cream around the edge of the cake. Spike each with chocolate leaves or flakes.

SEED CAKE
Císte Síol Cearbhais
Caraway seeds were enormously popular from the sixteenth to the end of the nineteenth century for flavouring biscuits and cakes. However, from the twentieth century, they went out of favour and are seldom used today, mainly because of their very strong flavour. In Ireland seed cake is also known as carvie cake and a number of different recipes and methods are used for making it. Some rub the fat into the flour, others, where the proportion of fat is more than half fat to flour, use the creaming method. Also, 25 g (1 oz) mixed peel plus 100 g (4 oz) cherries or sultanas make an excellent addition and, if the caraway seeds are not to your taste, the additional fruit can enable them to be omitted. In the grand Irish houses, seed cake was offered wih a glass of port to lady visitors if they called in the morning or afternoon.

225 g (8 oz) butter
225 g (8 oz) caster sugar
4 eggs, size 3, whisked until frothy
275 g (10 oz) plain flour
1 × 2.5 ml ($\frac{1}{2}$ teaspoon) baking powder
1 × 1.25 ($\frac{1}{4}$ teaspoon) ground cinnamon
1 × 1.25 ml ($\frac{1}{4}$ teaspoon) ground nutmeg
4 × 15 ml (4 tablespoons) caraway seeds
1 × 20 cm (8 in) round or 18 cm (7 in) square, deep cake tin
OVEN TEMPERATURE 160°C (325°F, gas mark 3)
OVEN TIME 1$\frac{1}{2}$ hours

Line the bottom and sides of the cake tin with greaseproof paper and lightly grease with melted butter. Cream the butter and sugar together until very pale in colour and light and fluffy in texture. Sieve the flour, baking powder and spices together. Gradually beat the eggs into the creamed mixture, adding a little flour after each addition if the creamed mixture begins to curdle. Fold in the remaining flour with the caraway seeds and, if necessary, a little milk to give a soft dropping consistency. Put into the prepared tin, level the top and bake in the pre-heated oven. The cake is cooked when it is firm to the touch and a pale golden colour. Leave to cool in the tin for about 10 minutes before turning on to a wire rack to cool. Remove the paper when cold.

SAFFRON CAKE
Círte Cróch

Along with the many spices, fruits and other luxury goods coming into Ireland from the East was a spice grown in Cornwall, called saffron. Saffron, the stamen of a very special crocus, is highly prized for its flavour and yellow colour, and it was used as a dye, particularly for wool and in baking. One of the most popular ways of using saffron in Ireland in the eighteenth and nineteenth centuries was in the making of cakes. There are many recipes for these in the 'receipt' manuscript books of the time, most of which probably came from Cornwall along with the saffron.

The original Cornish saffron cakes were not sweetened, but made from a basic white bread dough, which made them more like a bread than a cake in texture. Often dried fruits such as sultanas and raisins were added, producing a

saffron-flavoured currant bread, which is delicious with plenty of butter.

The following 'receipt' is an adaptation of a number of saffron cake recipes I have found in eighteenth-century Irish 'receipt' manuscript books, all of which were not quite complete.

75 g (3 oz) butter
75 g (3 oz) lard
450 g (1 lb) plain flour
100 g (4 oz) caster sugar
Pinch of salt
25 g (1 oz) yeast
2 eggs
150 ml (5 fl oz) milk, warmed
Generous pinch of saffron powder
100 g (4 oz) currants
100 g (4 oz) sultanas
2 × 15 ml (2 tablespoons) caraway seeds
2 × 450 g (1 lb) tins, 19 × 8.5 × 5 cm (7$\frac{1}{2}$ × 3$\frac{1}{2}$ × 2 in), the bottom lined with a piece of greaseproof paper and lightly greased with oil or white fat
OVEN TEMPERATURE 190°C (375°F, gas mark 5)
OVEN TIME 30–35 minutes

Rub the butter and lard into the flour until as fine as breadcrumbs, then add the sugar and salt. Mix the yeast with the tepid milk and saffron. Make a well in the centre of the flour mixture and pour in the yeast liquid, followed by the beaten eggs. Cover with a damp cloth and leave in a warm place for 30–40 minutes until the mixture has doubled in size. Stir in the fruit and caraway seeds. Turn on to a lightly-floured work surface and knead until smooth, about 4–5 minutes. Return to the bowl, cover with a damp cloth and leave in a warm place until it has once again doubled in size. Knead again and place in the prepared tin. Leave in a warm place to rise, without covering; this will take 25–35 minutes. Brush with a mixture of beaten egg, water and salt. Bake in the pre-heated oven for 30 minutes.

When cooked, leave in the tin to set for a few minutes before turning on to a cooling rack. Serve in slices with butter.

ALMOND CHEESE CAKES
Cístí Almóinne agus Cáis

These little cakes, although called almond cheese cakes, are in fact made without cheese.

They appear frequently in manuscript cookery books of the eighteenth century and are still popular throughout Ireland today, being baked in many homes as well as being sold in most bakeries. They consist of a pastry case topped with a rich almond sponge, which can be flavoured with almond essence, rose water or powdered mace. A spot of jam is sometimes put on the bottom of the pastry and flaked almonds sprinkled on the sponge before baking.

This recipe has been adapted from the eighteenth-century manuscript book of Charles Echlin from County Down, 1709, currently in the possession of John A. Gamble.

MAKES 18 small cakes
FOR 100 g (4 oz) QUANTITY RICH SHORTCRUST PASTRY
100 g (4 oz) plain flour
Pinch of salt
50 g (2 oz) butter or hard margarine
1 × 15 ml (1 tablespoon) caster sugar
1 egg yolk
2–3 × 15 ml (2–3 tablespoons) cold water
FOR THE ALMOND TOPPING
100 g (4 oz) butter or 'cake' margarine
100 g (4 oz) caster sugar
2 eggs, size 3, lightly beaten
1 × 2.5 ml ($\frac{1}{2}$ teaspoon) almond essence
100 g (4 oz) ground almonds
25 g (1 oz) plain flour
FILLING
Raspberry jam
TOPPING
Flaked almonds
18 patty tins
7.5 cm (3 in) fluted pastry cutter
OVEN TEMPERATURE 190°C (375°F, gas mark 5)
OVEN TIME 20–25 minutes

First make the pastry cases. Sieve the flour and salt into a bowl. Cut the fat into small pieces and rub into the flour until the mixture resembles fine breadcrumbs. Stir into the caster sugar. Mix the egg yolk and water together and sprinkle on top of the crumbed mixture. Stir, using a broad-bladed knife, to form a stiff dough, adding a little extra water if necessary. Turn on to a lightly-floured work surface and knead very lightly. Roll out into a circle about 2 mm ($\frac{1}{16}$ in) thick and cut into rounds with the fluted cutter. Place a round in each patty tin and put approximately $\frac{1}{4}$ teaspoon raspberry jam into the centre of each.

Prepare the almond topping by creaming the butter and sugar together until light and fluffy and pale cream in colour. Very gradually add the eggs, beating well between each addition. Stir in the almond essence, ground almonds and flour. Put a generous heaped teaspoonful on top of each pastry case to cover the raspberry jam. Sprinkle a few slivered almonds on top and bake in the pre-heated oven until well risen and pale golden brown.

CURD CAKE
Císte Grutha

Curds (gruth) not only played an important part in the Irish diet, but were used in the payment of rent, fines and even sick maintenance. They were formed by the souring of milk and their texture was probably similar to what is known today as cottage cheese. When these curds were pressed, either by hand or in a mould, they produced the simplest type of cheese.

Curd cake is a form of cheesecake, baked in a pastry case and flavoured with lemon, mace, rose water or sherry. It appeared to be very popular in the eighteenth century, appearing frequently in manuscripts of that time.

The following recipe has been adapted from the manuscript book of Lady Rivers, County Cavan, 1750, currently in the possession of The Ulster Folk and Transport Museum.

SERVES 6–8
FOR THE PASTRY CASE
100 g (4 oz) plain flour
Pinch of salt
50 g (2 oz) butter or hard margarine
1 × 15 ml (1 tablespoon) caster sugar
1 egg yolk
2–3 × 15 ml (2–3 tablespoons) cold water
FOR THE CURD FILLING
275 g (10 oz) cottage cheese
50 g (2 oz) caster sugar
50 g (2 oz) softened butter
Rind of 1 large lemon
Juice of $\frac{1}{2}$ lemon
Pinch of ground mace
3 eggs, separated

Curd cake.

3 × 15 ml (3 tablespoons) plain flour
FOR THE TOPPING
1 egg
1 × 15 ml (1 tablespoon) caster sugar
1 × 15 ml (1 tablespoon) butter, melted
1 × 15 ml (1 tablespoon) plain flour
1 × 20.5 cm (8 in) diameter metal quiche tin, or loose-bottomed flan tin or ring, 3.5 cm (1$\frac{1}{2}$ in) deep
OVEN TEMPERATURE 160°C (325°F, gas mark 3)
OVEN TIME 1 hour 10 mins (approximately)

FOR THE PASTRY CASE Sieve the flour and salt into a bowl. Cut the fat into small pieces and rub into the flour until the mixture resembles fine breadcrumbs. Stir in the caster sugar. Mix the egg yolk and water together and sprinkle on top of the crumbed mixture. Stir, using a broad-bladed knife, to form a stiff dough, adding a little extra water if necessary. Turn on to a lightly-floured work surface. Knead very lightly and roll out into a circle, about 3–4 mm ($\frac{1}{8}$ in) thick. Set the tin on a baking sheet. Roll the pastry over a floured rolling pin and use to line the tin, easing the pastry into the curve without stretching it. Press the pastry against the sides of the tin, keeping it an even thickness all the way round. Neaten the edge of the pastry by trimming with a knife. If the pastry has been rolled out to the correct thickness there will be very little excess. Prick the bottom of the pastry with a fork and line with grease-proof paper, or aluminium foil, and baking beans. Leave in a cold place to chill while preparing the filling.

FOR THE CURD FILLING Sieve or part sieve the cottage cheese, depending on whether a smooth or grainy texture is desired. Cream the butter and sugar until light and fluffy, then beat in the lemon rind, juice, mace, egg yolks, flour and cheese. Beat in the egg whites until stiff and fold in the curd cheese mixture. Pour into the prepared pastry case.

FOR THE TOPPING Combine all the ingredients

for the topping, stirring in the flour at the end to prevent lumps from forming. Beat until smooth and well mixed. Pour on top of the filling, being careful to cover the entire surface evenly.

Bake in the pre-heated oven until the cake is a deep golden-brown colour. It will have slightly risen and feel spongy but firm to the touch. Remove from the oven and leave to settle for 10 minutes before removing from the tin. The curd cake will shrink back slightly to its own level as it cools. Serve warm, rather than hot, with cream or natural yoghurt.

NOTE 50–100 g (2–4 oz) currants, raisins or sultanas were sometimes added to the filling, along with a spoonful of rose water or sack (sherry).

CARROT TARTS
Toirtíní Meacan Dearg

Following the success of the carrot pudding recipe (see page 153) I now use the carrot filling for individual pastry tarts, which look most attractive when served either hot or cold and are equally delicious. The filling is exactly the same as for the carrot pudding, although I have included both the recipe and method here for convenience.

SERVES 8
FOR THE PASTRY
225 g (8 oz) rich shortcrust pastry (see page 142)
FOR THE CARROT FILLING
1–1½ large carrots
6 egg yolks
100 g (4 oz) caster sugar
100 g (4 oz) butter, softened
2 × 15 ml (2 tablespoons) double cream
50 g (2 oz) ground almonds
Icing sugar to serve
8 × 11 × 2 cm (4 × ¾ in) quiche tins
OVEN TEMPERATURE AND TIME
Pastry: 190°C (375°F, gas mark 5), 16–20 minutes
Filling: 160°C (325°F, gas mark 3), 25 minutes

Begin by lining the quiche tins. Divide the pastry into 8 pieces and roll each into a circle just larger than the tin. I find it easier to work this way, rather than rolling the pastry into one large circle and then dividing it up. Because the measurements are so accurate it is necessary to keep the pastry in a round shape when it is being rolled, otherwise there will be too much waste and the pastry will not be the correct thickness. When the circles are large enough to line the base and sides of the tin, roll them over the rolling pin, then carefully unroll over the quiche tin, allowing the same overlap all round. Ease the pastry into the tin without pulling or stretching, almost pushing down the sides to keep them an even thickness. Flatten and neaten the pastry by pressing down on the edge of the tin with a floured thumb and nipping off the pastry. The edge around the quiche tin should have straight sides of an even thickness. The thickness should be no more than 6 mm (¼ in). Prick the base of the pastry with a fork, and line with a circle of aluminium foil to support the sides and stop the base from rising. Fill this with baking beans and repeat with the remaining tins.

Set the prepared pastry cases on a baking tray and bake in the pre-heated oven until set and very lightly coloured. Take care that the pastry does not scorch, otherwise it will taste bitter. The tart shells are now ready for filling. They will keep unfilled like this for several days in a metal or plastic box, or in a rigid container in the deepfreeze for several months.

While the pastry is cooking, prepare the filling. Wash and peel the carrots and cook in boiling water until just tender, then drain and grate on a coarse grater. Beat together the yolks and sugar, using a hand or electric whisk, until pale in colour and thick in texture. This will take about 3 minutes. Soften the butter to a consistency of thick cream, but do not melt, then add with the cream to the egg yolk mixture. Stir in the carrots, beating well to combine. Fold in the ground almonds and divide between the pastry cases. Return the pastry shells to a slightly cooler oven for 25 minutes until the filling is set. Remove from the tins, set on individual plates, dust with icing sugar and serve hot or cold with thick cream.

RICH SHORTCRUST PASTRY
Taosrán

This recipe is sufficient to line 2 × 20 × 4 cm (8 × 1½ in) quiche tins, to make 1 × 20 cm (8 in) double-crust tart or 8 × 11 cm (4½ × ¾ in) individual quiches.

25 g (8 oz) plain flour
Pinch of salt
100 g (4 oz) butter or block margarine
50 g (2 oz) solid white fat
2 egg yolks
2 × 15 ml (2 tablespoons) cold water

HAND-MADE METHOD Traditionally this pastry is made by sieving the flour and salt into a bowl, then cutting the fats into pieces the size of a walnut and rubbing these into the flour with the fingertips until the mixture resembles fine breadcrumbs. The egg yolks and water are mixed together with a fork and sprinkled on top of the crumbed mixture. This is then mixed together with a knife to form a firm dough. The pastry is generally chilled before rolling.

FOOD PROCESSOR METHOD The other method for making this pastry is in the food processor. Nowadays it is the method I generally prefer because of its convenience. Use the sharp metal blade to mix the fat and flour together to form crumbs. When doing this I use the 'pulse' mechanism on the machine to make sure that the mixture is not over-processed. It only takes a few seconds and is ready when the crumbs are fairly small but before the mixture starts to bind together. At this stage remove the processor lid, sprinkle on the egg yolk and water mixture and then process until the mixture is just beginning to stick together. At this stage, while it is still in a fairly loose crumbly state, turn on to a lightly-floured work surface and gather gently together by hand to form a dough. The pastry is now ready to use as required, although it does benefit from chilling for at least 30 minutes before use.

OATIES
Brioscaí Coirce

Oats in Ireland were not only used for making porridge. They were used for coating fish, making soup and a variety of biscuits including the famous Irish oatcakes (see page 136). This recipe is one of the very quick and easy oat biscuit recipes used in many houses today.

MAKES 24 biscuits
100 g (4 oz) butter
100 g (4 oz) caster sugar

100 g (4 oz) plain flour
100 g (4 oz) flake meal or porridge oats
25–50 g (1–2 oz) coconut
1 × 18 × 28 × 4 cm (7 × 11 × 1½ in) tin
OVEN TEMPERATURE AND TIME
180°C (350°F, gas mark 4) for 10 minutes, then
lower to 160°C (325°F, gas mark 3) for a further
20–25 minutes

Lightly grease the tin with a little oil or butter. Cream the butter and sugar until light and pale in colour. Stir in the remaining dry ingredients. Turn into the greased tin and flatten, pressing down with a fork. Bake in the pre-heated oven for 10 minutes to give the mixture a light colour, then reduce the temperature and continue for a further 20–25 minutes.

Remove the tin from the oven and cut into approximately 24 biscuits. Dust with caster sugar and leave to go completely cold before removing from the tin. Store in an airtight tin.

IRISH SHORTBREAD BISCUITS
Brioscaráin

These short buttery biscuits, of Scottish origin, have been a feature of Irish cookery for many hundreds of years and are one of the very popular biscuits served on tea tables all over the country. To cook thoroughly and retain their delicate pale colour, they require long slow cooking.

MAKES 20 finger biscuits, 8.5 cm × 2.5 cm (3½
× 1 in)
225 g (8 oz) butter
100 g (4 oz) caster sugar
50 g (2 oz) cornflour
275 g (10 oz) plain flour
Caster sugar for dusting
1 × oblong tin, 27 × 18 cm (10¾ × 7 in)
OVEN TEMPERATURE AND TIME
140°C (275°F, gas mark 1) for 30 minutes, then
reduce to 120°C (250°F, gas mark ½) for a further
1–1½ hours

Cream the butter and sugar together until light and fluffy in texture and pale in colour. Sieve in the cornflour and plain flour and mix well to combine. Press into the oblong tin and prick lightly all over with the prongs of a fork. Bake in the pre-heated oven for 30 minutes, then

reduce the temperature and continue cooking for a further 1–1½ hours, depending on whether a light or dark colour is required.

Remove from the oven, sprinkle with caster sugar and cut into 20 finger shaped biscuits. Leave to cool slightly in the tin before transferring to a cooling rack to go hard. Store in an airtight tin.

HONEY BISCUITS
Brioscaí Meala

These fine crisp biscuits with their rich taste of honey are similar to brandy snaps, but are not quite so hard.

MAKES 22 biscuits
100 g (4 oz) butter
6 × 15 ml (6 tablespoons) liquid honey
50 g (2 oz) caster sugar
1 × 5 ml (1 teaspoon) bicarbonate of soda
1 egg yolk
100 g (4 oz) plain flour
50 g (2 oz) granulated sugar
OVEN TEMPERATURE 180°C (350°F, gas mark 4)
OVEN TIME 15–20 minutes

Grease two baking sheets with oil or white fat. Melt the butter and pour into a large bowl. Stir in the honey, caster sugar, bicarbonate of soda and egg yolk. Gradually sieve in the flour and mix to form a firm dough. Wrap in foil and rest in the refrigerator for 5–10 minutes. Roll teaspoons of the mixture into balls on a lightly-floured work surface. Set 4 cm (1½ in) apart on the baking sheets to allow for expansion. Bake in the pre-heated oven until the biscuits are pale golden in colour. Remove from the baking tray immediately and leave to cool on a wire rack before storing in an airtight container.

CARAWAY BISCUITS
Brioscaí Cearbhais

Caraway, a popular spice in eighteenth-century Ireland, was used to make cakes and biscuits. For those who enjoy the taste, these crisp biscuits are delicious.

MAKES 18 biscuits
100 g (4 oz) butter
50 g (2 oz) caster sugar
1 egg, separated

2 × 15 ml (2 tablespoons) milk
225 g (8 oz) plain flour
2 × 15 ml (2 tablespoons) caraway seeds
Extra caster sugar to dust
A 6 cm (2½ in) cutter
OVEN TEMPERATURE 160°C (325°F, gas mark 3)
OVEN TIME 20–25 minutes

Cream the butter and sugar until pale in colour and light in texture. Beat in the egg yolk and milk then work in the flour and caraway seeds with your hand to make a stiff dough. Roll out on a lightly-floured work surface until about 3 mm (⅛ in) thick and cut into biscuits. Place these on a baking tray. Lightly beat the egg white and brush the top of each biscuit, dust with caster sugar and bake in the oven until lightly coloured. Remove the biscuits from the tray to a cooling rack. When cold store in an airtight tin.

SAFFRON BISCUITS
Brioscaí Cróch

Saffron was a popular spice in the eighteenth century and was used not only for its flavour but also for its colour. In this recipe from the 'receipt' book of Bishop Story of Clogher, 1742, it is used along with caraway seeds to make afternoon-tea biscuits.

MAKES 20 biscuits
100 g (4 oz) butter
75 g (3 oz) caster sugar
225 g (8 oz) plain flour
A generous pinch of powdered saffron or a 0.1 g
sachet
1 × 1.25 (¼ teaspoon) caraway seeds
1 × 15 ml (1 tablespoon) milk to bind
A 6 cm (2½ in) cutter
OVEN TEMPERATURE 180°C (350°F, gas mark 4)
OVEN TIME 20–25 minutes

Lightly grease a baking tray with oil or white fat. Cream the butter and sugar until pale in colour. Stir in the flour and caraway seeds. Dissolve the saffron in the milk and add to the other ingredients, mixing to a stiff dough by hand. Roll out to 3 mm (⅛ in) thick on a lightly-floured work surface and cut into biscuits. Transfer to the baking tray and bake in the pre-heated oven for 20–25 minutes.

PUDDING
AND DESSERT
RECIPES

CLOCKWISE, FROM TOP: *Saffron pudding (page 146), Irish apple cake (page 150), bread and butter pudding (page 146) and a little apple tart (page 150).*

In Ireland, just as no dish is complete without meat and potatoes, no meal is complete without the pudding or dessert – no matter how simple. Over the years both the style and the variety of these has changed. Today, in addition to the so-called traditional puddings and desserts, there are many which have found their way into Ireland along with the invaders and visitors who have settled here over the centuries.

Wild fruits and berries such as blackberries, raspberries, strawberries, sloes, elderberries, bilberries, cranberries and rowan berries have long been gathered and eaten with relish, either simply on their own, with honey or cream, or made into pastry pies. Walnuts, hazelnuts and filberts were also gathered and enjoyed in their natural state, as well as being made into biscuits and cakes. Apple orchards were introduced by the Normans in the twelfth century to the south-east of the country, and flourished in Counties Armagh, Down and Fermanagh. Apples were used principally in pastry tarts and pies, as a filling for potato bread, as a topping and ingredient in fruit bread and cakes, and baked whole and served like the other fruits with honey and cream.

Many poets and storytellers describe Ireland as a land of milk and honey, and both were abundantly found and widely used in many puddings and desserts. Milk was combined with oats to make stirabout (porridge), which was served not only for breakfast but for dessert, supper and often at other times of the day with cream and honey. Milk or cream was combined with eggs, flavoured with saffron, cinnamon, honey and nutmeg, and mixed into plain custards; baked with bread and dried fruit for bread pudding; and added to rice and made into blancmange. Cream was also combined with fruit to make fools, mousses and soufflés and with carrageen to make jelly creams, often sweetened and flavoured with heather-flavoured honey.

Suet and sponge puddings, either plain or rich with fruit or jam, were wrapped up in a cloth or packed into a basin and boiled for many hours until spongy and moist. Ice creams were mixed and frozen; pastry cases were made and filled with thick rich curd cheese; and possets, syllabubs and jellies were created. Whether it be for family supper or celebration feast, there was always a pudding to suit the occasion.

SAFFRON PUDDING
Maróg Chróch

This rich rice pudding, flavoured and coloured with saffron and enriched with eggs and milk, is a far cry from the tinned variety more commonly used today. This recipe is an adaptation from the eighteenth-century manuscript of Bishop Story from County Down and is a wonderful combination of rice pudding and egg custard.

SERVES 4–6
100 g (4 oz) short-grain pudding rice
900 ml (1½ pints) full cream milk
Large pinch of saffron powder
50 g (2 oz) butter
75 g (3 oz) caster sugar
1 lemon, grated rind
Pinch of ground cloves
2 eggs, size 3, beaten
Grated nutmeg
1 × 15 ml (1 tablespoon) lemon peel, cut in very thin strips
1 × 1 litre (2 pint) baking dish, well buttered
OVEN TEMPERATURE 150°C (300°F, gas mark 2)
OVEN TIME 40–45 minutes

Put the rice and milk into a saucepan with the saffron powder and slowly bring to simmering point. Cook very gently for 10–15 minutes until the rice is almost tender. Add the butter, sugar, lemon rind and cloves, stirring until the sugar has dissolved and the butter melted. Leave until cold before stirring in the beaten eggs. Pour into the well-buttered ovenproof dish, sprinkle with a little nutmeg and bake in the pre-heated oven for 30 minutes, then reduce the temperature to 120°C (250°F, gas mark ½) for the last 10–15 minutes until the custard is lightly set. Serve hot or cold, decorated with fine shreds of lemon peel and a little cream.

BREAD AND BUTTER PUDDING
Maróg aráin agus Ime

A popular recipe in the eighteenth- and nineteenth-century manuscript 'receipt' books, which makes full use of the excellent dairy produce so readily available throughout Ireland. This is my adaptation of the recipe from Lady Rivers' manuscript 'receipt' book, 1750, from County Cavan.

SERVES 4
350 ml (12 fl oz) milk
300 ml (10 fl oz) double cream
Pinch of salt
1 × 5 ml (1 teaspoon) vanilla essence
5 eggs, size 2
75 g (3 oz) caster sugar
3–4 small bread rolls, 150–175 g (5–6 oz)
15 g (½ oz) butter, melted
25 g (1 oz) sultanas, soaked in 2 × 15 ml (2
tablespoons) cold water
4 × 15 ml (4 tablespoons) apricot jam
1 × 15 ml (1 tablespoon) water
Icing sugar to dust
1 × ovenproof dish, 1.5 litre (2½ pint) capacity,
approx. 4–5 cm (1½–2 in) deep
OVEN TEMPERATURE 150°C (300°F, gas mark 2)
OVEN TIME 25–30 minutes

Combine the milk, cream and salt in a saucepan and heat to simmering. Stir in the vanilla essence. Mix together the eggs and caster sugar in a large bowl until well blended. Add the simmering milk and cream, stirring continually to form a smooth creamy mixture.

Cut the rolls into 5 mm (¼ in) slices and arrange these slightly overlapping in a lightly-buttered ovenproof dish. Sprinkle the drained and soaked sultanas on top. Melt the butter and brush over the bread. Pour on the milk, cream and egg mixture and place the dish in a roasting tin of simmering water and cook in the pre-heated oven for 25–35 minutes until the custard is just set. When cooked, remove from the water bath. Melt the apricot jam with 1 × 15 ml (1 tablespoon) water in a small saucepan, sieve and brush on top of the pudding. Sprinkle with icing sugar and serve warm, either on its own or with poached or bottled fruit, or ice cream.

FRUIT FOOLS

The original fool goes back as far as the fifteenth and sixteenth centuries and consists of crushed fruit mixed with cream. Any kind of fresh fruit, such as apricots, blackberries, damsons, plums, raspberries, rhubarb and gooseberries, can be made into a pulp and used as the base for a fool. However, the water and sugar quantities must be adjusted to allow for the varying levels of acidity, natural sugar and water content in individual fruits. Some recipes combine the

fruit with cream only, which gives a very loose texture; others combine the fruit with a rich egg custard, which I personally prefer. These light creamy concoctions are presented chilled, usually arranged in tall individual glass dishes, and served with sponge fingers or shortbread biscuits.

GOOSEBERRY FOOL
Spionán ar Uachtar

SERVES 6
900 g (2 lb) gooseberries
65 ml (2½ fl oz) water
175–225 g (6–8 oz) caster sugar
2 sprigs elderflower or 2 × 15 ml (2 tablespoons)
orange-flower water or elderberry wine
300 ml (10 fl oz) double cream
FOR THE CUSTARD
250 ml (8 fl oz) milk
3 egg yolks
2 × 15 ml (2 tablespoons) caster sugar
1 × 15 ml (1 tablespoon) cornflour
TO DECORATE
Elderflowers

Bread and butter pudding.

Top and tail the gooseberries and simmer in the water with the elderflowers until soft. I generally do this in the microwave oven at 60 per cent power for 10–12 minutes. Remove the elderflowers and pour the fruit into a sieve, set over a bowl, to remove the excess juice. This is no longer required but does make a refreshing drink when slightly sweetened. Transfer the fruit to a bowl and stir in the sugar to sweeten according to taste. Leave to go cold.

While the fruit is cooling, prepare the egg custard. Bring the milk to boiling point. Mix together the egg yolks, sugar and cornflour, then pour on the hot milk, stirring continuously. Return to a clean saucepan and cook gently over a medium heat until the custard thickens. Pour into a bowl and leave to go cold.

Mix the gooseberry pulp with the custard, whip the cream until thick and holding its shape, then gently fold into the fruit mixture. Spoon into small glasses or dishes and chill well before decorating with elderflowers. Serve with shortbread biscuits (see page 143).

RHUBARB FOOL
Biabhóg ar Uachtar

SERVES 6
900 g (2 lb) rhubarb
50 g (2 oz) caster sugar
1 × 5 ml (1 teaspoon) ground ginger
300 ml (10 fl oz) double cream
FOR THE CUSTARD
250 ml (8 fl oz) milk
3 egg yolks
1 × 15 ml (1 tablespoon) caster sugar
1 × 15 ml (1 tablespoon) cornflour
TO DECORATE
4 pieces of preserved ginger, cut into chunks

Trim and wipe the rhubarb and cut into 1 cm (½ in) chunks. Put into a large saucepan with the caster sugar and ginger. Cover with a lid and cook very gently over a low heat until the rhubarb is soft but not mushy. I generally do this in the microwave oven at 60 per cent power for 10–12 minutes. Place the rhubarb in a plastic sieve over a bowl to drain off the juice; this is no longer required. Transfer the rhubarb to a bowl and leave to go cold.

While the rhubarb is cooling, prepare the custard. Bring the milk to boiling point. Mix together the yolks, sugar and cornflour until pale and smooth, then pour on the milk, stirring continuously. Return the liquid to the saucepan and cook gently over a medium heat until it thickens. Pour into a bowl and also leave to go cold. Mix the rhubarb with the cold custard. Whip the cream until it is thick and holds its shape, then gently fold into the fruit mixture. Spoon into small glasses or dishes and chill well before decorating with pieces of ginger.

LEMON POSSET
Milseog Liomóide

Although traditionally served as a light meal to invalids, these nutritious drinks found their way into many of the elegant eighteenth-century dining rooms where, with a few additions, they

CLOCKWISE, FROM TOP RIGHT: *Carrageen mould with rhubarb compote, carrageen mould with blackcurrant compote, St Brendan's syllabub and lemon posset.*

were served for dessert. They were generally served in specially-made china posset dishes with covers, or elegant glasses.

SERVES 6
300 ml (10 fl oz) double cream
1 large lemon, grated rind and juice
50 ml (2 fl oz) dry white wine
2 egg whites
50 g (2 oz) caster sugar
Crystallised lemon slices to garnish

Put the cream in a large mixing bowl and whisk until just beginning to thicken, then very gradually add the lemon rind and juice along with the wine, taking care not to over beat as the mixture will curdle. When the mixture forms a trail across the surface, beat together the egg whites and sugar until very thick and solid like a meringue mixture. Gently fold into the cream mixture until well mixed. Spoon into individual glass dishes and decorate with crystallised lemon slices.

NOTE This mixture is so stable it will hold in the refrigerator for 3 days without separating.

LEMON SYLLABUB
Siollabab Liomóide
The syllabub dessert dates from medieval times and originated in England. It appears in a number of Irish manuscript 'receipt' books of the eighteenth and nineteenth centuries and was obviously a popular dessert at this time. Syllabub is made with cream whipped until thick with fruit juice, brandy and wine.

SERVES 4
120 ml (4 fl oz) Sauterne or sweet white wine
2 × 15 ml (2 tablespoons) whiskey or brandy
3 × 15 ml (3 tablespoons) lemon juice
100 g (4 oz) caster sugar
300 ml (10 fl oz) double cream
1 × 5 ml (1 teaspoon) ground cinnamon
A few lemon slices to garnish

Combine the wine, whiskey, or brandy, and sugar in a bowl. Whisk with an electric beater for a minute to dissolve the sugar, then gradually add the cream, whisking all the time until the mixture begins to thicken and forms peaks and a heavy trail across the surface. This takes about 3–4 minutes. It is important not to over beat as the mixture will curdle and go grainy in texture. Spoon into long-stemmed glasses or dishes and cover and chill for 4–24 hours to develop the flavours. Just before serving, dust with a light sprinkling of cinnamon and decorate with a thin slice of lemon.

NOTE Orange can be used instead of lemon for flavouring. However, since it is not so strong, the grated rind of the orange needs to be added along with the juice.

ST BRENDAN'S SYLLABUB
Siollabab Naomh Breandáin
This is one of the new Irish desserts – a variation on the popular medieval syllabub – made from one of Ireland's most popular cream liqueurs, St Brendan's.

SERVES 4
50 ml (2 fl oz) Sauterne or sweet white wine
120 ml (4 fl oz) St Brendan's or Baileys liqueur
Juice of 1 lemon
50 g (2 oz) caster sugar
300 ml (10 fl oz) double cream
Slices of lemon to decorate

Combine the wine, liqueur, lemon juice and sugar in a bowl. Whisk with an electric beater for a minute to dissolve the sugar, then gradually add the cream, whisking all the time until the liquid begins to thicken. This mixture will look curdled at first, but with whisking will improve in texture. However, it cannot be whisked as stiffly as the true syllabub as it will return to its curdled state. When the mixture holds its own shape, spoon into long-stemmed glasses or dishes, cover and chill for 4–24 hours to develop the flavours. Before serving, decorate with thin slices of lemon.

CARRAGEEN MOULD
Múnla Carraigín
Carrageen is a branching mucilaginous seaweed found on the rocks all over Ireland. In some areas, particularly on the northern and southern coasts round Donegal and Cork, it is gathered and sold as 'Irish moss', 'sea moss', or simply carrageen. It is picked from the farthest rocks at low water, during the spring tides in May and June, where it is almost always covered by the sea. It is then spread on the rocks, or the short grass of the cliff tops, where it is dried and its dark green or purple colour bleached in the sun.

Carrageen is a rich source of agar jelly and is used for thickening sweet and savoury dishes. It is available from health food and other specialist shops.

SERVES 4–6
40 g (1½ oz) dried carrageen moss
3 strips lemon rind
900 ml (1½ pints) milk
1 egg, separated
2–3 × 15 ml (2–3 tablespoons) caster sugar
1 × 1.25 ml (¼ teaspoon) vanilla essence
1 glass, china or metal mould of 900 ml (1½ pint) capacity, or 8 × 85 ml (3 fl oz) individual moulds

Put the carrageen moss, lemon rind and milk into a saucepan and slowly bring to the boil. Reduce the heat and simmer gently for 15–20 minutes until the carrageen exudes jelly. Meanwhile mix the egg yolk and caster sugar together until pale in colour and add the vanilla essence. Pour the carrageen and milk mixture through a sieve on to the sugar and egg yolks, stirring all the time and pushing the jelly through the sieve. Transfer this mixture to a clean saucepan, return to a gentle heat and cook like a custard until the mixture coats the back of a wooden spoon. Transfer to a bowl and leave until cold. Whisk the egg white until very stiff and gently fold into the cold carrageen mixture. Pour into the wetted mould, or moulds, and leave to set in the refrigerator. Turn out of the mould on to a decorative plate or individual serving plates and serve with a fruit *compote* made from rhubarb or berry fruits, or an Irish whiskey sauce (see page 153). **FOR HONEY CARRAGEEN** substitute 3 × 15 ml (3 tablespoons) liquid honey for the sugar.

GOOSEBERRY CRUMBLE
Grabhar Spíonán
Fruit crumbles are one of the most popular family puddings and are served throughout the year. They are particularly good when made with fresh local fruit like rhubarb, apples and gooseberries. If rhubarb is being used, trim, wash and cut it into 1 cm (½ in) pieces before

putting it in the pie dish with the sugar. For an apple crumble, peel and core Bramley apples, then slice thinly.

SERVES 6
450 g (1 lb) gooseberries
50–75 g (2–3 oz) caster sugar
FOR THE CRUMBLE TOPPING
225 g (8 oz) plain or wholewheat flour
50 g (2 oz) jumbo or porridge oats
100 g (4 oz) butter
100 g (4 oz) soft brown sugar
1 × 800 ml (1½ pint) capacity ovenproof pie dish
OVEN TEMPERATURE 180°C (350°F, gas mark 4)
OVEN TIME 40–45 minutes

Top and tail the gooseberries, place them in the pie dish and sprinkle the caster sugar over them. Put the flour into a mixing bowl and rub in the butter until the mixture looks crumbly and the fat has been dispersed fairly evenly. Stir in the oats and brown sugar and mix well. Sprinkle on top of the fruit in an even layer. Bake in the pre-heated oven for 40–45 minutes until the top is very pale gold. Serve with cream.

IRISH APPLE CAKE
Císte Úll

This fruit tart or 'cake', as it is often called in Ireland, is made from rich shortcrust pastry and packed with Bramley apples. It is enjoyed throughout the year in most Irish homes, but is traditionally eaten at Hallowe'en on 31 October, when 'charms' such as rings and coins are wrapped in paper and buried in the middle of the cake.

This quantity is sufficient to make a 25 cm (10 in) double-crust tart on a 25 cm (10 in) enamel, glass or china plate. I prefer to bake pastry tarts on an enamel plate as the metal conducts the heat better and ensures that the pastry is cooked and crisp.

SERVES 6–8
FOR THE RICH SHORTCRUST PASTRY
250 g (10 oz) plain flour
Pinch of salt
150 g (5 oz) butter or hard margarine
75 g (3 oz) hard white fat
1 × 15 ml (1 tablespoon) caster sugar
1 egg yolk (reserve the egg white for glazing the top of the cake)
4–5 × 15 ml (4–5 tablespoons) cold water
FOR THE FILLING
1–1.5 kg (2–3 lb) Bramley cooking apples
5 × 15 ml (5 tablespoons) granulated sugar
6 whole cloves
A dust of cinnamon powder
'Charms' (rings or small coins wrapped in greaseproof paper)
OVEN TEMPERATURE 200°C (400°F, gas mark 6)
OVEN TIME 30–40 minutes

Begin by making the pastry: sieve the flour and salt into a large mixing bowl, then cut the fat into the flour and rub in until as fine as breadcrumbs. Stir in the sugar. Mix the egg yolk with water, sprinkle over the top of the crumbed mixture and mix with a knife to form a dough. Work only long enough to form a ball, wrap this in polythene and allow to rest in the refrigerator for about 30 minutes.

Divide the pastry in two, use one half to line the plate and the other to make the lid. Roll out the pastry for the base into a circle, about 4 cm (1½ in) larger than the diameter of the plate. Cut a circular strip, about 2.5 cm (1 in) in diameter, from around the outer edge of the pastry disc. Line the plate with the large circle of pastry, easing it into the plate without stretching it. Brush the edges with lightly beaten egg white (reserved from making the pastry) and lay the 2.5 cm (1 in) pastry strip on top, both pastry edges meeting. Press the edges together. Roll out the second half of the pastry until just large enough to cover the top of the pie.

Now prepare the filling: peel, core and thinly slice the apples, then layer on top of the pastry base, leaving the rim of the pastry round the edge of the plate free from apples. Sprinkle a mixture of sugar and cinnamon between the layers, finishing with a layer of apples. Arrange the 'charms', wrapped in paper, along with the cloves among the apples. Brush the top of the pastry with the remaining egg white and sprinkle with caster sugar. Make a slit in the centre of the pastry and bake in a hot oven for 30–40 minutes until the apples are tender and the pastry is golden brown. Remove the tart from the oven, sprinkle with more caster sugar and serve hot or cold with whipped cream.

RHUBARB TART This is made in exactly the same way. The rhubarb is cut into 2 cm (¾ in) lengths and tossed in 2 × 15 ml (2 tablespoons) cornflour before being used to fill the tart. The cornflour helps to thicken the rhubarb juice.

LITTLE APPLE TARTS
Toirtíní Aonair Úll

These little tarts are delicious. A rich shortcrust pastry base holds a mixture of scented Bramley apples and dried fruit and is served on a pool of butterscotch sauce. Although this dish could not, as yet, be described as traditionally Irish, it forms part of the new style of Irish cooking which uses the indigenous produce of the country and a light and modern style of cooking and presentation.

SERVES 4
100 g (4 oz) rich shortcrust pastry (see page 142)
FOR THE FILLING
350 g (12 oz) Bramley apples, peeled and cored
3 × 15 ml (3 tablespoons) apricot jam
Grated rind of 1 lemon
1 × 15 ml (1 tablespoon) orange peel, finely chopped
Juice of ½ orange
2 × 15 ml (2 tablespoons) sultanas
2 × 15 ml (2 tablespoons) currants
FOR THE BUTTERSCOTCH SAUCE
50 g (2 oz) demerara sugar
25 g (1 oz) unsalted butter
300 ml (10 fl oz) double cream
TO FINISH
A few very thin slices of red-skinned dessert apple
A few mint sprigs
2 × 15 ml (2 tablespoons) double cream, whipped until thick
Icing sugar, to dust
4 × 11 × 2 cm (4½ × ¾ in) quiche tins
OVEN TEMPERATURE 190°C (375°F, gas mark 5)
OVEN TIME 16–20 minutes

Use the pastry to line the individual quiche tins and bake 'blind' until completely cooked and dried out (for detailed instructions see page 142, carrot tarts). Leave to go cold.

While the tart shells are cooking, prepare the apple filling and butterscotch sauce. Quarter the apples and slice them thinly. Put into a pan

CLOCKWISE, FROM TOP RIGHT: *Rhubarb fool (page 148), gooseberry fool (page 147), stewed gooseberries and lemon syllabub (page 149).*

with the apricot jam, lemon rind, orange peel and juice, sultanas and raisins. Cook over a gentle heat until the apples are soft but still holding their shape. Remove the pan from the heat and allow to go cold.

Prepare the butterscotch sauce by first melt-

ing the butter in a heavy saucepan, then add the demerara sugar and continue to cook over a very gentle heat, stirring with a wooden spoon until the sugar dissolves and the syrup begins to turn a pale straw colour. This will take about 1 minute. The mixture may look slightly curdled. Very gradually add the cream, stirring all the time to combine with the sugar. Bring gently to simmering point, making sure all the sugar has completely dissolved. Remove the pan from the heat, pour the sauce into a bowl and leave in the

refrigerator until cold before using as a base for the apple tarts.

Use individual medium-sized flat plates to serve the tarts. To assemble the dish, place 2–3 tablespoons of butterscotch sauce at one side of each of four plates. Remove the pastry shells from their tins and set on the plates, half on and half off the sauce. Fill each tart shell with the fruit mixture, decorating each with a few small slices of sweet red apple and a piece of variegated mint or other herb for colour. Dust the tart and the side of the plate with a little icing sugar (this will only show up if using a dark-coloured plate for service).

Fill a homemade paper icing bag with a few tablespoons of cream or thick natural yoghurt and pipe a fine line round the butterscotch sauce, about 1 cm ($\frac{1}{2}$ in) from the edge. Then, using a skewer or cocktail stick, make 'comma' shapes through the cream to give a feathered effect. Serve chilled.

BLACKBERRY AND APPLE TART
Toirtín Úll agus Sméara Dubh

Blackberries and Bramley apples, two of the most popular autumn fruits, are combined in one of Ireland's most popular desserts, a rich shortcrust-pastry tart. This quantity is sufficient to make a 25 cm (10 in) double-crust tart on a 25 cm (10 in) enamel or glass plate.

SERVES 6–8
FOR THE RICH SHORTCRUST PASTRY
250 g (10 oz) plain flour
Pinch of salt
150 g (5 oz) butter or hard margarine
75 g (3 oz) hard white fat
1 × 15 ml (1 tablespoon) caster sugar
1 egg yolk (reserve the egg white for glazing the top of the cake)
4–5 × 15 ml (4–5 tablespoons) cold water
FOR THE FILLING
2 large cooking apples, or about 675 g (1$\frac{1}{2}$ lb) windfalls
450 g (1 lb) blackberries
5 × 15 ml (5 tablespoons) granulated sugar
OVEN TEMPERATURE 200°C (400°F, gas mark 6)
OVEN TIME 30–40 minutes

Begin by making the pastry: sieve the flour and salt into a large mixing bowl, then cut the fat

Blackberry mousse.

into the flour and rub in until as fine as breadcrumbs. Stir in the sugar. Mix the egg yolk with water, sprinkle over the top of the crumbed mixture and mix with a knife to form a dough. Work only long enough to form a ball, wrap in polythene and allow to rest in the refrigerator for about 30 minutes.

Divide the pastry in two, using one half to line the plate and the other to make the lid. Roll out the pastry for the base into a circle, about 4 cm (1½ in) larger than the diameter of the plate, and cut a circular strip about 2.5 cm (1 in) in diameter from around the outer edge of the pastry disc. Line the plate with the large circle of pastry, easing it on to the plate without stretching. Brush the edges with lightly beaten egg white and lay the 2.5 cm (1 in) pastry strip on top, both pastry edges meeting. Press the edges together. Roll out the second half of the pastry until just large enough to cover the top of the pie.

Now prepare the filling: peel, core and thinly slice the apples. Wash and pick over the blackberries carefully, then drain and dry well on absorbent kitchen paper. Arrange a mixture of the apples and blackberries together on top of the pastry base, sprinkling with sugar. Cover with the second circle of pastry, sealing the edges together with a little of the egg white. Brush the top of the pastry lightly with the remaining egg white and dust with caster sugar. Make a slit in the centre of the pastry and bake in the pre-heated oven until the fruit is tender and the pastry crisp and a light golden colour. Sprinkle with caster sugar and serve hot or cold with pouring cream.

BLACKBERRY MOUSSE
Cúr Sméara Dubh

When the autumn blackberries are at the height of their season, they can quickly be made into this simple mousse or frozen to be used at another time. The mousse itself is best not frozen because it contains gelatin, which becomes rubbery when subjected to extreme cold.

SERVES 8
450 g (1 lb) blackberries
100 g (4 oz) caster sugar
Juice of a small lemon
15 g (½ oz) powdered gelatin
4 × 15 ml (4 tablespoons) water
150 ml (5 fl oz) double cream, whipped
2 egg whites

Put the blackberries, carefully picked and cleaned, into a saucepan with the caster sugar and lemon juice. Place over a low heat and simmer gently for about 10 minutes. As the fruit heats, the juices will flow. Cool and then press through a nylon sieve into a large mixing bowl. This purée can be prepared in advance and frozen if required.

Put the gelatin in a teacup with the water and leave to soak for about 5 minutes, then put the teacup into a small saucepan containing a little boiling water. Stir the gelatin until dissolved, then slowly pour into the blackberry purée, whisking all the time. Just as the purée shows signs of thickening, whisk the egg whites until beginning to hold their shape but not too stiff. Fold the lightly whipped cream into the purée and then the egg whites until evenly blended. Pour into individual serving dishes and chill until set. Decorate each with a rosette of cream and a whole blackberry.

BLACKBERRY SAUCE
Anlann Sméara Dubh

This delicious blackberry sauce should be made from the best blackberries of the season, gathered before they become hard and woody and 'have the devil in them'. The sauce can be either sweet or savoury and is the perfect accompaniment to dishes like lemon soufflé, tarragon jelly and breast of duck, pheasant or venison.

SERVES 6–8
SAVOURY BLACKBERRY SAUCE
750 g (1½ lb) large ripe blackberries
8 × 15 ml (8 tablespoons) wine vinegar
8 × 15 ml (8 tablespoons) red wine (Cabernet Sauvignon is ideal as it has a strong fruity flavour)
150 ml (5 fl oz) stock
Salt and milled black pepper
Pinch of sugar

Pick over the blackberries, removing any discoloured or bad ones. Put into a bowl with the wine vinegar and the wine. Crush the berries and leave to stand in a cool place overnight. Next day rub through a nylon sieve. Add the stock and the seasoning with a pinch of sugar to counteract the sharpness. Transfer to a saucepan, bring to the boil and serve hot with duck, pheasant, rabbit or venison.

SWEET BLACKBERRY SAUCE
750 g (1½ lb) large ripe blackberries
350 g (12 oz) icing sugar, sieved
2 × 15 ml (2 tablespoons) Crème de Cassis
(blackcurrant liqueur)
Juice of ½ lemon

Pick over the blackberries, removing any discoloured or bad ones. Purée the fruit with the sieved icing sugar, then force through a fine nylon sieve. Add more sieved icing sugar if necessary, along with the lemon juice and liqueur. Serve with hot or cold fruit soufflés, meringues and fresh berry fruits.

HONEY WHISKEY SAUCE
Anlann Meala agus Uisce Beatha
This is a delicious accompaniment to Carrageen mould (see page 149).

SERVES 4
MAKES 250 ml (8 fl oz)
4 oz cottage cheese, sieved
50 ml (2 fl oz) whiskey
2 × 15 ml (2 tablespoons) liquid honey
100 ml (4 fl oz) double cream

Bring the whiskey and honey to the boil. Stir in the cream while still hot, remove from the heat and cool to room temperature before pouring on top of the sieved cheese a little at a time, whisking between additions.

CARROT PUDDING
Maróg Mheacan Dearg
In the 1700s a popular way to use carrots was in a sweet pie or pudding. This one comes from the 1709 'receipt' book of Charles Echlin from County Down.

Take three large carrots give them a good warming in boiling water then take them out and grate them take the yolk of twelve eggs very well beat half a pound of sugar half a pound of butter melted three or four spoonfuls of sweet cream beat all the ingredients together you must put puff pastry round your dish you may improve

it by putting in a quarter of a pound of blanched almonds pounded let the sugar be the last thing going in.

In testing this recipe, I found that the quantities were sufficient to make two pies in 750 ml (1¼ pint) pie dishes. The mixture is very rich and would serve 8–12 people. For this reason I have halved the recipe.

SERVES 4–6
FOR THE CARROT PUDDING FILLING
2 medium carrots, approx. 350 g (12 oz)
6 egg yolks
100 g (4 oz) butter
2 × 15 ml (2 tablespoons) double cream
50 g (2 oz) ground almonds
FOR THE PASTRY
225 g (8 oz) puff or flaky pastry
1 small egg, to glaze
1 × 750 ml (1¼ pint) pie dish with rim
OVEN TEMPERATURE AND TIME
200°C (400°F, gas mark 6) for 20 minutes, then reduce to 180°C (350°F, gas mark 4) for a further 35 minutes

Wash and peel the carrots, leave whole and cook in boiling water until just tender. This will take about 8 minutes. Drain the carrots and dry off any excess moisture. Grate on a coarse grater. Beat together the egg yolks and sugar with an electric whisk until rich and thick in texture and pale cream in colour. Beat in the cream. Soften the butter until the consistency of thick cream, but not melted. Beat into the egg and sugar mixture along with the carrots. Stir in the ground almonds. A few drops of orange-flower water can also be added. Pile into the pie dish.

Roll out the pastry thinly into a rectangle. Cut an oval, the same shape as the top of the pie dish but 2 cm (¾ in) bigger. Cut an oval out of the centre of the pastry, the exact size of the pie dish, leaving a 2 cm (¾ in) ring of pastry. Moisten the edge of the pie dish with water or beaten egg. Set the pastry ring on top and brush this with water or egg. Lift the pastry lid on top. Press the pastry edges together and seal with a knife. Flute or decorate the edges, brush the pastry top with beaten egg to glaze. Make a cut in the centre of the pie to allow the steam to

escape and set on a baking tray. Bake in the pre-heated oven for 20 minutes, then reduce the temperature and bake for a further 35 minutes until the pastry is risen and golden. By this time the pudding should be set.

The pudding is delicious, with a texture somewhere between an almond cake and a custard. It is very rich, so only small servings are required.

STIRABOUT OR PORRIDGE
Brachán
Up until the introduction of the potato, the staple food of the vast majority of the Irish people was 'stirabout', better known as porridge. Stirabout was made from oatmeal, wheatmeal and barley meal: oatmeal was the most generally used, followed by wheatmeal, while porridge made from barley meal was considered to be greatly inferior. Poor people made their porridge with water or a combination of buttermilk and water, while those who were better off made it from cow's or sheep's milk, the latter being considered a great delicacy.

The porridge of the poor was eaten with sour milk, while those of greater means enjoyed it with fresh milk, butter and honey. It was always made very thick and with salt. Nowadays, the type of oats, liquid ingredients, flavourings and consistency are all a matter of personal preference. I like to use a medium oatmeal along with fresh milk and salt to give a thick but not solid consistency. I serve it with honey or sugar and fresh milk. Occasionally I would make it with cream, if there was an excess in the fridge.

300 ml (10 fl oz) milk
Pinch of salt
25 g (1 oz) medium oatmeal, or approx. 5 × 15 ml
(5 tablespoons)
Milk and sugar, or honey, for serving.

Bring the milk to the boil in a small saucepan, add the salt and oatmeal. Return to the boil, stirring all the time. Then reduce the heat and simmer for about 5–6 minutes, stirring occasionally. Some people prefer a well-cooked porridge and allow about 10–15 minutes. If it seems too thick, add a little more liquid.

RECIPE NOTES

Follow either imperial or metric measures for the recipes, not a combination of each.

All spoon measures given are for either imperial or metric measuring spoons. Such spoons are readily available and give accurate measurements for small quantities. Spoons should be level.

Vegetables used in the recipes are either described by size or weight.
i.e. onions, carrots and parsnips

large: 225 g (8 oz)
medium: 175 g (6 oz)
small: 100 g (4 oz)

The fat traditionally used in Irish cooking is lard, dripping, bacon fat, goose fat or butter. The use of polyunsaturated oils such as sunflower and olive oil are recent introductions. Such oils can be substituted for frying, where suitable, along with solid vegetable margarines. However, the results may differ slightly, as will the flavour.

Plain flour has been used in the recipes unless otherwise stated.

Salt is used in most of the savoury recipes as a flavour enhancer, but it can obviously be omitted for those on a low- or no-salt diet.

Where sizes of cartons, packets or tins have been given, they have been taken directly off the products used in testing the recipes. Use the nearest size available to you.

250–300 ml (8–10 fl oz) soup is allowed per serving.

The following is a guide to the number of servings obtained from a joint of meat:

1–1.5 kg (2–3 lb) joint of meat serves approximately 4
1.5–2 kg (3–4 lb) joint of meat serves approximately 6–8
2–3 kg (4–6 lb) joint of meat serves approximately 12
1.75–2 kg ($3\frac{1}{2}$–4 lb) chicken serves 4

Bouquet garni: a bunch of herbs consisting of a bay leaf, a sprig of thyme and a few parsley stalks used for flavouring stocks, soups and stews.

1 × 15 ml (1 tablespoon) plain flour or 1 × 15 ml (1 tablespoon) fat will thicken 200 ml (7 fl oz) of liquid.

BIBLIOGRAPHY

BELL JONATHAN, 'Hiring Fairs in Ulster', *Ulster Folk Life*, vol. 25, 1979

BELL, JONATHAN & WATSON, MERVYN, *Irish Farming Implements and Techniques 1750–1900*, John Donald, Edinburgh 1986
Farming in Ulster: Historic Photographs of Ulster Farming and Food, Friar's Bush Press, Belfast 1988

BOLGER, PATRICK, *The Irish Co-Operative Movement*, The Institute of Public Administration, Dublin 1977

BUCHANAN, DONALD H., 'Calendar Customs', *Ulster Folk Life*, vols 7–9, 1961–3

BURDY, SAMUEL A. B., *The Life of Philip Skelton*, The Clarendon Press, Oxford 1814

CAMBRENSIS, GIRALDUS, *Topography of Ireland* (Trans. by John O'Meard), Dundalgan Press, Dundalk 1951

CARBERY, MARY, *The Farm by Lough Gur*, Cathone Book Club, London 1938

COSMOPOLITE, A., *The Sportsman in Ireland*, vol. I and II, Henry Colburn, London 1897

COYNE, WILLIAM P. (ed.), *Ireland, Industrial and Agricultural*, Browne & Nolan, Dublin, Cork, Belfast 1902

CRAWFORD, DR W. H., 'The Patron, or Festival of St. Kevin at the Seven Churches, Glendalough, Co. Wicklow, 1813', *Ulster Folk Life*, vol. 32, 1986

CROHAN, TOMÁS Ó, *The Islandman* (trans. by Robin Flower), Oxford University Press, Oxford 1978

CULLEN, L. M., *Life in Ireland*, Batsford, London 1968
The Emergence of Modern Ireland, 1600–1900, Gill & Macmillan, Dublin 1983

CULLEN, NUALA, 'Women and the Preparation of Food in Eighteenth-Century Ireland', *Woman in Early Modern Ireland*, MacCurtain & O'Dowd (eds), Edinburgh University Press, Edinburgh 1991

DANAHER, KEVIN, *The Quarter Days in Irish Tradition*, Mercier Press, Cork and Dublin 1959
In Ireland Long Ago, Mercier Press, Cork and Dublin 1962
The Pleasant Land of Ireland, Mercier Press, Cork and Dublin 1970
The Year in Ireland, Mercier Press, Cork and Dublin 1972
The Hearth and Stool and All: Irish Rural Households, Mercier Press, Cork and Dublin 1985

DAY, ANGELIQUE (ed.), *Letters from Georgian Ireland*, Friar's Bush Press, Belfast 1991

DERRICKE, JOHN, *The Image of Ireland*, John Day, London 1581

DONNELLY, JAMES S., Jr., 'Cork Market: Its Role in the Nineteenth Century Irish Butter Trade', *Studia Hibernica* No. 11, 1971

DUBOURDIEU, REV. JOHN, *Statistical Survey of the County of Down*, Graisberry & Campbell, Dublin 1802

EVANS, E. ESTYN, *Mourne Country*, Dundalgan Press, Dundalk 1951
  'The Ulster Farmhouse', *Ulster Folk Life*, vol. 1, 1955
  Irish Folk Ways, Routledge & Kegan, London 1957
FEDER & SCHRANK (eds), *Literature and Folk Culture, Ireland and Newfoundland*, Memorial University of Newfoundland, Newfoundland 1977
FENTON & OWEN (eds), *Food in Perspective*, John Donald, Edinburgh 1981
FITZGIBBON, THEODORA, *Irish Traditional Food*, Gill & Macmillan, Dublin 1983
FOX, ROBIN *The Tory Islanders*, Cambridge University Press, London 1978
GAILEY, DR ALAN, 'A House, from Gloverstown to Lismacloskey', *Ulster Folk Life*, vol. 20, 1974
  'Cultural Connections and Cheese', *Ulster Folk Life*, vol. 25, 1986–7
GINNELL, *The Brehon Laws*, T. Fisher Unwin, London 1914
GLASSIE, HENRY, *Irish Folk History*, O'Brien Press, Dublin 1982
HALL, MR AND MRS C. S., *Ireland, Its Scenery and Character*, 3 vols, How and Parsons, London 1841–3
HUGHES, P. H., *The Sea Fishing Industries of Northern Ireland*, HMSO, London 1970
IRWIN, FLORENCE, *The Cookin' Woman*, Oliver & Boyd, Edinburgh 1949
JOYCE P. W., *A Social History of Ancient Ireland*, vols I and II, M. H. Gill & Son, Dublin 1920
  'Corn, Milk and Staples', *Journal of the Royal Society of Antiquaries of Ireland*, vol. 74, 1944
  'Old Irish Cheeses and other Milk Products', *Journal of the Cork Historical and Agricultural Society*, vol. 53, 1948
  'Old Irish Buttermaking', *Journal of the Cork Historical and Agricultural Society*, vol. 54, 1949
LAVERTY, MAURA, *Never No More*, Virago, London 1985
LOGAN, PATRICK, *Tan Day*, Appletree Press, Belfast 1986
LOUGHREY, PATRICK (ed.), *The People of Ireland*, Appletree Press, Belfast 1989
LUCAS, A. L., 'Nettles and Charlock as Famine Food', *Breifne*, vol. 1, no. 2, Cumann Seanchais Bhreifne, 1958
  'Irish Food Before the Potato, *Gwerin*, vol. iii, no. 3, Denbigh, Gee and Son, 1960–2
LYSAGHT, PATRICIA, 'When I makes Tea, I makes Tea . . .', *Ulster Folk Life*, vol. 33, 1987
MCKINNEY, JACK, 'They came in Cars and Carts: A History of the Fairs and Markets of Ballyclare', Area Resource Centre, Antrim 1989
MacLYSAGHT, E., *Irish Life in the Seventeenth Century*, Cork University Press, Cork 1939
MacNEILL, MAIRE, *The Festival of Lughnasa*, Oxford University Press, Oxford 1962
MAGUIRE, W. A., *Caught in Time*, Friar's Bush Press, Belfast 1986
MASON, CHARLOTTE, *The Lady's Assistant*, Dublin 1778
MAXWELL, CONSTANTIA, *The Stranger in Ireland*, Jonathan Cape, London 1954
MAXWELL W. H., *Wild Sports of the West*, Richard Bentley, London 1843
MEYER, RONO (ed.), *The Vision of MacConglinne* (trans. by Aisling MacConglinne), Lemma Publishing Corporation, New York 1974
MITCHEL, N. C., 'The Lower Bann Fisheries', *Ulster Folk Life*, vols 10–12, 1964–6
MITCHELL, FRANK, *The Shell Guide to reading the Irish Landscape*, Country House, Dublin 1986

MITCHELL, FRANK (ed.) *The Book of the Irish Countryside*, Blackstaff Press, Belfast 1987
MORYSON, FEYNES, *Itinerary, 1605*, John Beale, London 1617
MOURNE LOCAL STUDIES GROUP, *12 Miles of Mourne*, vol. 41
MURPHY, MICHAEL J., *Ulster Folk of Field and Fireside*, Dundalgan Press, Dundalk 1983
NICHOLSON A., *Ireland's Welcome to the Stranger: Excursions through Ireland*, Charles Gilpen, London 1847
NI DHOIBHNE, EILIS, 'The Land of Cokaygne – A Middle English Source for Irish Food Historians', *Ulster Folk Life*, vol. 34, 1988
O'CURRY, EUGENE, *Manners and Customs of the Ancient Irish*, vols I–III, London 1873
O'DONOVAN, JOHN, *The Economic History of Livestock in Ireland*, Cork University Press, Cork 1940
O'FLANAGAN, FERGUSON, WHELAN (eds), *Rural Ireland 1600–1900: Modernisation and Change*, Cork University Press, Cork 1987
O'NEILL, THOMAS, 'Food Problems during the Great Irish Famine', *Journal of the Royal Society of Antiquaries of Ireland*, vol. 82, 1952
O'NEILL, TIMOTHY P., *Life and Tradition in Rural Ireland*, J. M. Dent & Sons, London 1977
O'SE, PROF. MICHEAL, 'Irish Cheese Making', *Journal of Cork Historical and Archaeological Society*, vol. 411
OREL, B. (ed.), *Irish History and Culture*, Wolfhound Press, Dublin 1979
PAOR, LIAM DE, *The Peoples of Ireland*, Hutchinson, London 1932
  Portrait of Ireland, Rainbow Publications, 1985
PATTERSON T. G. F., 'T. G. F. Patterson Memorial Fund Committee', *The Armagh County Museum*
  'Blayeberry Sunday', *Ulster Folk Life*, vol. 2, 1956
PETTY, SIR WILLIAM, *The Political Anatomy of Ireland*, Irish University Press, 1691
REID, THOMAS, *Travels in Ireland in the Year 1822*, Longman, Hurst, Rees, Orme and Brown, London 1823
RYAN, MICHAEL (ed), *Treasures of Ireland*, Royal Irish Academy, Dublin 1983
SALAMAN, REDCLIFFE, *The History and Social Influence of the Potato*, Cambridge University Press, Cambridge 1949
  Ancient Laws of Ireland, vols 1–6, Alexander Thom, Dublin 1865–1901
SAYERS, PEIG, *Machnamh Sean-Mhna – An Old Woman's Reflections*, Oxford University Press, Oxford, 1962
SHARKEY, OLIVE, *Old Days – Old Ways*, O'Brien Press, Dublin 1985
SIMON, ANDRE, *Cheese of the World*, Faber & Faber, London 1956
STRINGER, ARTHUR, *The Experienced Huntsman*, Blackstaff Press, Belfast 1977
SYNGE, J. M., *Riders to the Sea*, J. M. Dent & Sons, London 1941
THACKERAY, WILLIAM MAKEPEACE, *The Irish Sketch Book*, vol. XVIII, Smith Elder & Co., London 1879
TROW-SMITH, ROBERT, *Life from the Land*, Longman, London 1957
WAKEFIELD, EDWARD, *An Account of Ireland, Statistical and Political*, vols I and II, London 1812
WATSON, MERVYN, 'Standardisation of Pig Production: The Case of the Large White Ulster', *Ulster Folk Life*, vol. 34, 1988
WENT, ARTHUR E. J., 'The Irish Hake Fishery 1504–1824, *Journal of The Cork Historical and Archaeological Society*, vol. 51, 1946
WHITLEY, STOKES, 'Lives of the Saints', *The Book of Lismore*, Oxford 1980
WILSON, ANNE, *Food and Drink in Britain*, Constable, London 1973
YOUNG, ARTHUR, *A Tour in Ireland*, vols I and II, Cadell, London

INDEX